AF469913

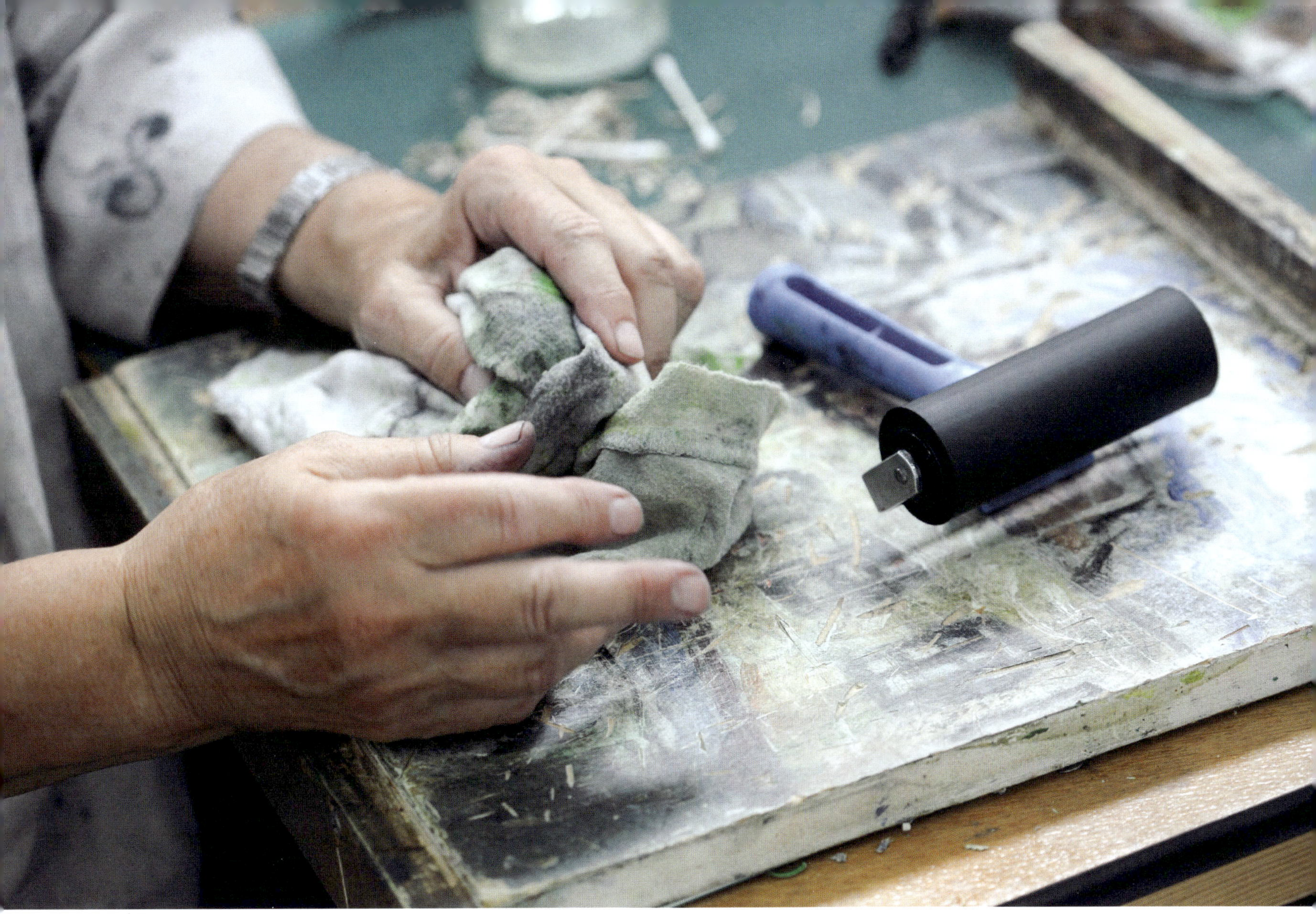

MAKING
NOWHERE
SOMEWHERE

A MONOGRAPH OF
ORIGINAL PRINTS
BY GAIL MALLATRATT

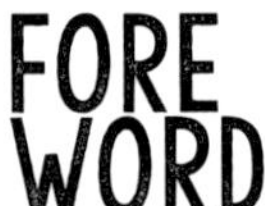

FORE WORD

I AM AT MY TABLE, LOOKING UP AT ONE OF GAIL'S PRINTS. Gail is standing in the centre with classmates on either side of her. They are maybe 15 or 16 and they appear to be in their best clothes, as if on ceremony. The print is black and white, apart from Gail, who is a just-detectable pale colour of pink. There is definitely a sense of tension in the print – as if they were being instructed to stand so straight.

For me, as in so much of Gail's work, it's a story waiting to be told. There's a sense of occasion and what I call an edgy energy about it. That energy is partly about her drive. I also think it's also about her need for the things she sees to be recognised and brought to life.

I've known Gail for over 30 years. When I was living in London, we worked together, became best friends and, it seemed, stormed about the city, consuming the arts. When we met, one of the first things I noticed was that her house was full of paintings. They spoke to her eclectic taste and assured eye. She introduced me to art really. One time she handed me a short book on Rothko and said '*read that and learn about colour*'. As if it was the most obvious thing to do. I barely knew who he was.

We holidayed in the US and Spain and much later she visited me in Australia.

It was on one of our first trips together in the 1980s that I bought my first painting. We were in Baton Rouge, Louisiana in a Cajun restaurant that had a dance floor. After bloody marys and some traditional Cajun food, we danced (tentatively) on a raised dance floor that looked like a boxing ring.

The walls of the restaurant were covered in paintings. The few that stood out were by a local artist called Frances Xavier Pavy. We called up next day and asked about the artist and were given his phone number and he invited us over to his place, which was teeming with paintings. For some reason, we couldn't decide on anything that day and left empty handed. Back In London, we regretted that, got in touch and ordered two paintings. Weeks later they arrived.

Mine is of a smoking, accordion-playing cowboy, looking cool and inscrutable. Gail's was of a cowboy wrestling with an alligator. And how fitting was that?

I should explain that comment. When I first met Gail, she'd not long completed a degree in graphic design as a mature student and before that she'd trained as a teacher, married and had three sons. She seemed to take on massive tasks (restoring houses, learning new skills) with gusto and what looked to me like fearlessness - in effect reinventing herself. After a few years in graphic design, she went back to painting and then did a course in printmaking at St Martin's.

That took her work in a new direction, into her family history and their role in the early days of the US, battling it out as people moved West. All of the above are examples of wrestling the alligator.

In all of her work, she captures and gives an edge to a situation, or a place or some aspect of history or of a relationship. And she uses colour in a dramatic and at times surreal way. You can see it in her prints of London, where her use of colour makes the familiar seem startlingly new.

In *Cacti with iphone, Arizona* (photo-taking man dwarfed by massive cactus shapes) and *Kachinas, Arizona #1*, there's an almost graphic simplicity to the imagery. In *Evening Lake* (a

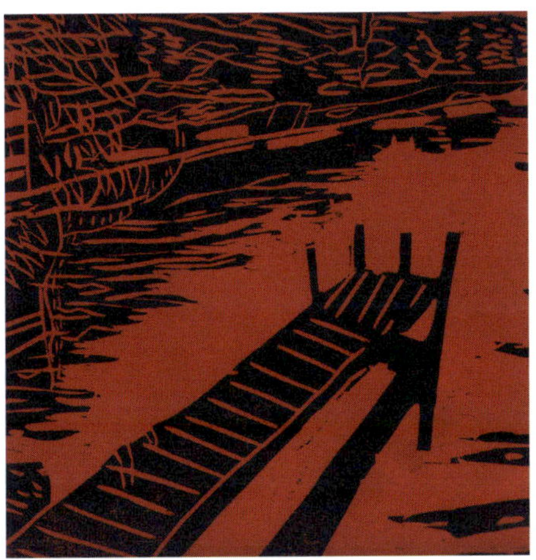

print that I covet), a blazing red moonlight illuminates a small wharf jutting out into a lake. The emptiness of the scene reminds me of a time in Louisiana when we were in a cabin in an otherwise empty and slightly spooky waterside park. I'd stupidly dropped the keys to our car (mercifully retrieved the next morning) when earlier walking down a lakeside path. That night, the countryside looked, like that print, stunningly beautiful and fraught with anxiety.

Yet I think it's in her 'Wild West' work that I perhaps see her most powerful story telling. Her family history has provided the background for a great deal of her print making. They left London/England in the 1830s, travelled to the US and journeyed west to California. They would have experienced huge uncertainty, adventure and surely danger.

These stories look like very personal experiences. Hardships are exposed. *Cowboys at the Water Hole: On the Hot Weary Trail* is as playful as it is bleak. Her *Log Cabins in the Woods* are no romantic cabins in the landscape. They are a testament to brutal hard work and effort. And there's no human presence in it.

Struggles are witnessed. In *The Cowboy Watch*, there's real threat. In *Indian Camp*, technology is outstripping traditional life. And in *Last Chance Gulch*, we're in the Gold Rush and the scramble for prosperity, which I assume her family was part of. Sometimes it feels as if secrets are being unearthed.

In Gail's work, I see everywhere her curiosity, her love of a good story and, in no small measure, her famed bluntness combined with a striking sense of style and elegance.

I love that she and her work are being celebrated in this book.

Sandy Belford
Sydney, Australia

FORE WORD

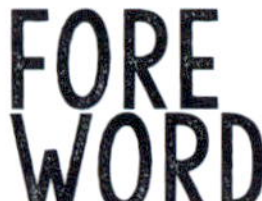

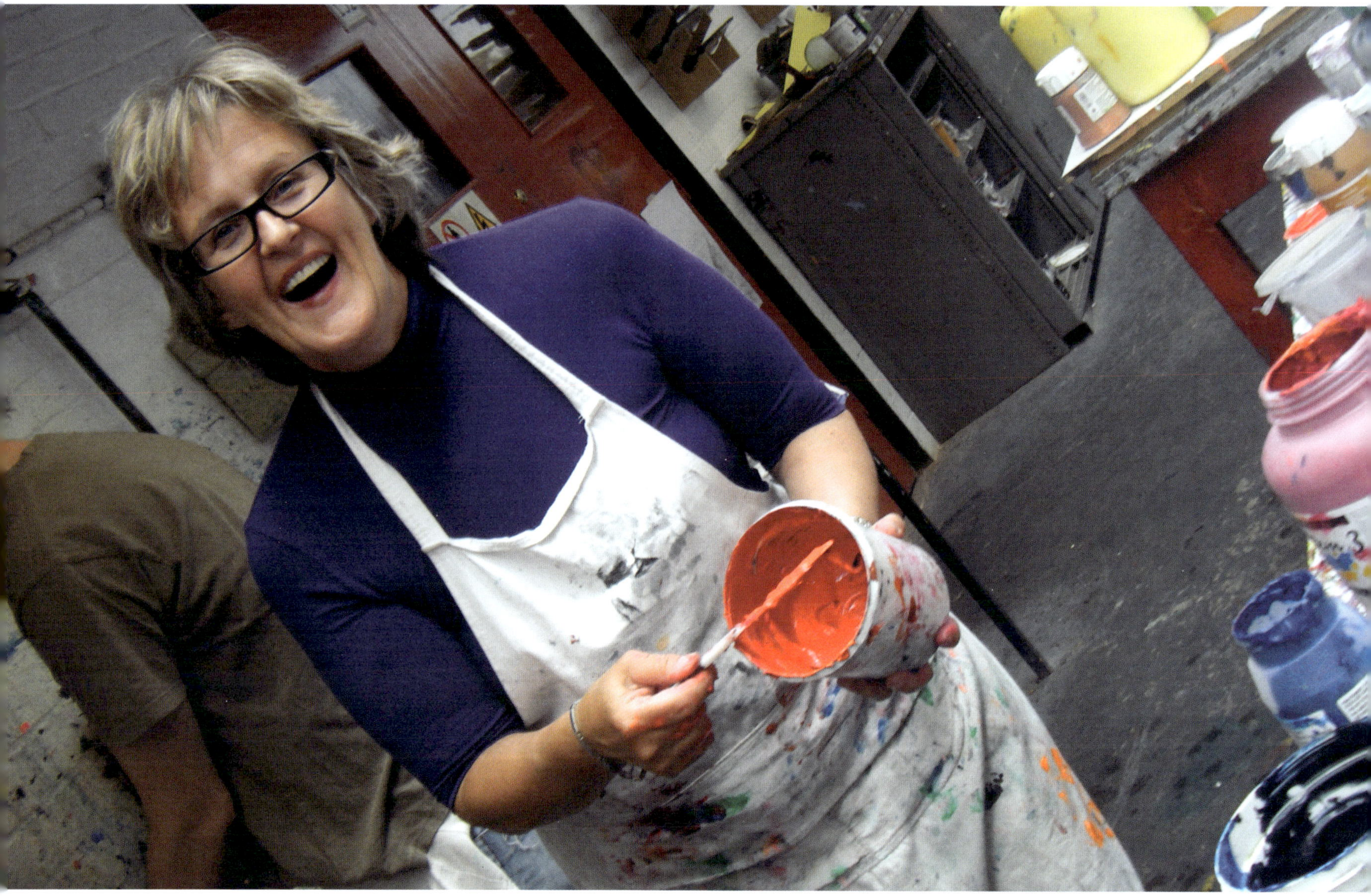

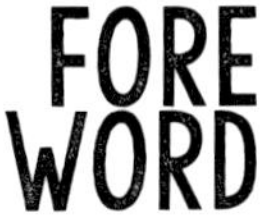

THE DRIVE TO CREATE IS IN ALL OF US, varied only by how we create and what our inspiration is. For Gail Mallatratt the impetus behind her artwork has been the drive to find herself. The need to do this comes partly from her family background – her ancestors left London to emigrate to California in the mid 1800s to take part in the Gold Rush. She was born in the USA and came to live in England when she married her first husband. She has felt a stranger in the UK, and like those ancestors has harnessed a sense of restlessness as the foundation of her creative process.

This book offers a way of assessing her output in the context of its historical narrative, and shows her striving to make experience meaningful and honest. The way she has developed her art connects her to the Gold Rush era with empathy and fascination, even a certain romance, and she takes us with her on that journey. She connects with these things as a way of processing the past and expressing it, conscious of how hard those early emigrés must have found it. Periods of stress and sorrow in her own life have enabled her to bring that understanding to her prints.

Gail is a printmaker who mainly focuses on woodcuts. Perhaps a love for working with wood comes from her father, who also whittled and carved as a hobby as no doubt the Gold Rush diggers did. But, for Gail, there is an even deeper relationship with the material. Gail says *"I hold a dialogue with the print coming off the wood"*, and she would be the first to describe her love of the tactile nature of it, the smell, the grain, the way the knives and tools she uses make cuts in it and the way ink interacts with it, so that there is always an element of surprise in the results when prints are pulled off.

Many printmakers work in editions. Generally, such editions offer an exact replica of the original print, the same ink, colours, intensity etc. Today some printmakers work more with variable editions, so that an edition of 10 or 20 prints will have adaptations in colour or process. Gail does this, producing what she calls *'iterations of prints'*.

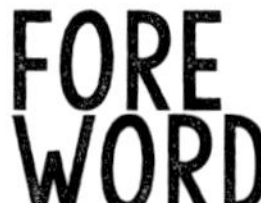

Her inspiration can come from photographs or drawings, where she begins by marking out the image and uses a jigsaw to make the initial cut. The photographic and filmic nature of her work is obvious, especially in the print of her mother from the 1930s, and in her representations of images from the Gold Rush – for example the prints of the railway coming, which altered the demographics of the living and working lives of the miners and their families, and all the Native Americans. It is clear from the Gold Rush prints that Gail has used her research of the difficult lifestyle in California to good effect. She feels it, so viewing her prints we feel it too.

The knife is like a pencil in her hand, she can change the sense of the cut according to the image. Thus, a forest can become edgy and feral by the use of jagged cuts; sweet flowery images are not for her. You can see this approach in **Come Closer, Tobago**, and **Wilton Woods, Connecticut**.

Usually her woodcuts are reduction prints. Her conversation with the print takes her into playing with colour. The iterative approach means she will change the ink – add a cut – alter the image – throughout the reduction process. At every level she can change a colour or tone, creating variable prints, instinctively knowing when she has achieved what she wants from it, when the energy has transmitted itself to the printed sheet. The way she cuts – be it quiet or noisy, rough or fine, textured or flat – is all designed to generate an emotional response in the viewer. Sometimes a sense of anger, or disappointment, or just an intense response to the subject matter gets on to the printed paper. The use of colour helps her do just that. As Matisse said, *"I do not literally paint the table but the emotion it produces in me."*

Her prints make for an art that draws you in, so you have to take time to reflect on your underlying response to it. This is figurative art that – with her use of vivid inking, decisive cutting, the sense of movement and its filmic quality – borders on the abstract but does not get there. When you look at her colourful prints, in the way the ink is laid down in flat swathes, you can see how some of her touchstones have influenced her stylistically, such as Kirchner, Gauguin, Daumier and Tom Hammick. The Japanese tradition of woodcutting is also evident with a modern twist.

The book takes us through her reaction to the Gold Rush, her family background and formative years in the States, and her many 'meanderings'. It provides a legacy of her work for her family and for her admirers. But in putting the book together, in redefining her work to date, one of the main things to emerge is a sense of surprise that she has physically ended up back where her ancestors set out from when they left to find gold.

In re-evaluating her prints, in collating this book, she has forged a new response to her own work and helped us to do the same; she can see her work in a more linear way, where the prints are not illustrative of a story but *are* the story.

In doing so she has found gold in her own creativity.

Tricia Henry
Cheltenham, Gloucestershire

MAKING NOWHERE SOMEWHERE: CONTENTS

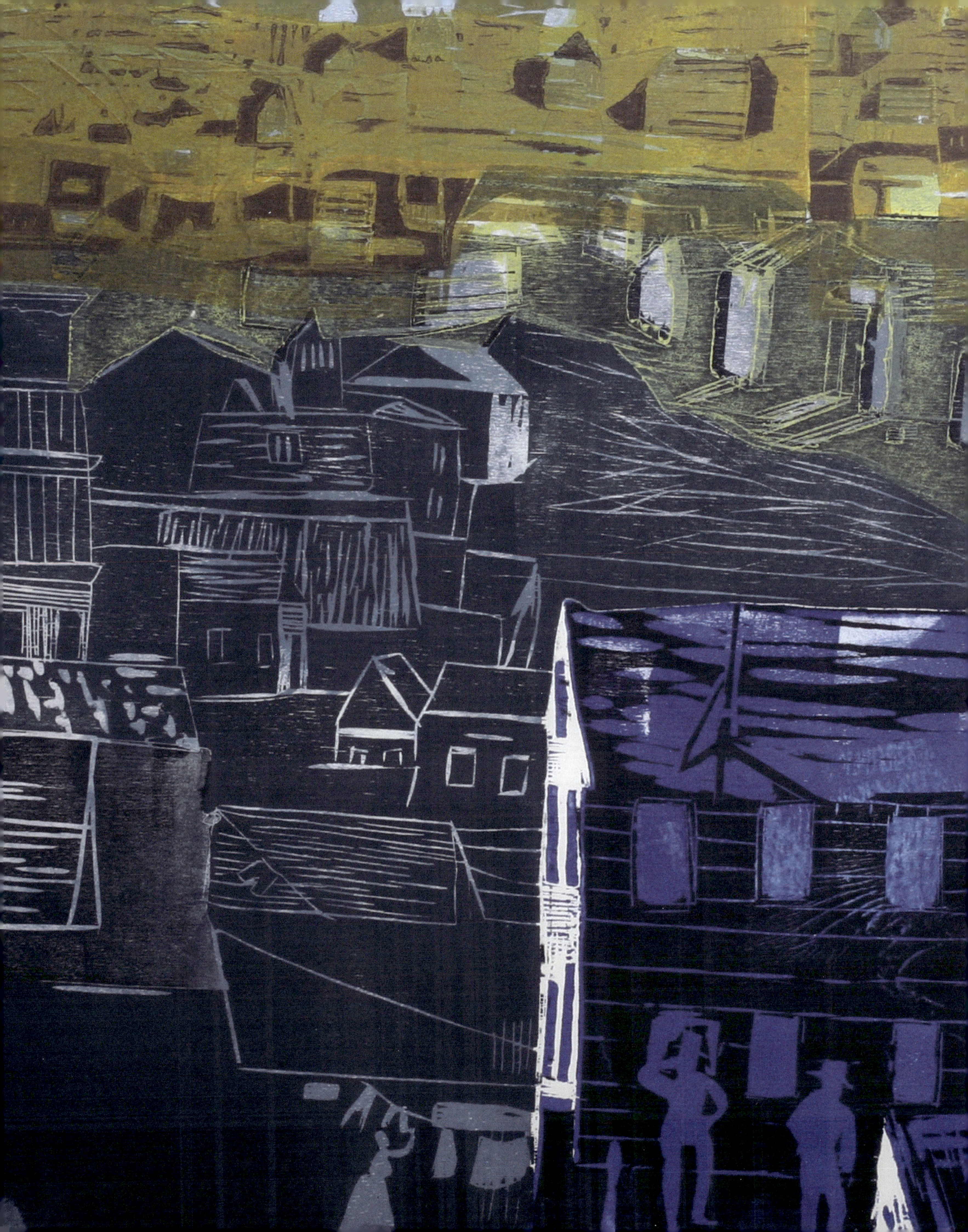

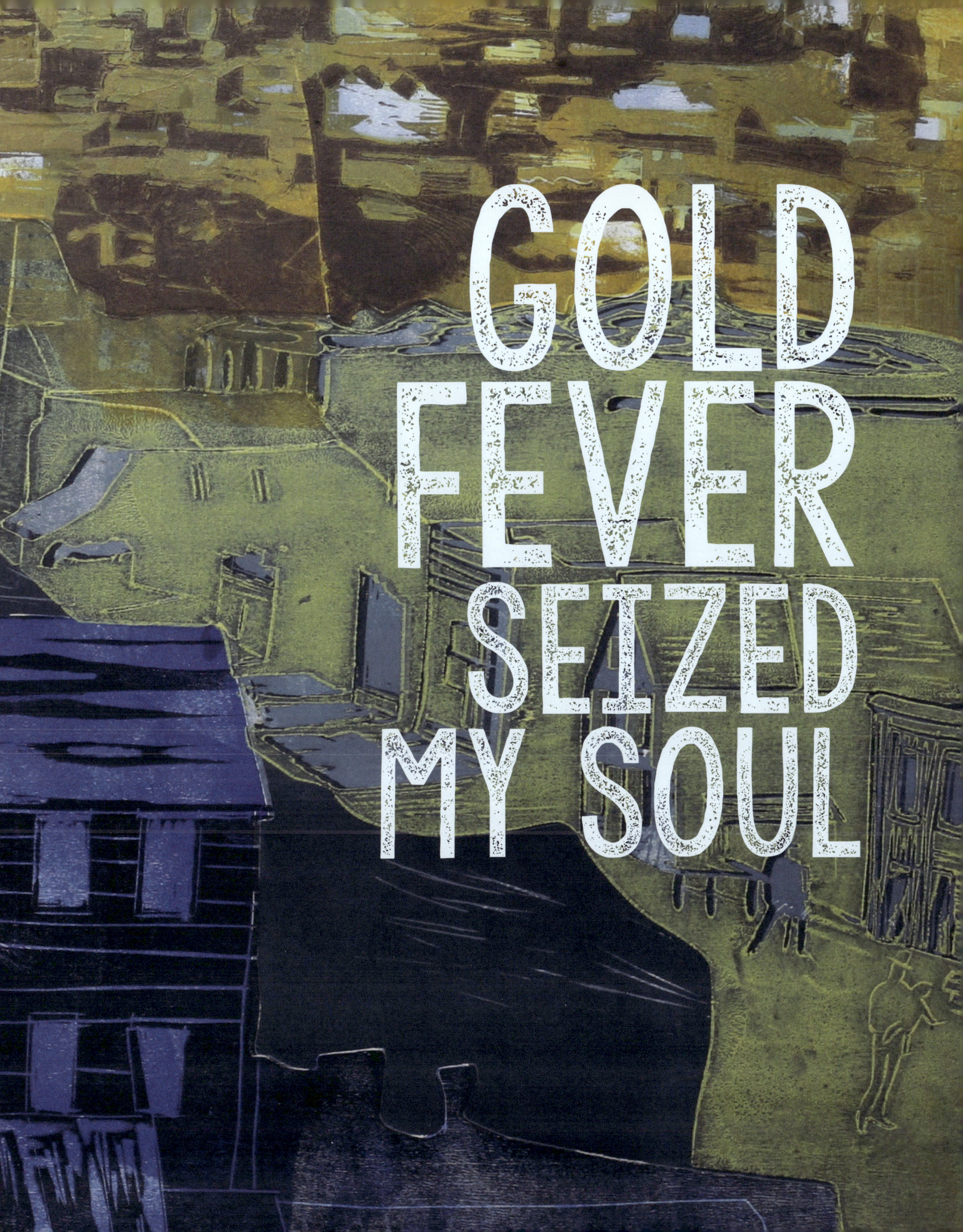

GOLD
FEVER
SEIZED
MY SOUL

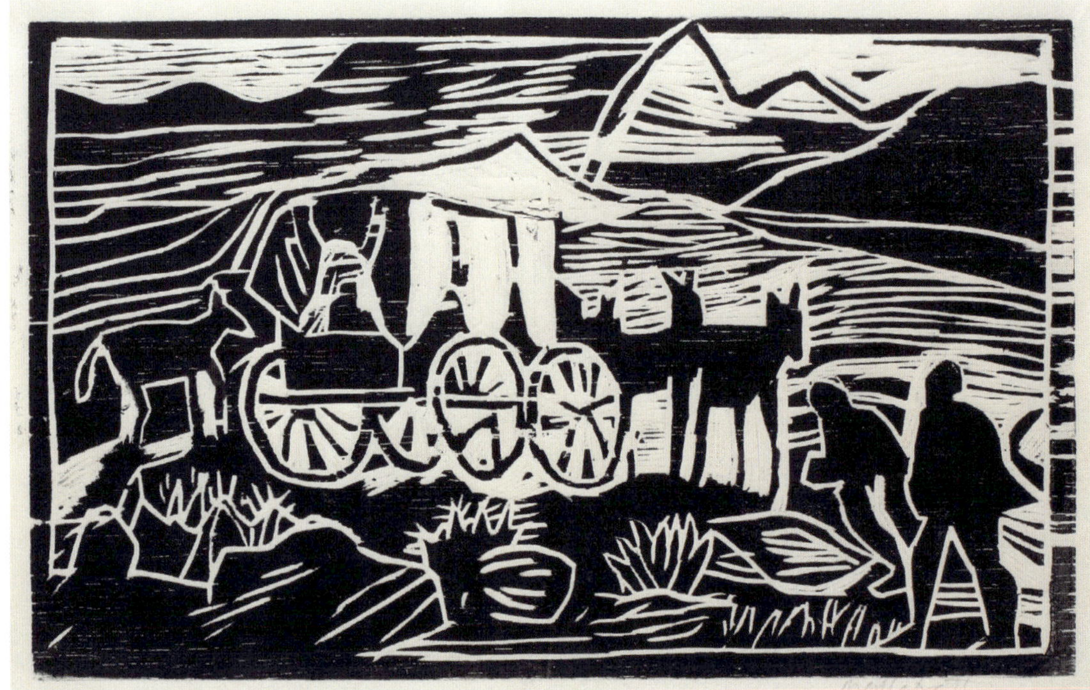

OFF WE GO
*A chaotic beginning
is shown here, with
rugged, uneven cuts*
[WC]

MY FAMILY, CALLED CROUCHER, originated in Shadwell, London, on the north bank of the Thames. When the cholera epidemic hit in the 1830s and one brother, working as a chemist, had died, they left. They followed the utopian philosopher and philanthropist Robert Owen to a community called New Harmony, Indiana, and settled there for seventeen years. My great-great grandmother, Esther Croucher Sweasey, died there before the Gold Rush. My great-great grandfather, William John Sweasey, decided to take the family on the Gold Rush to California. In January 1849 gold was discovered in the American River 50 miles north east of Sutters Fort, California. From there, the race was on.

There followed one of the largest mass migrations of all time for that era – approximately 100,000 people. They crossed the wilderness, prairie, rocky mountains and desert in the five-month gap between spring and the first snow – April to October 1850.

The wagon of my ancestors, the Sweasey Axton family, was part of that migration. They stayed in the San Francisco Bay area for five years until 1855, when they decided to travel north and take on the treacherous untried overland passage into Humboldt County, northern California.

That journey took five months, as long as the cross-continental trip, and involved lowering whole wagons and oxen down mountains with ropes.

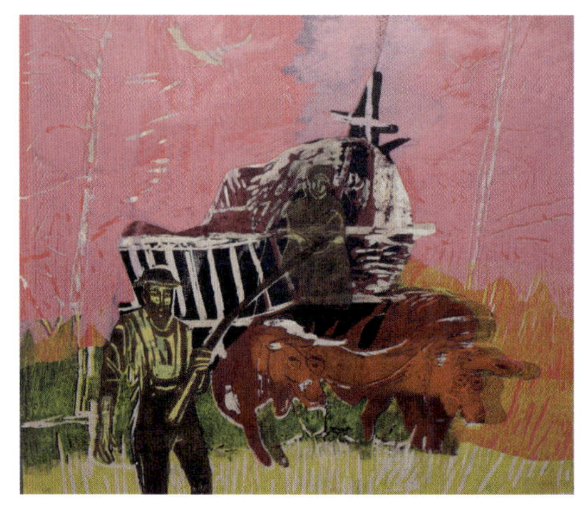

PULL UP YOUR BRITCHES BETSY, WE'RE OFF TO OREGON

This couple are setting off under chaotic circumstances, with the blind hope of getting rich. She is clutching her babe in arms, in disbelief of what is happening.

The husband tries to encourage and chivvy his confused wife and baby.
[RWC]

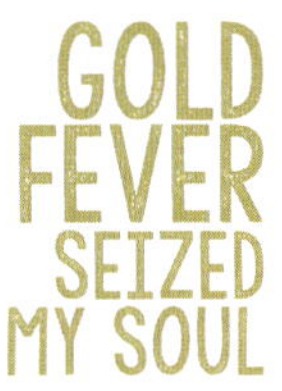

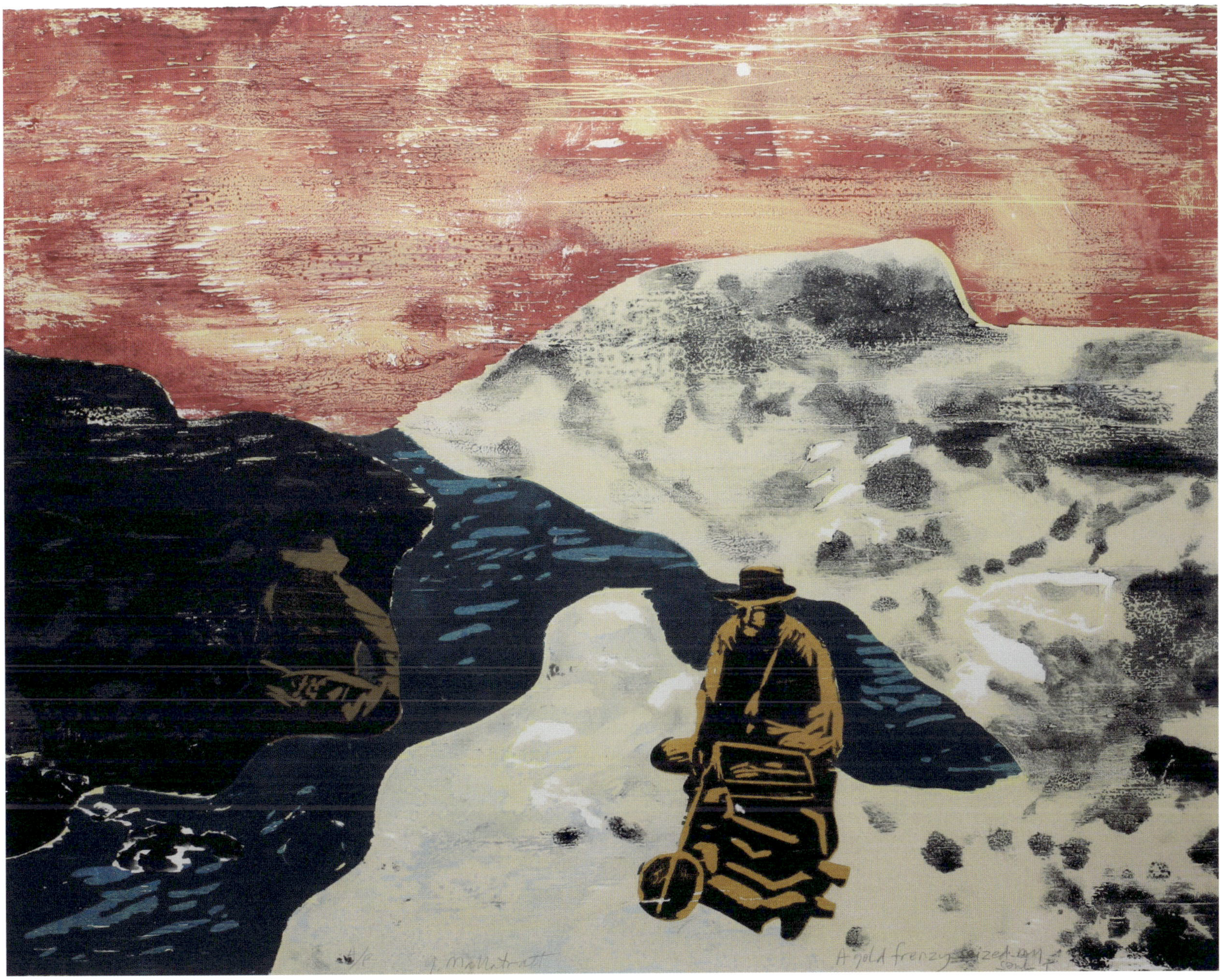

LONE PANNER

Surrounded by wilderness, each lone miner sets up his tent beside the river and stakes claims between posts. Then he begins searching.

[RWC]

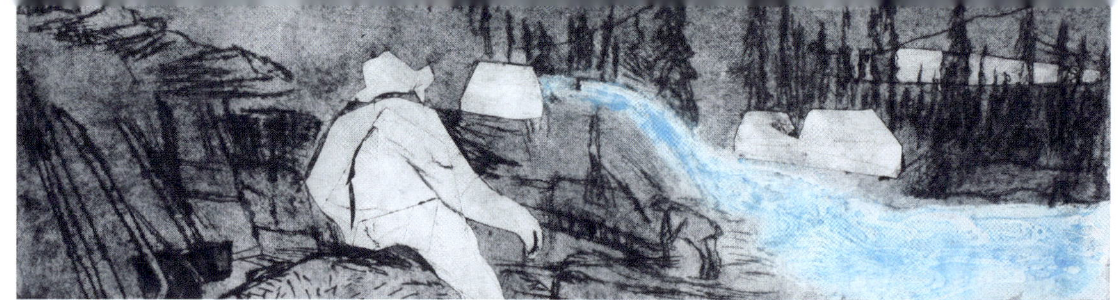

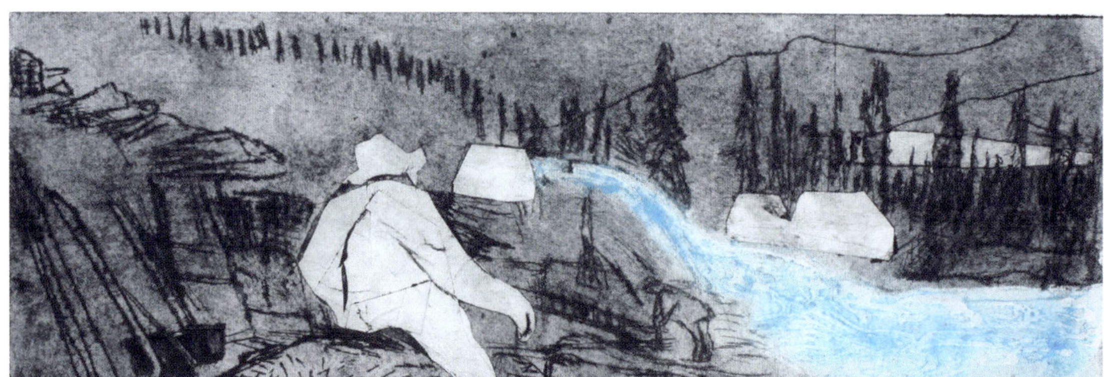

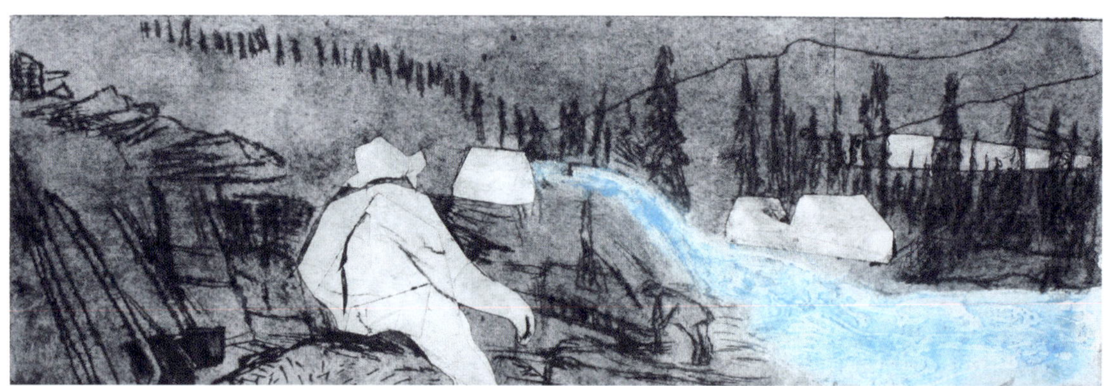

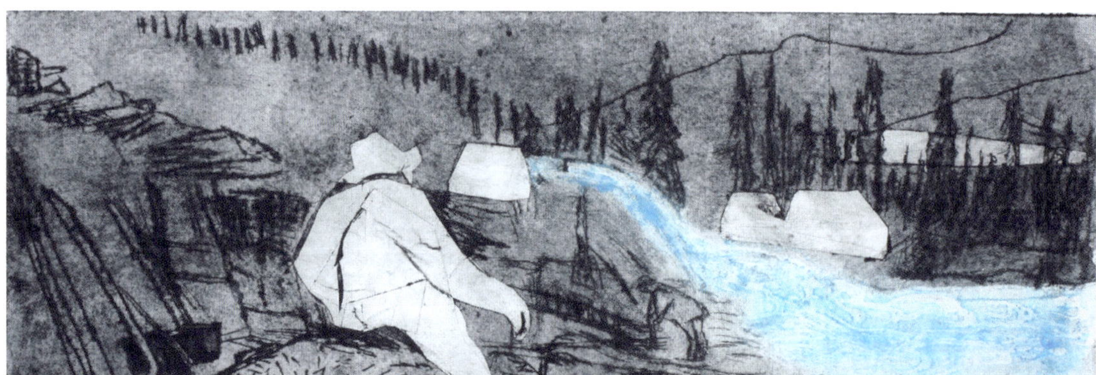

RUSH TO THE RIVER

This image originated from a still that I captured from a movie on afternoon TV. James Stewart was fighting for law and order in a mining camp in the California mountains.

[DP]

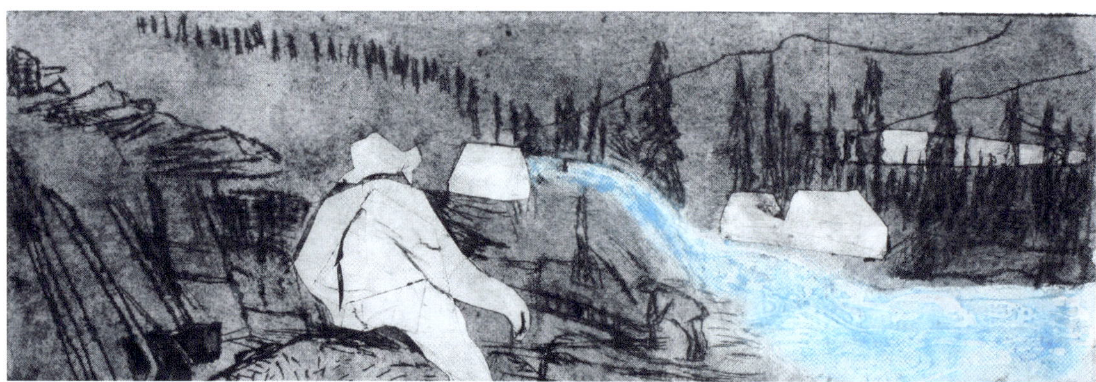

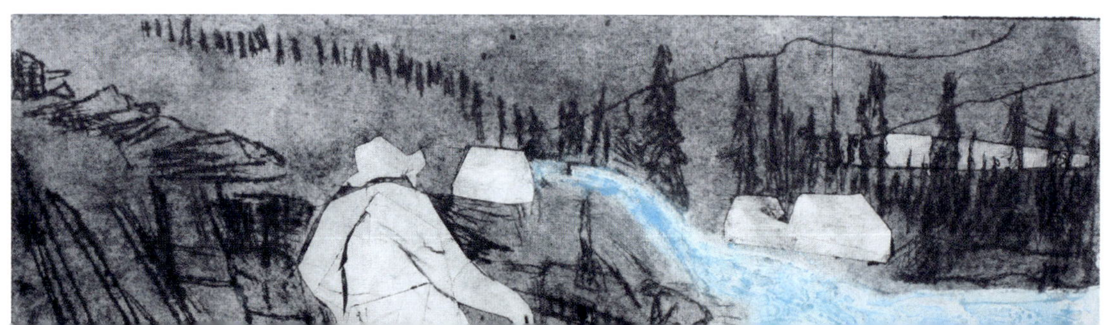

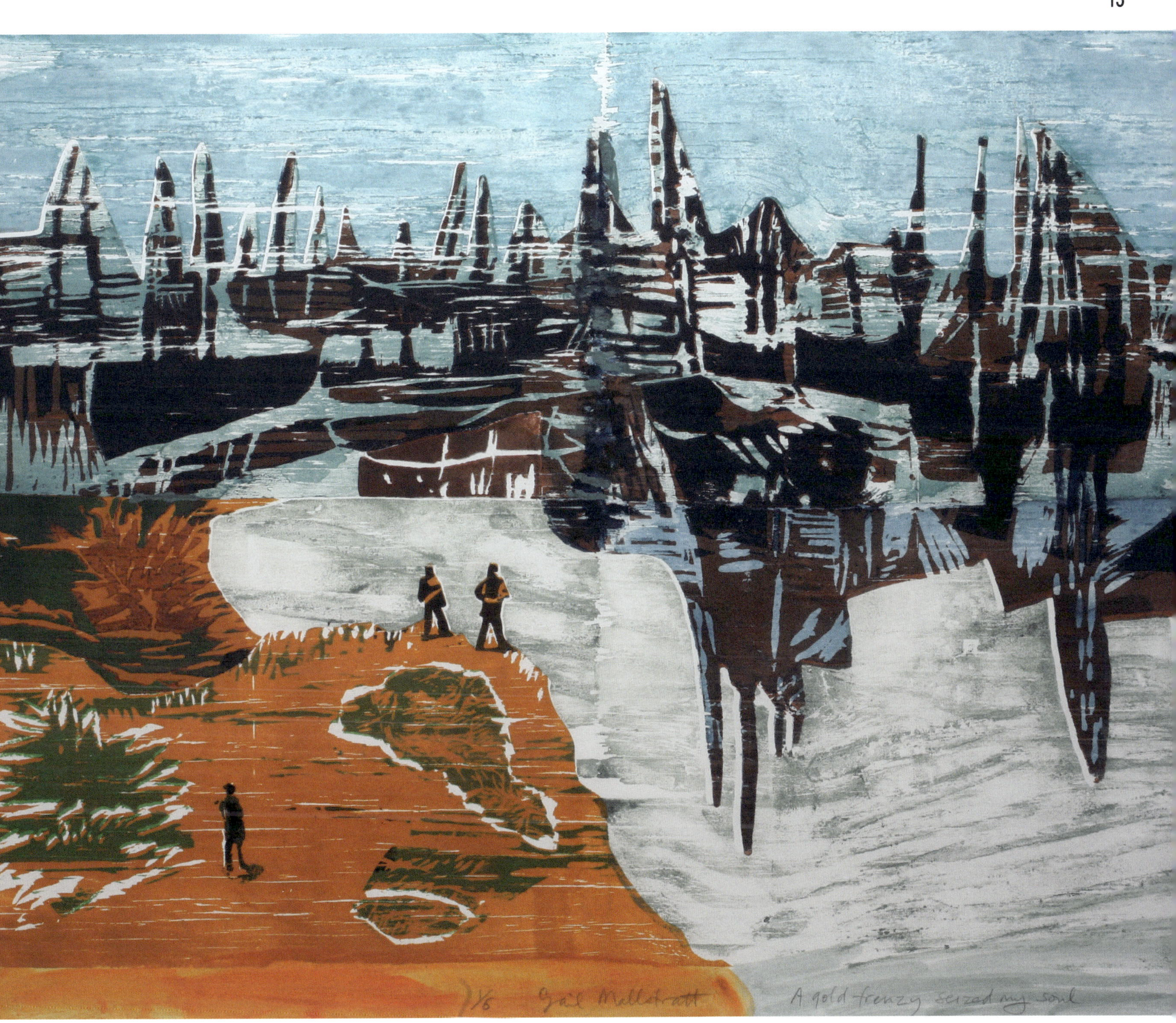

A GOLD FRENZY SEIZED MY SOUL

Entry to San Francisco Bay was clogged with deserted boats. Passengers jumped off the ships and rushed to the gold fields – there was no time to waste.

[RWC]

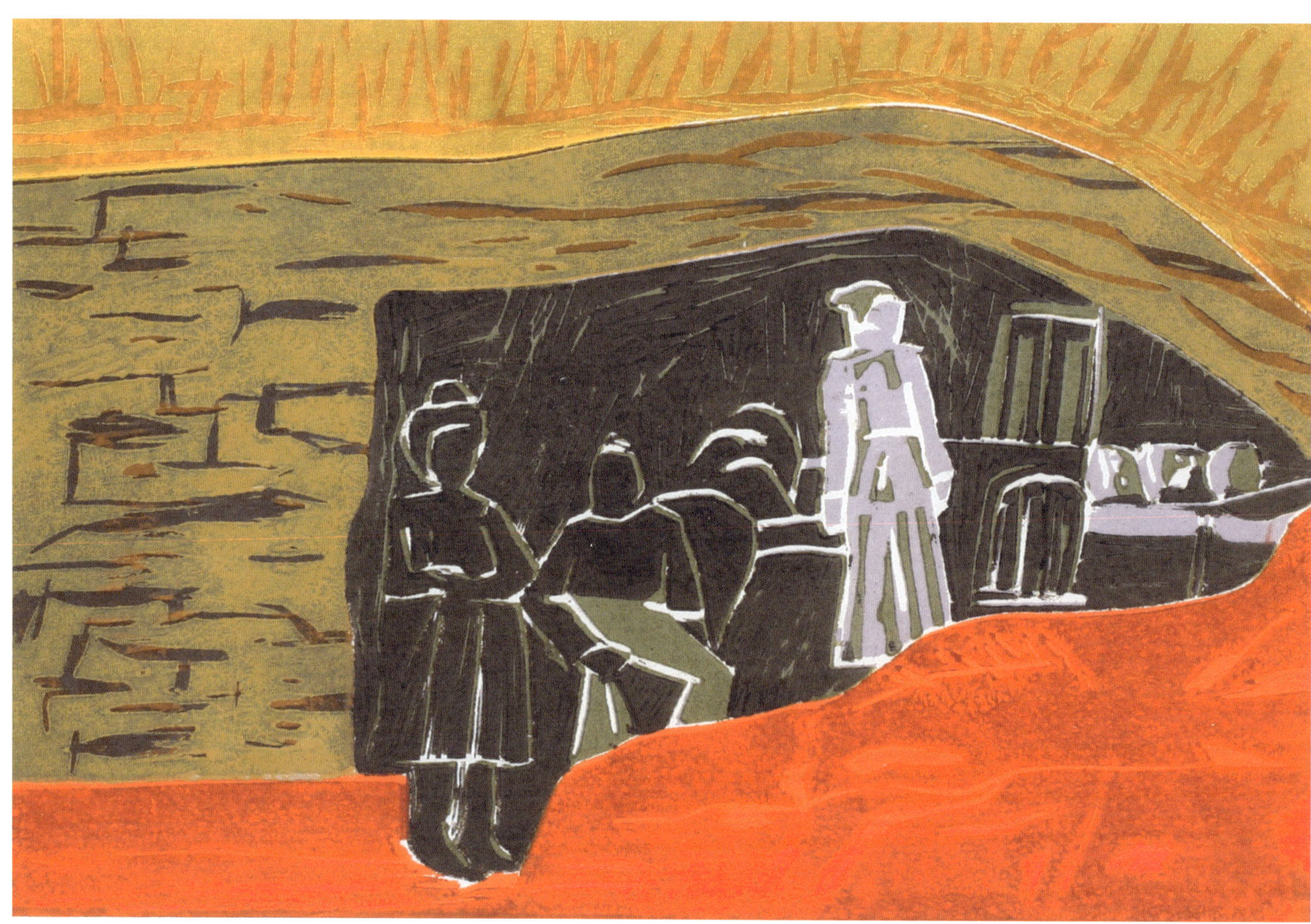

**THEN… OUT ON THE PRAIRIE:
THE DUGOUT**

*Travellers from Europe were sold
the idea of a bright new future and
a house. When they arrived – having
paid their life savings – they found
that what they had bought was a
dug-out hovel in a rise of earth.
There were no trees to build with.*

[RWC]

**THEN… OUT ON THE PRAIRIE:
GATHERING DUNG (opposite)**

*No trees on the prairie. For
firewood for cooking. For warmth in
the night, the women and children
were tasked with finding fuel.*

*These prints show the hardship,
want and suffering of the women
and families caught up in the frenzy.*

[RWC]

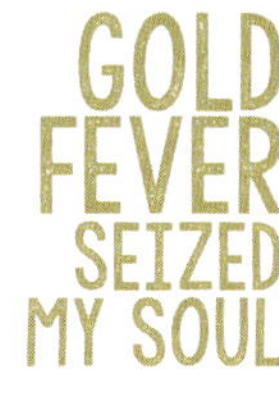

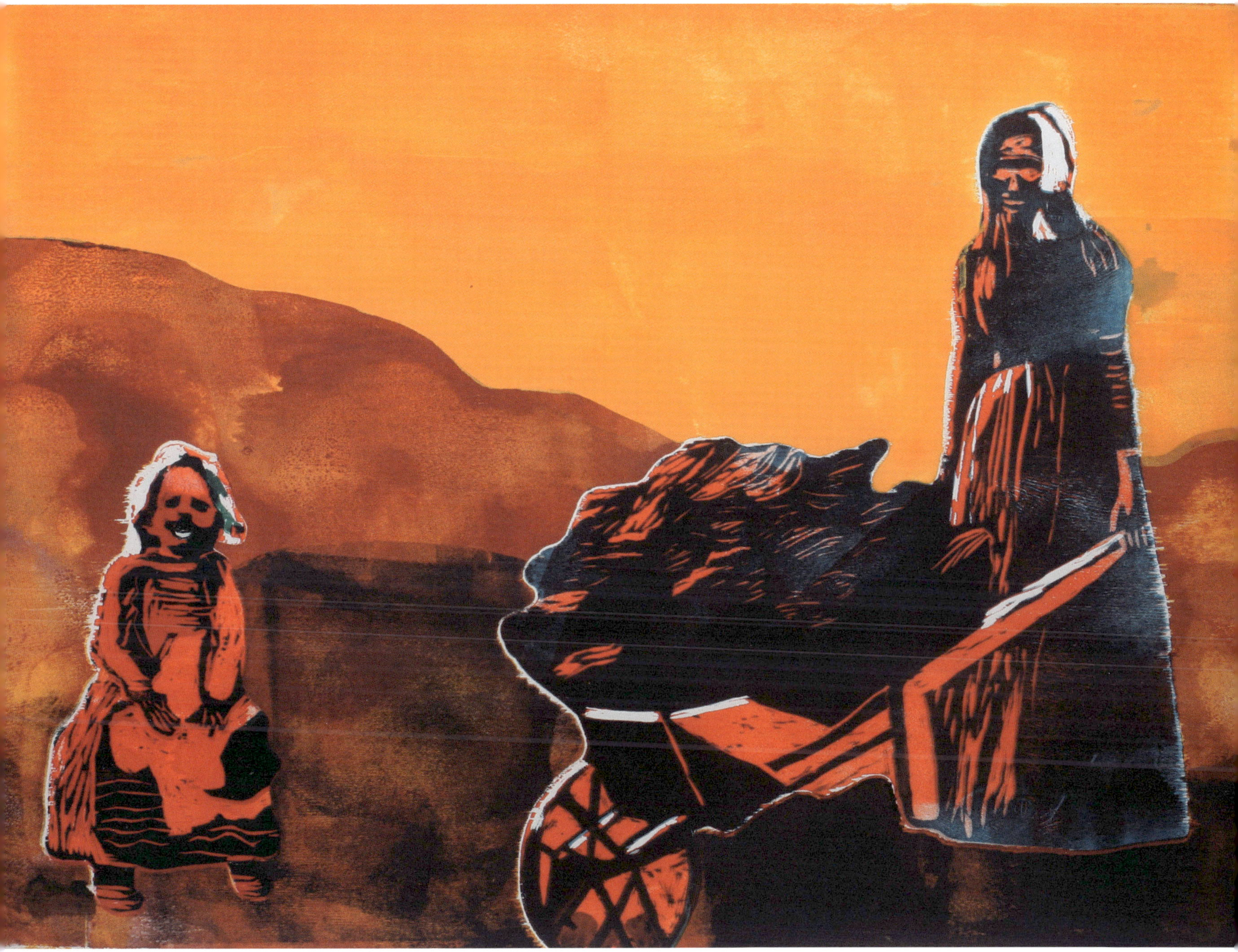

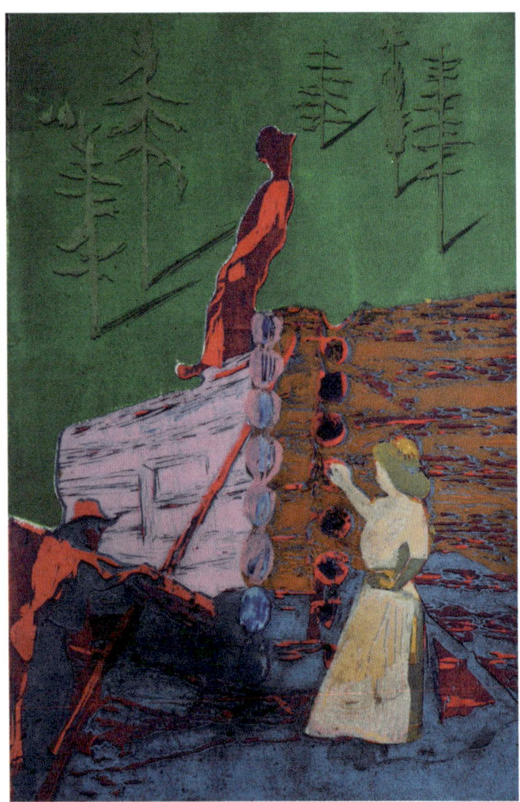

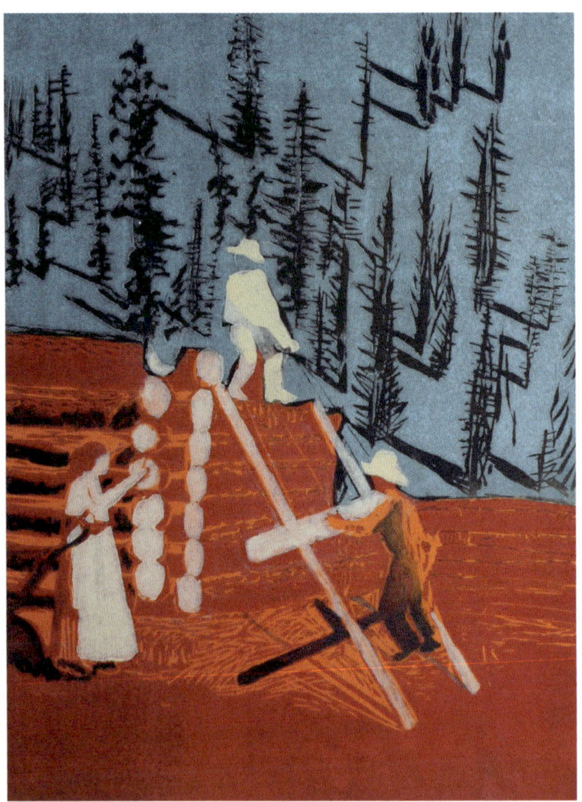

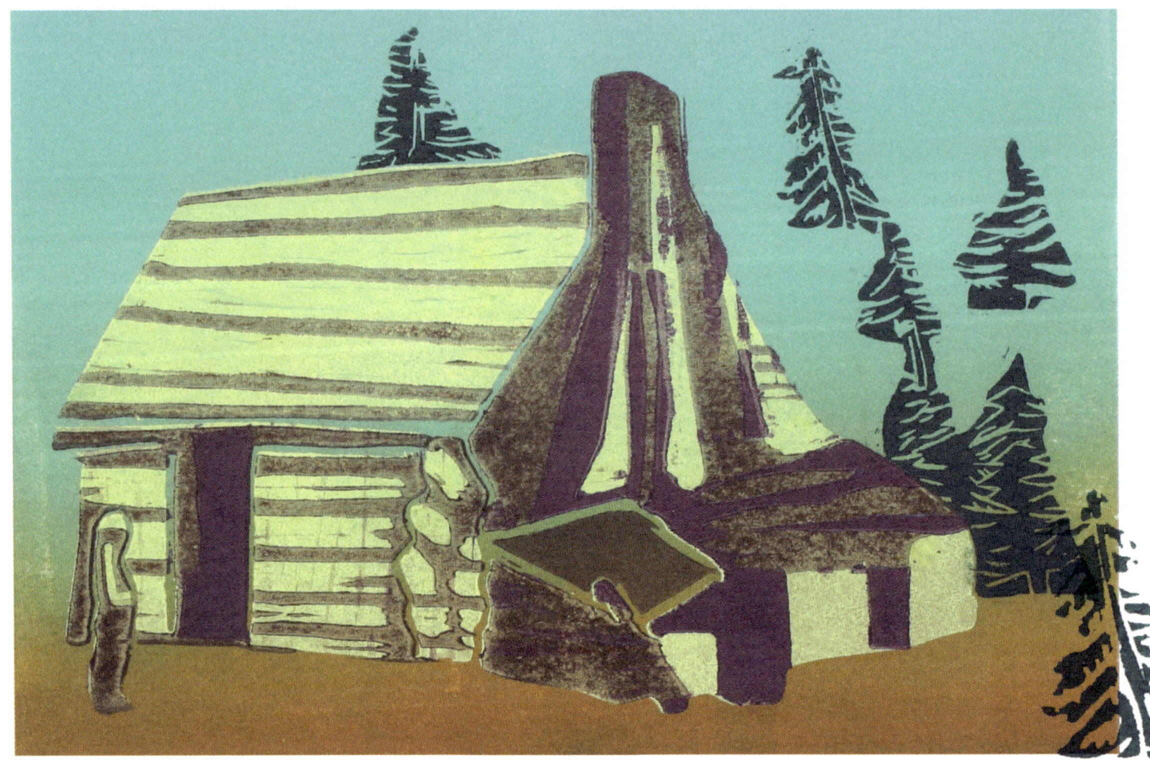

LOG CABINS IN THE WOODS

Families and communities worked together to build homes. Heavy logs had to be cut out of the forests and dragged to the homesteads.

[MWC]

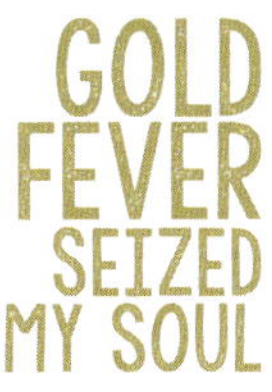

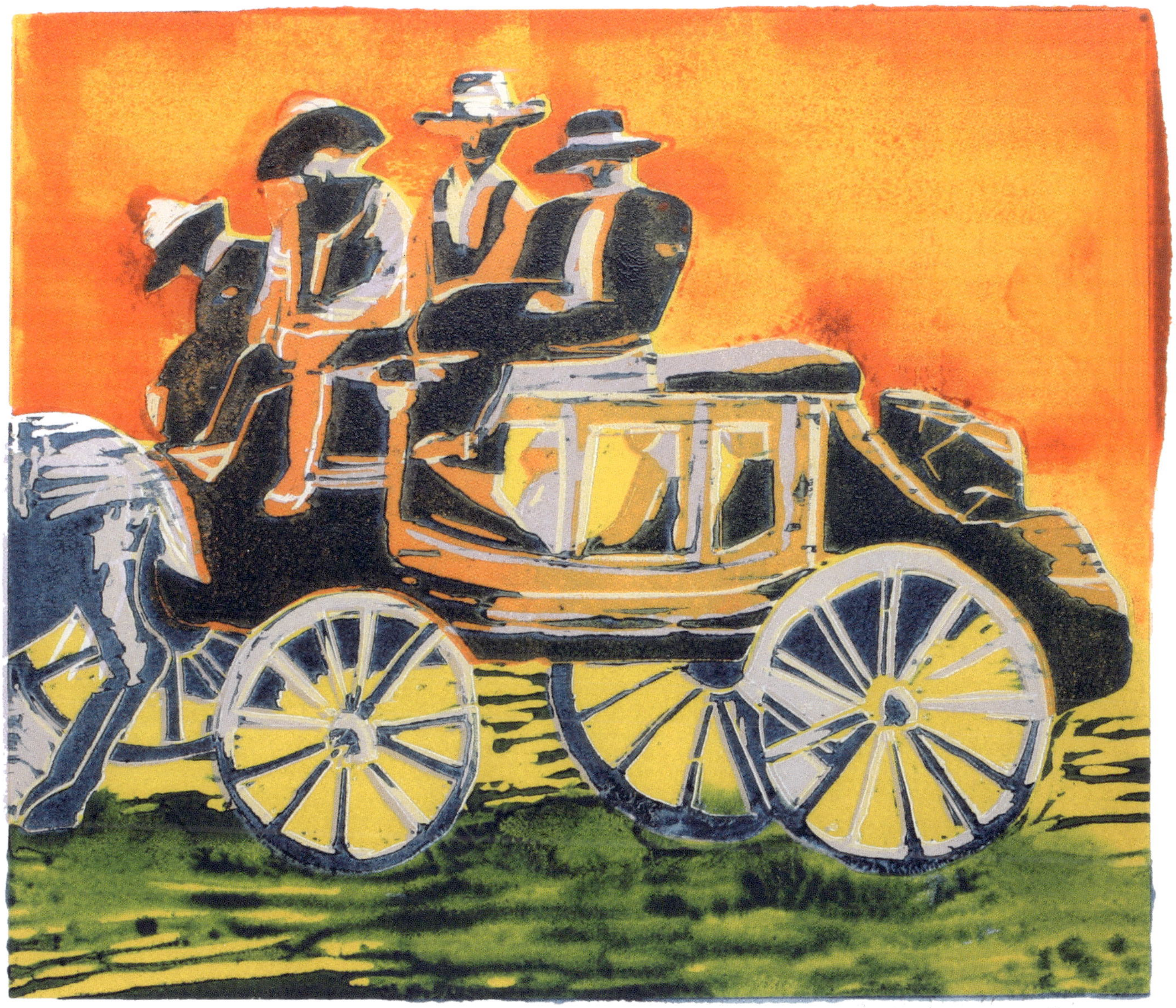

HOW WE GOT THERE

The stage coach provided transport for the elite. These workers didn't get to sit inside.

[RWC] [WS]

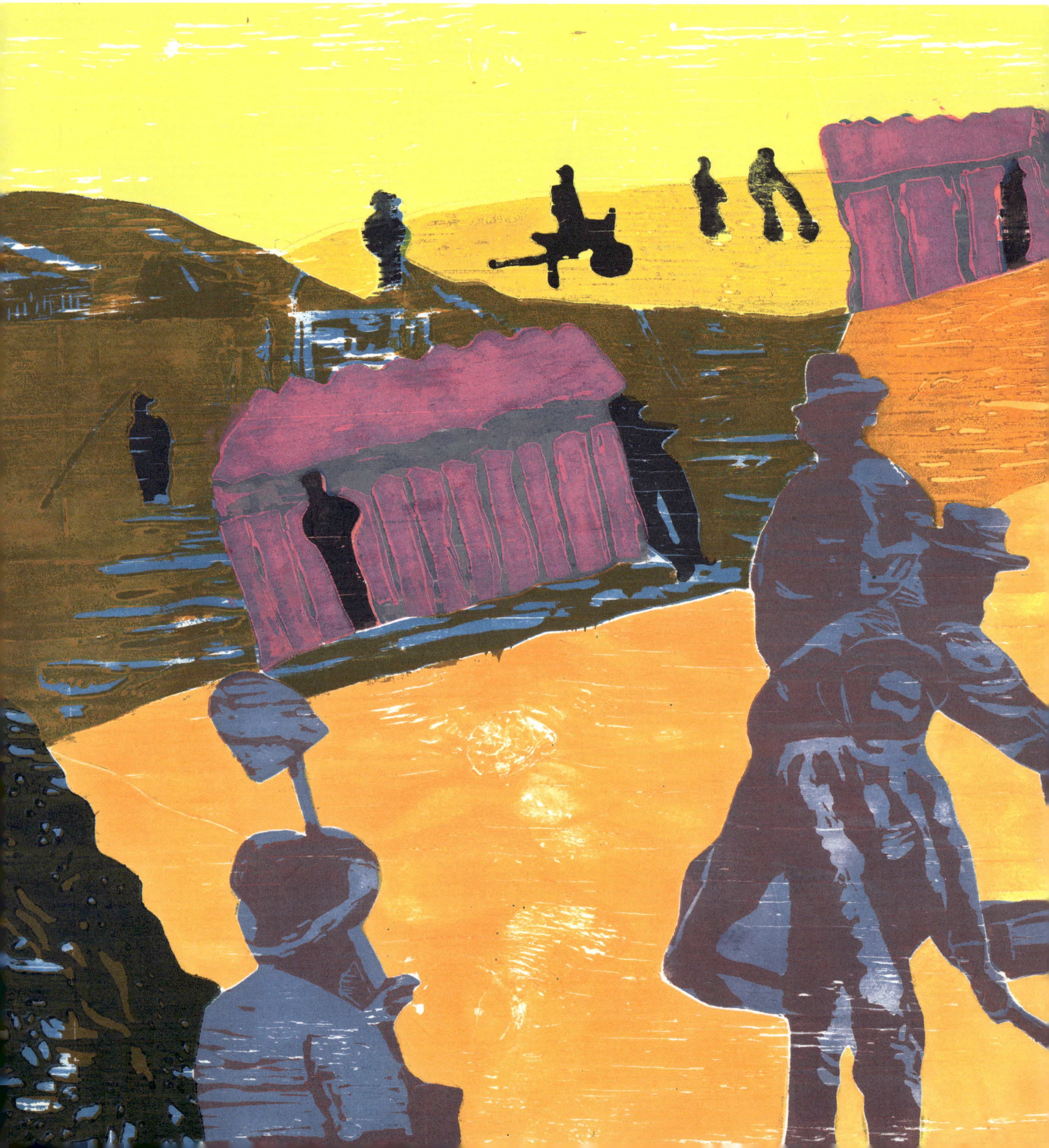

THE MINING CAMPS GROW

By 1852 thousands of miners had joined the rush, and momentum was growing. A new method called a sluice box – fed by water – washed through the mud to expose the gold nuggets, with a crew of shovellers who could process 100 cubic yards of gold-bearing gravel a day.

Team work had become the way to mine as the Gold Rush evolved to a full-blown, but chancy, industry by the end of the decade. Companies were formed to provide high-pressure hoses to wash down complete hillsides.

With this woodcut I opted for colours – pink and yellow – and varying sizes of figures to emphasise the hurry, rush, crowd and hot weather.

[RWC]

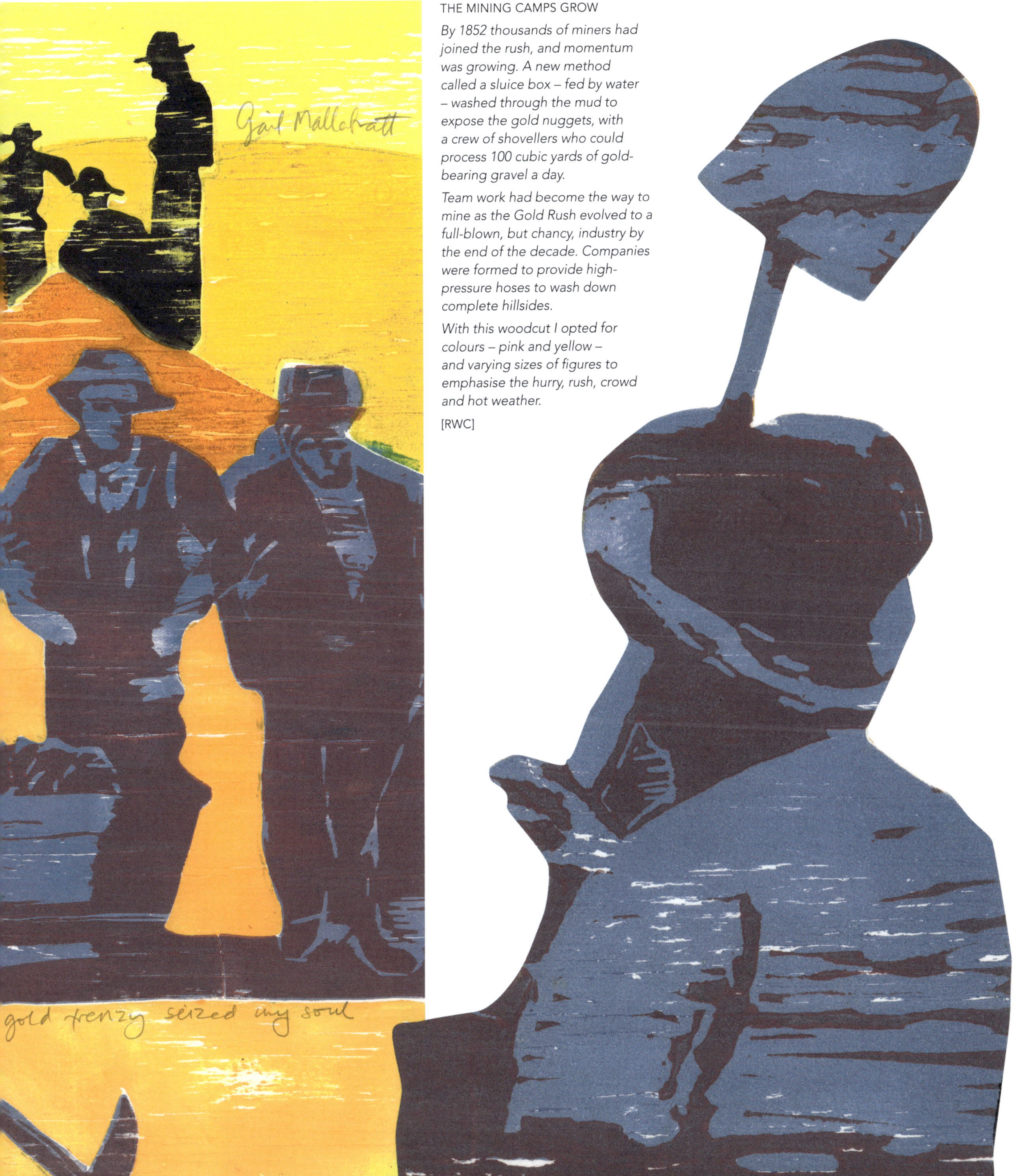

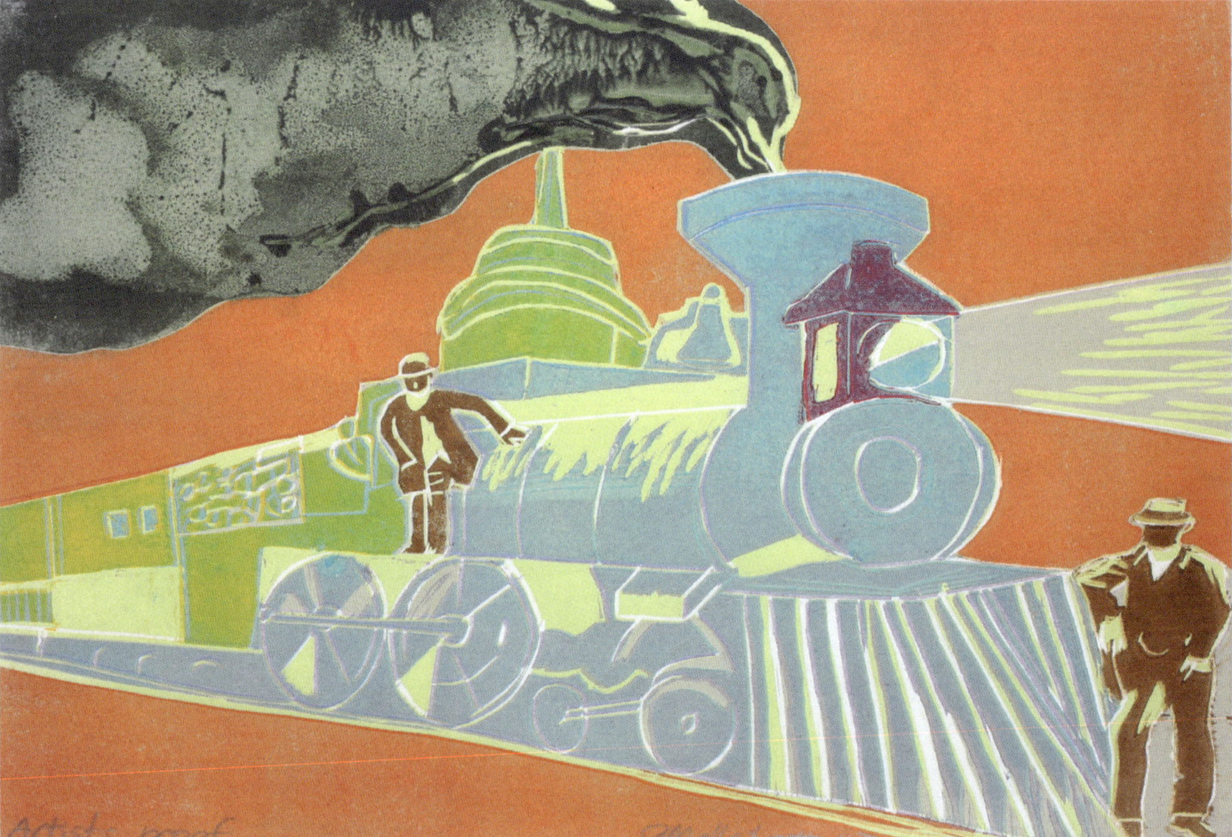

IRON HORSES

By 1869 the arrival of trains – iron horses as they were called by the native Americans – changed the landscape and the demographics permanently.

As they rumbled across the country bringing folks to prospect for gold, or settlers, and the life of the 'Old West', a transformation began.

I imagined the fear rising in the native. The whistle blowing. The rumble, roar, smell of coal burning, the steam and the foreignness of a man-made contraption.

[RWC] [WS]

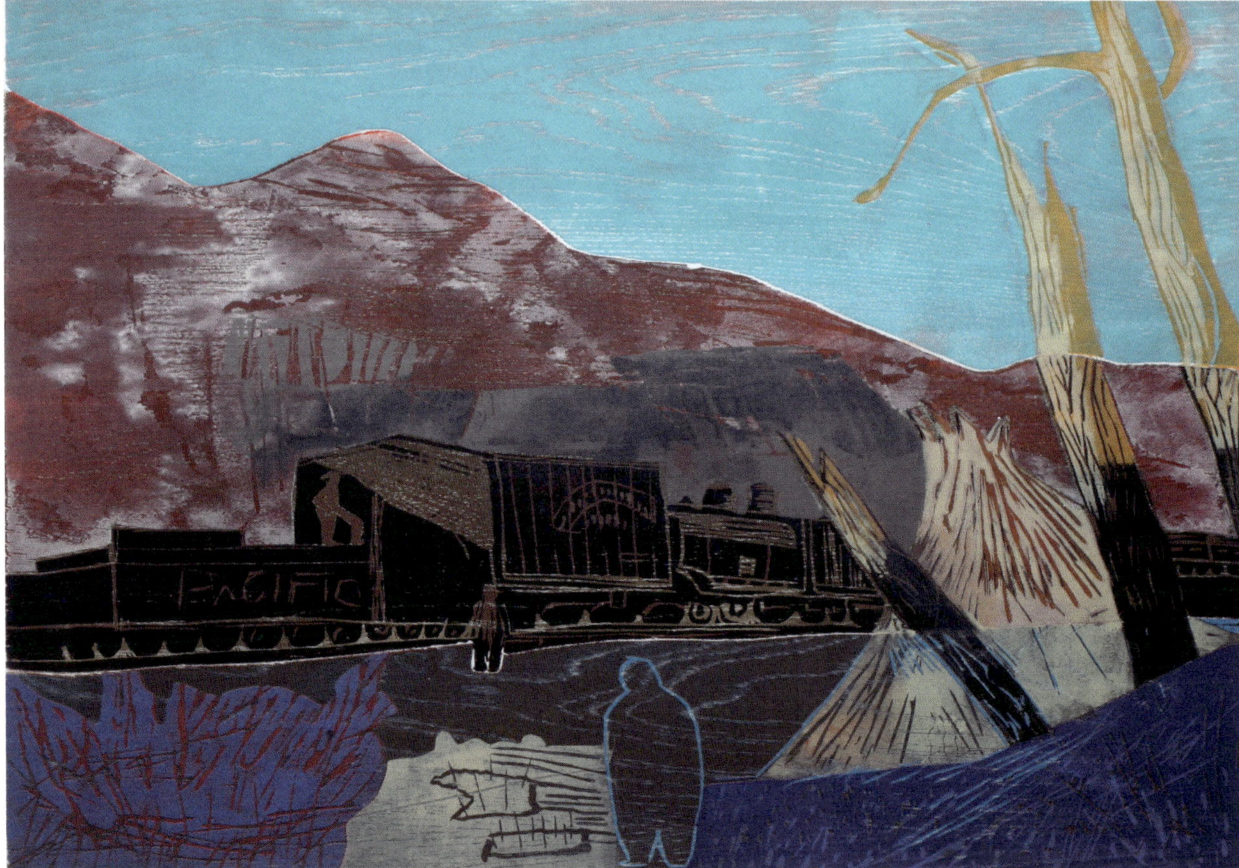

INDIAN CAMP

In this image I created a blue ghost outline of an Indian beside the skins he had just dried after hunting. He had pinned them out, as basic and natural as was possible.

And then... rhoom !... comes the train, breaking up the stillness. Shattering his natural world.

In the woodcut technique I use the natural grain of the wood in the sky.

[RWC] [WS]

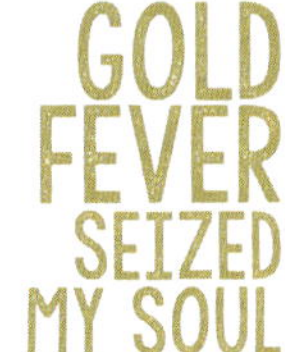

THE COWBOY WATCH:
THE LOOK-OUT
TO ROB THE TRAIN

The train was bringing money and mail and people into the wilderness – the perfect target for a robbery. This gang of cowboys is ready.

I wanted the perspective on this to be looking down from the lookout…

The layout was divided into sections for this, with the bandits up close and the train below. It emphasises the difficult terrain, the wilderness and the ruggedness. Steam from the train billows out as the figures stand awaiting their moment.

[RWC] [WS]

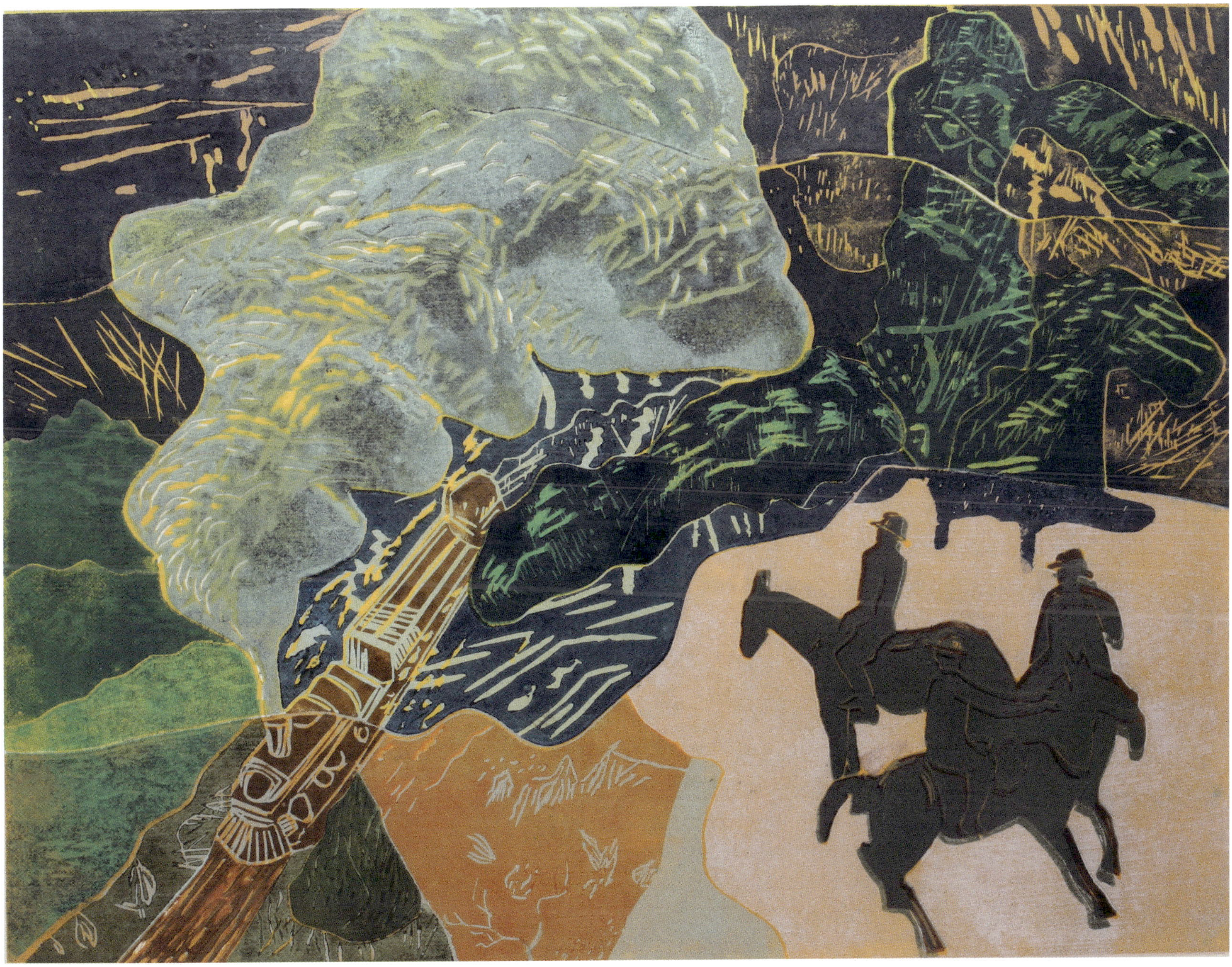

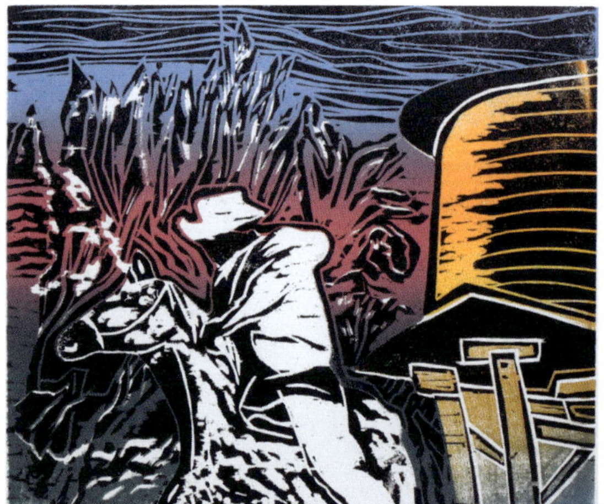

KNOCKING THE WATER BUTT #1 & #2

These action prints of cowboys knocking over a water butt are nearly identical, but they illustrate the effect of using more, or less, detail.

[RWC]

MORE WATCHING BANDITS
UNDER A PINE TREE *(opposite)*

This composition is designed to emote the ever-present unknown dangers and threats. A complex example of a reductive woodcut.

[RWC]

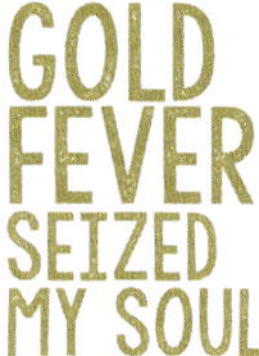

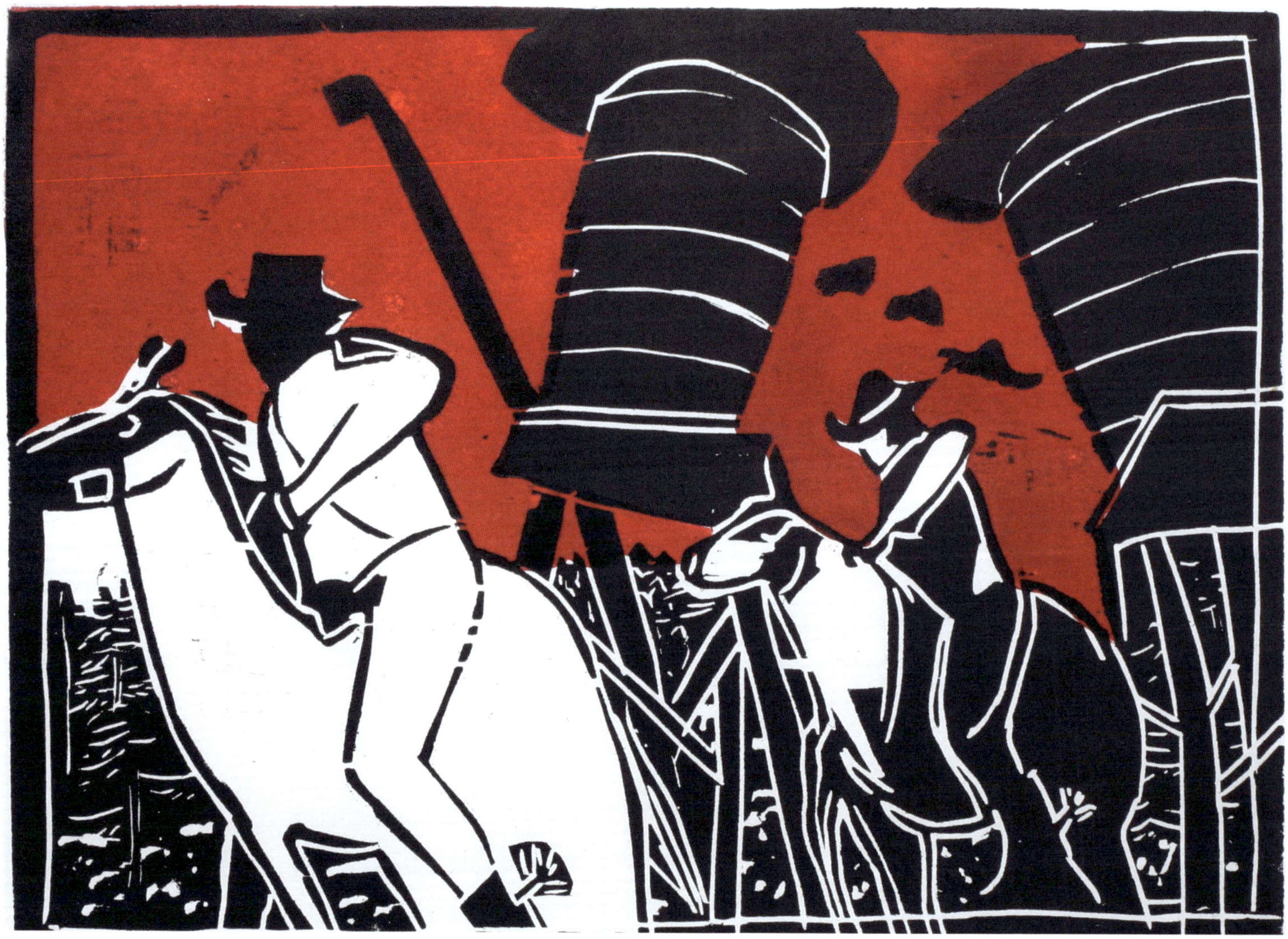

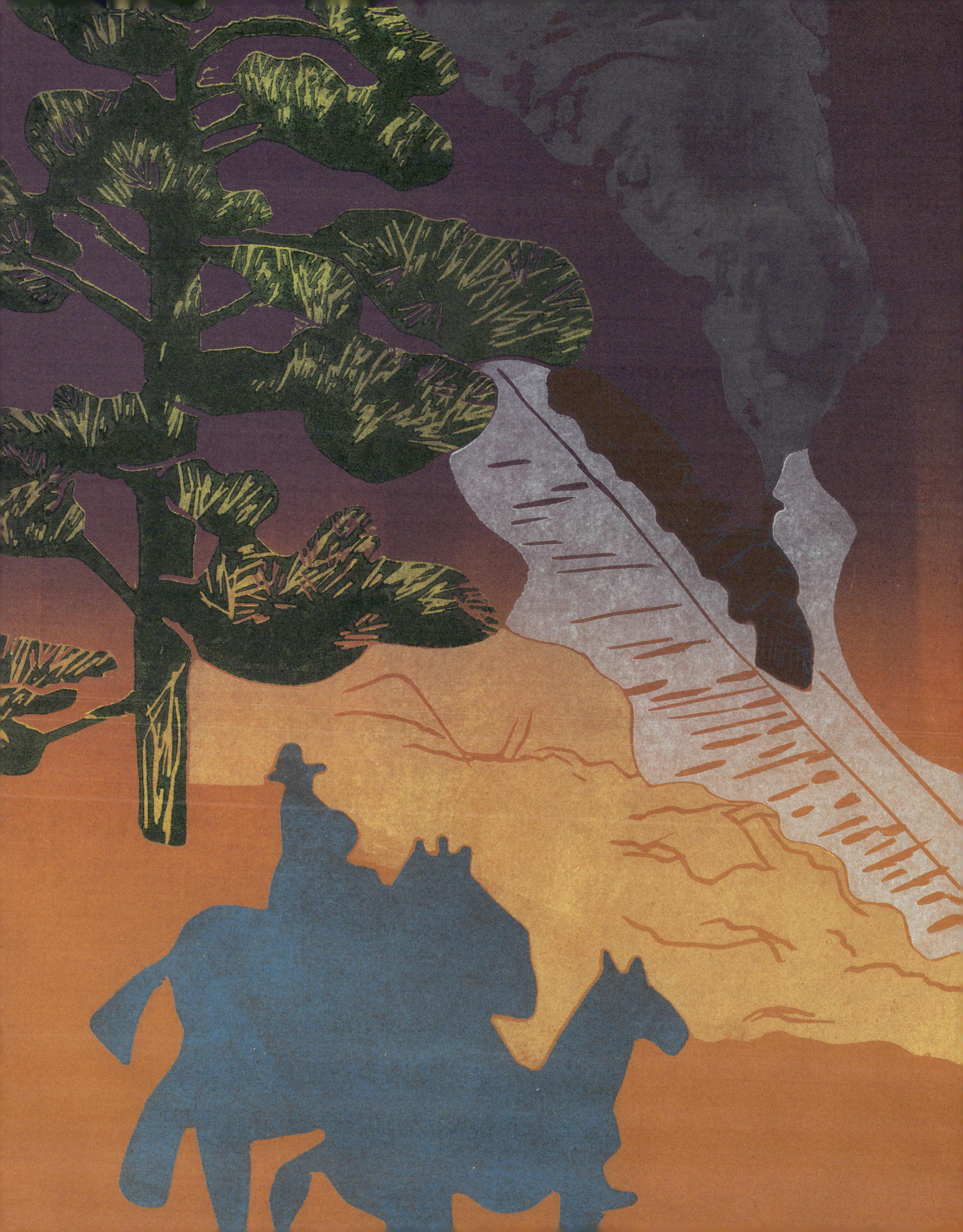

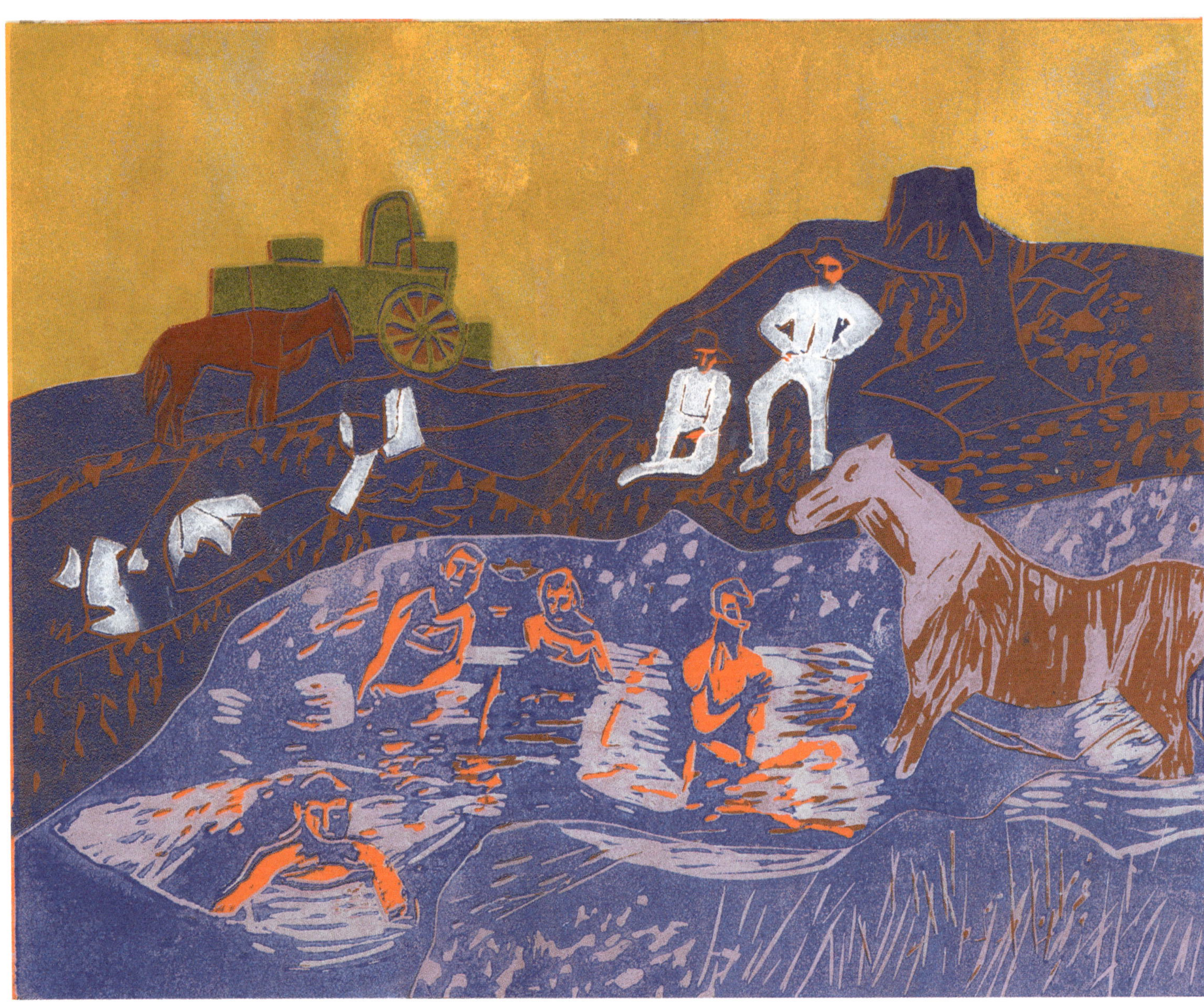

COWBOYS AT THE WATER HOLE

By the 1870s, thirteen or so cowboys would ride in positions around a herd of 2,500 cattle on a long haul from Texas to Chicago through prairie and Indian territory. Hot and dry, tired and thirsty, it was hard work all for $100 – the price of a new hat and boots.

This print aims to capture the hardships of life in the Wild West. The cowboys catch sight of a pool of water and stop, pull up the chuck wagon, strip down and jump in! What a relief!

I wanted to show the exhaustion of the men, how they flopped down in the bright morning sky.

[RWC]

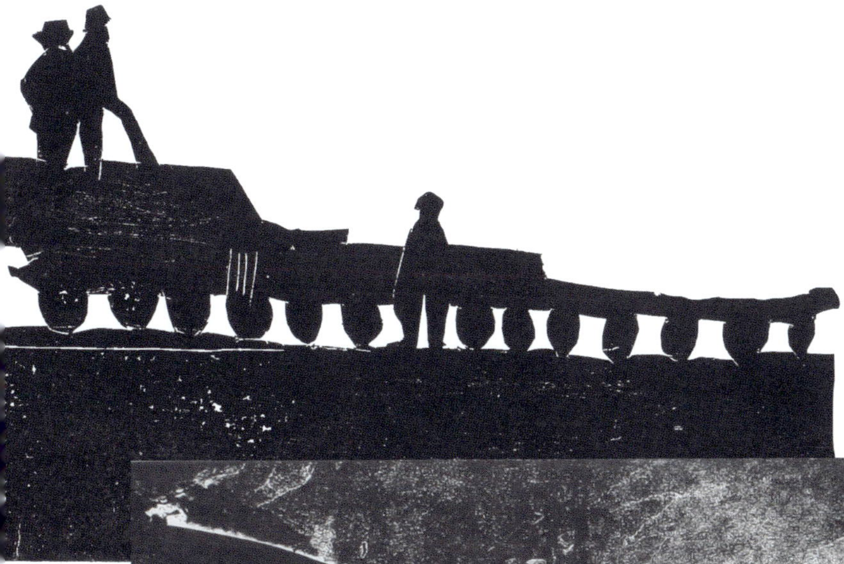

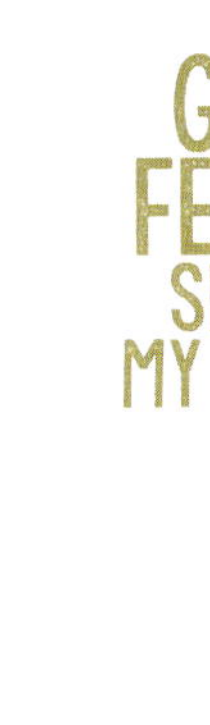

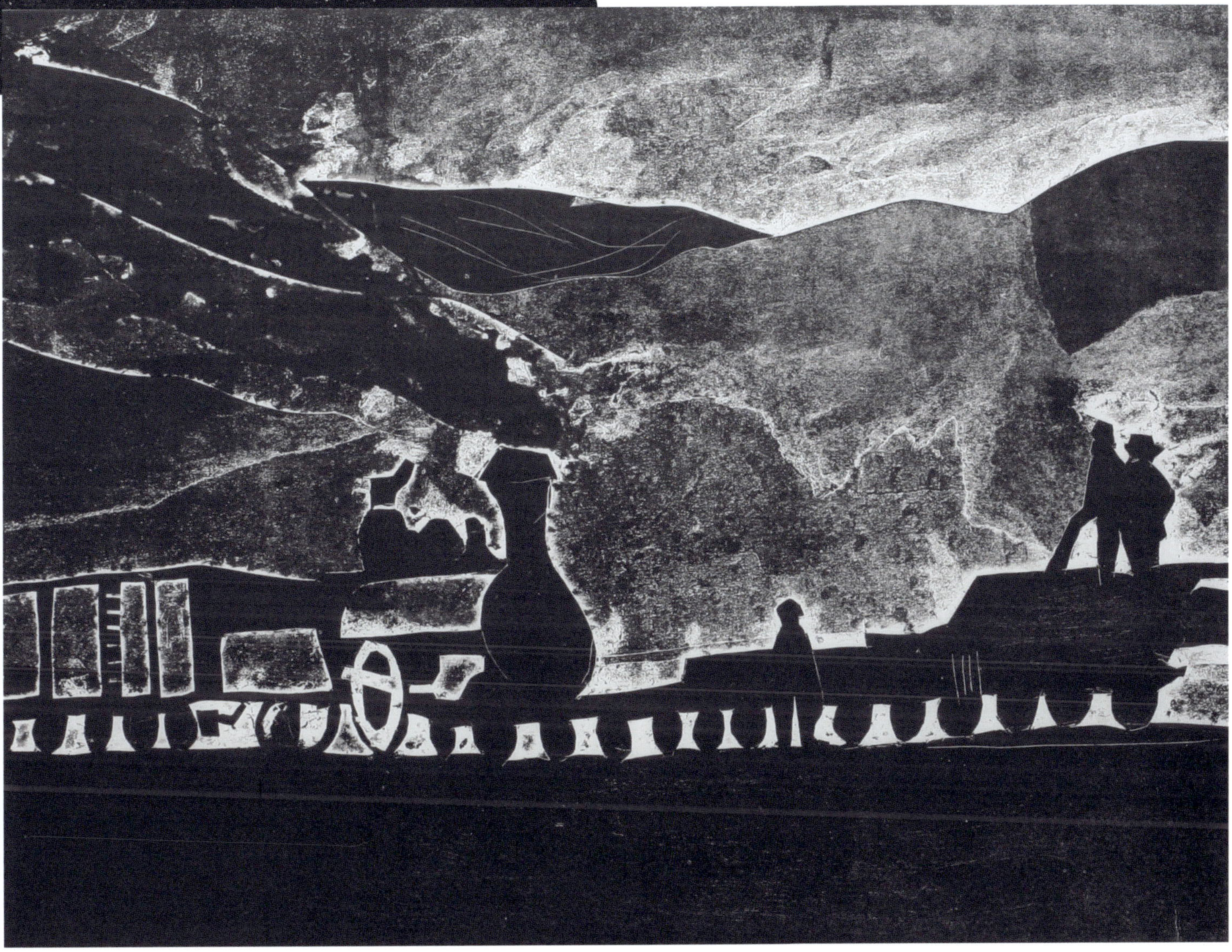

THE IRON HORSE AT DUSK

I wanted to express the menacing advance of the train which would change everything.

[WC]

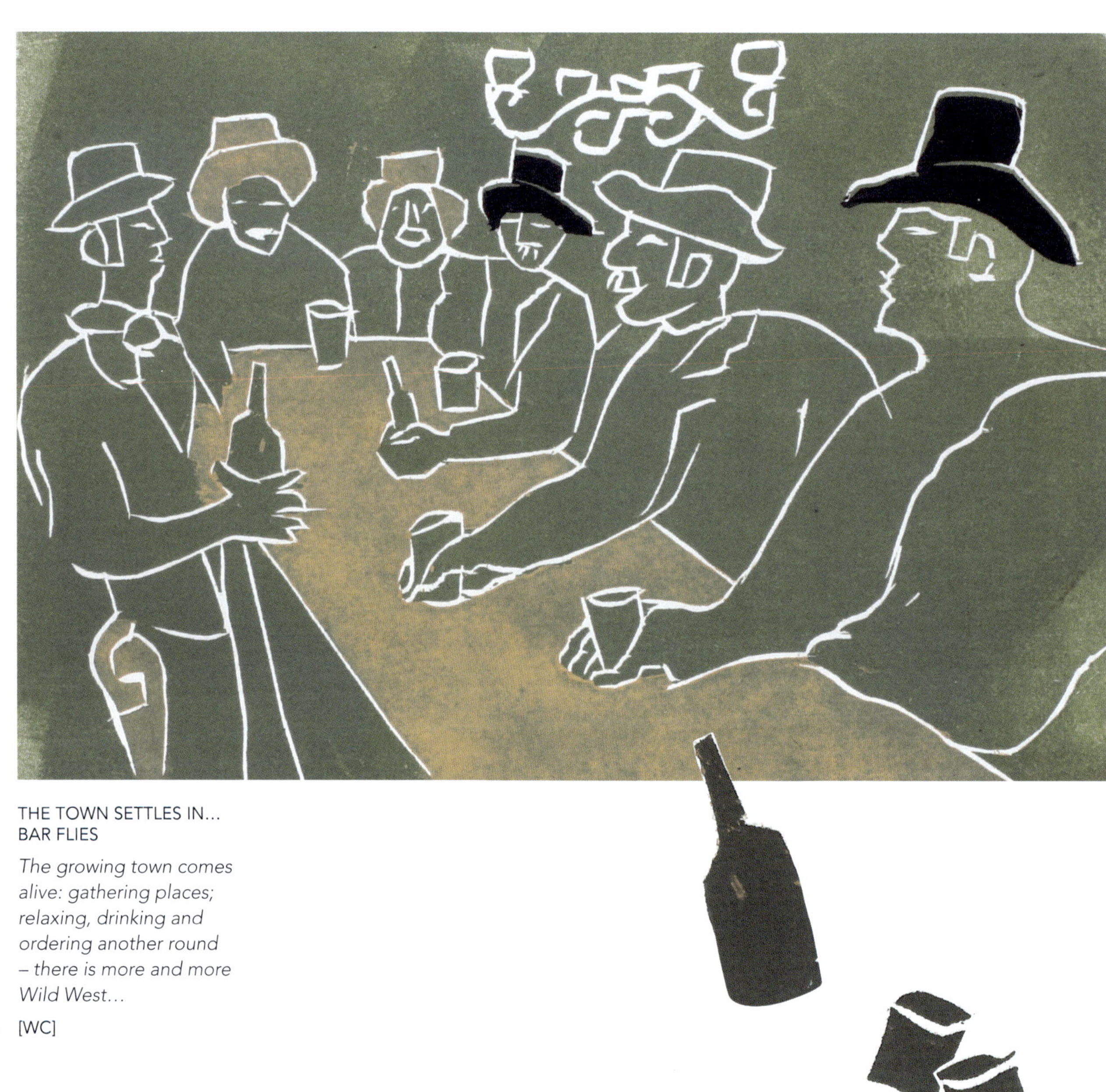

THE TOWN SETTLES IN…
BAR FLIES

The growing town comes alive: gathering places; relaxing, drinking and ordering another round – there is more and more Wild West…

[WC]

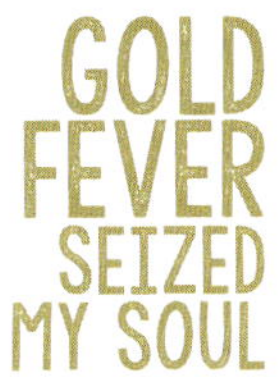

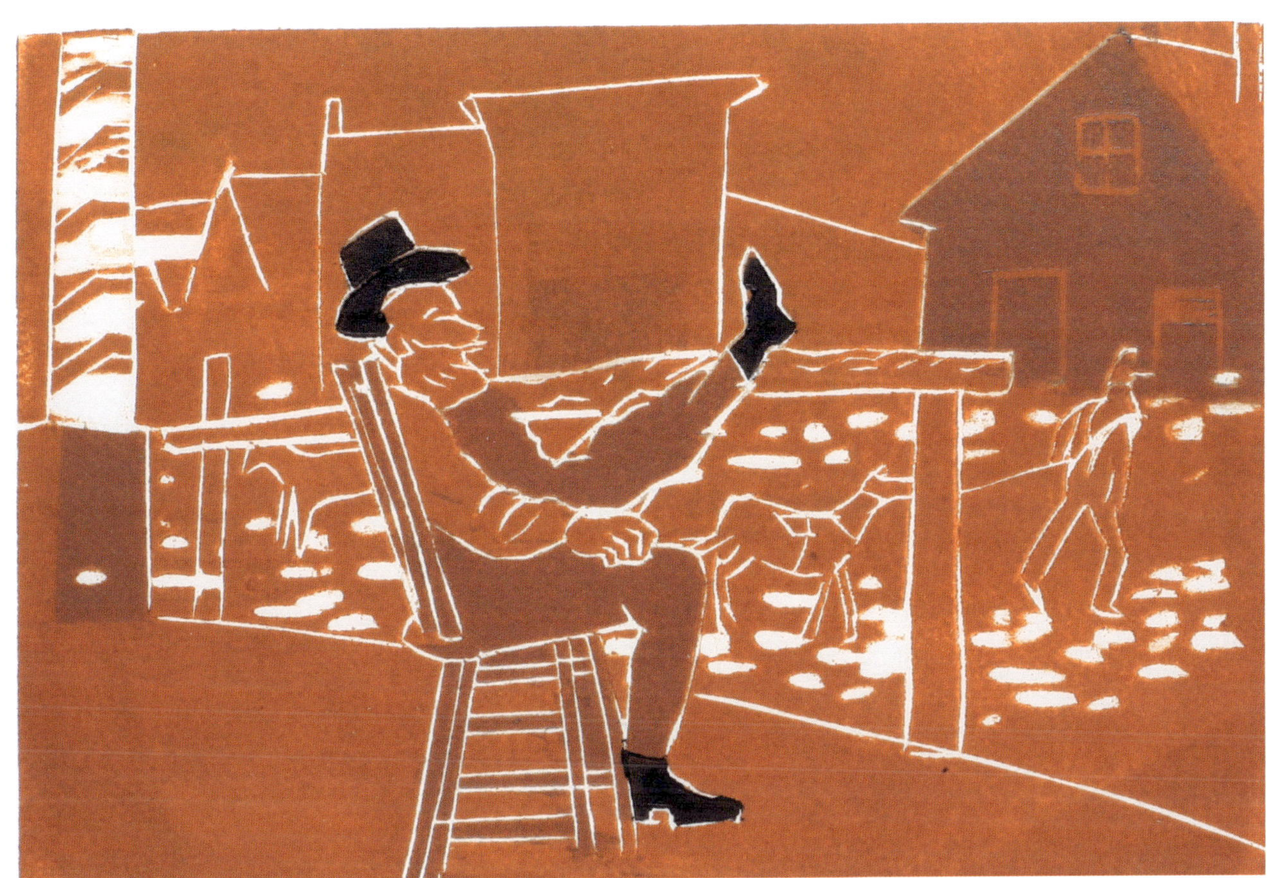

**THE TOWN SETTLES IN…
A GOOD STRETCH**

In the town folk settle in: watching the street with feet up – life becomes more comfortable.

[WC]

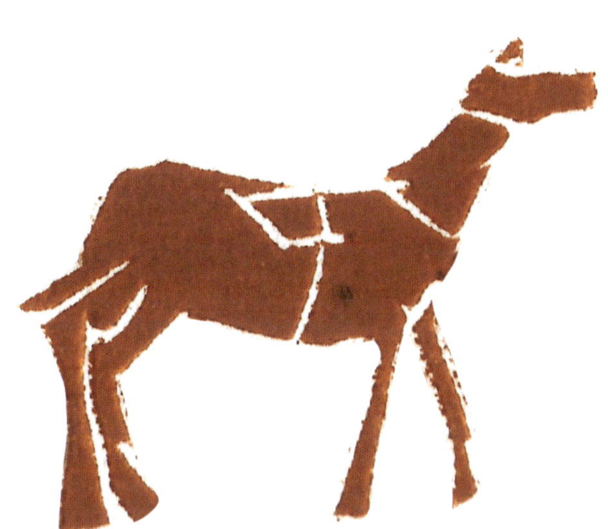

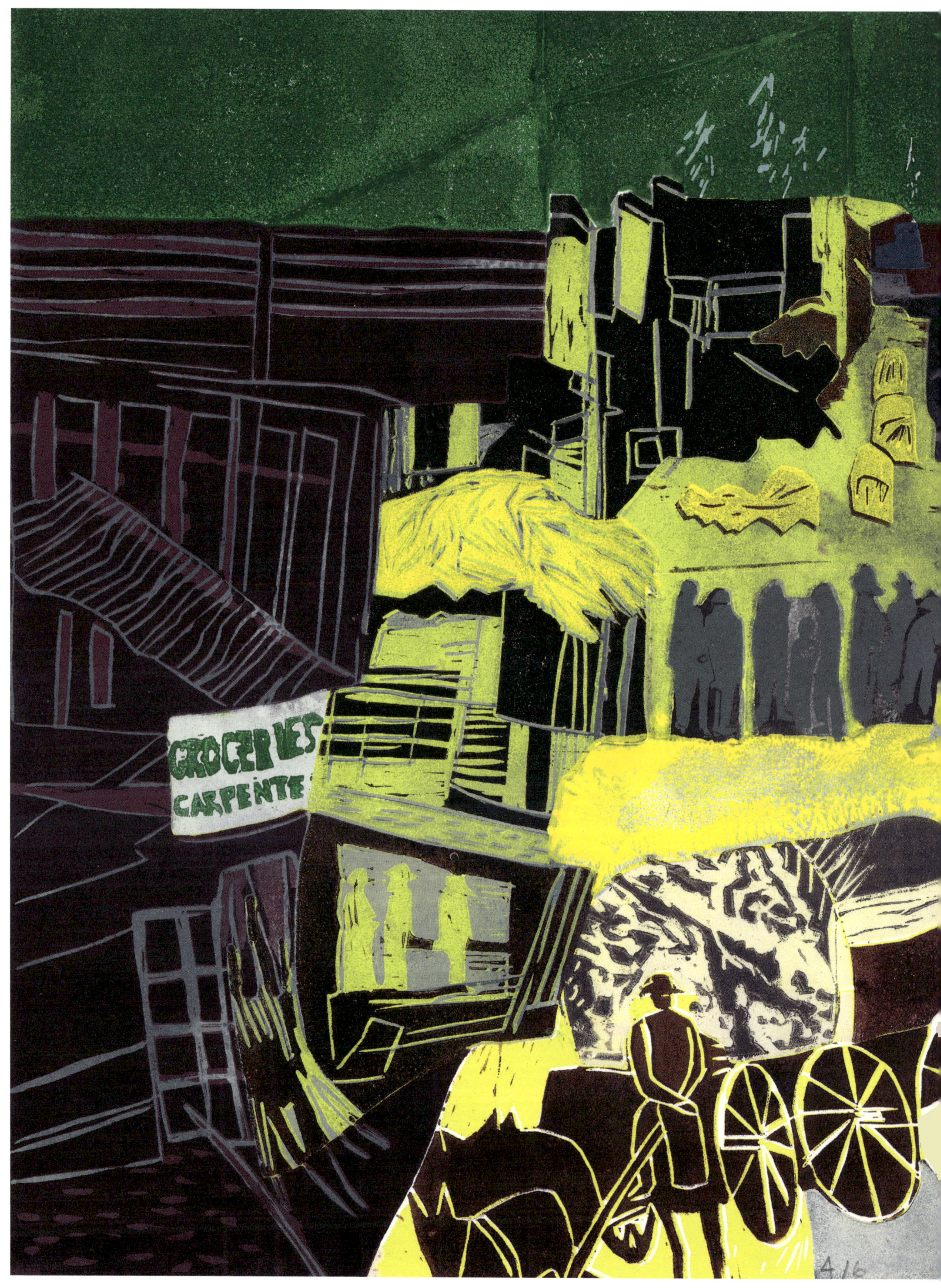
GROCERIES
CARPENTE

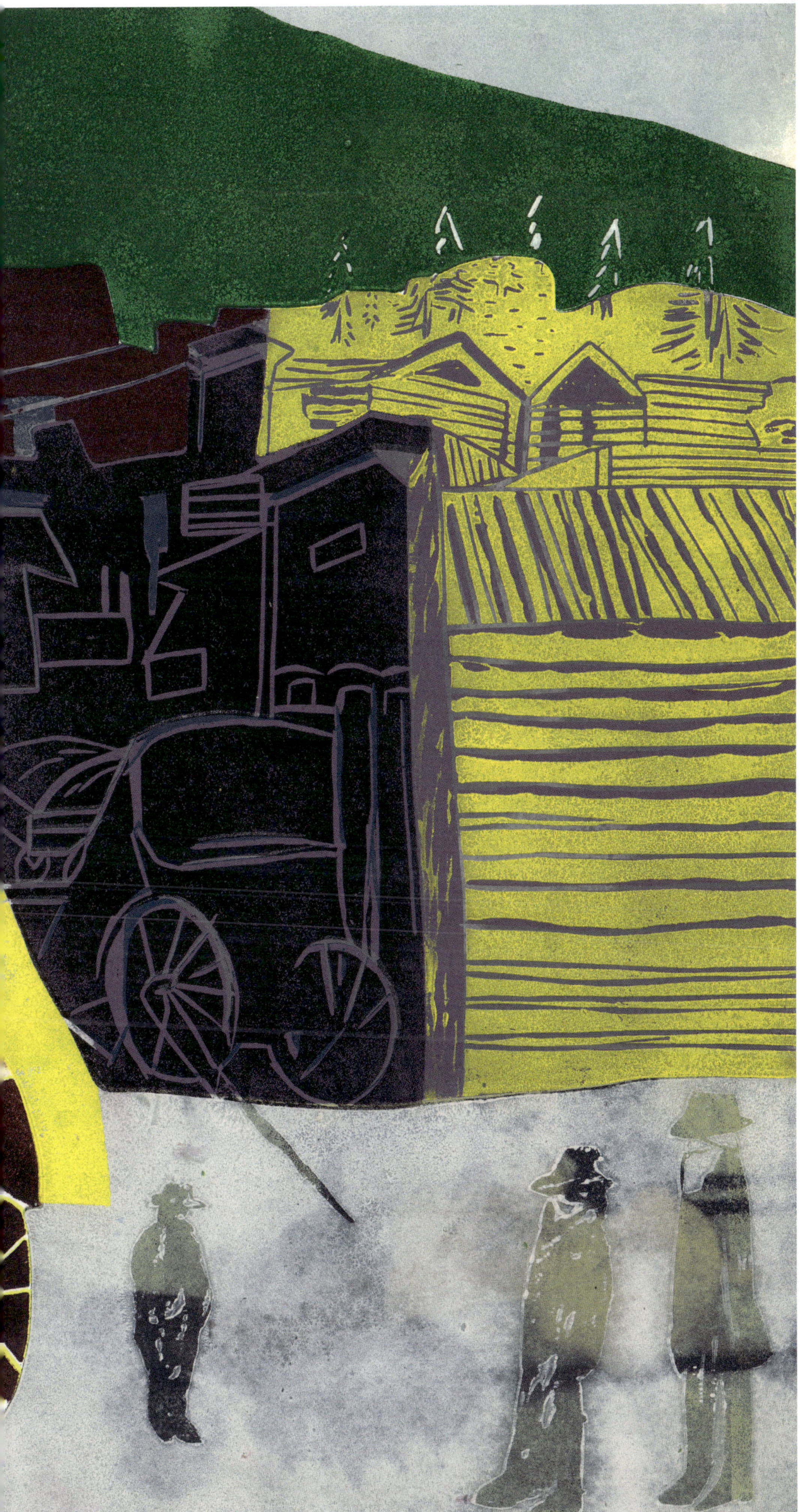

LAST CHANCE GULCH

One town was actually named Last Chance Gulch because if they didn't find gold there, they never would.

Showing the pervading California light – very bright sun or deep shadows – was my goal here, and a strong memory of my own childhood. It was in those contrasts that the drama was set.

Also the lurking shadowy figures of the men, who must have spent a lot of time waiting. Waiting for the wagons to be filled and ready, waiting for the other men to be ready, dreaming of the riches to be had!

[RWC]

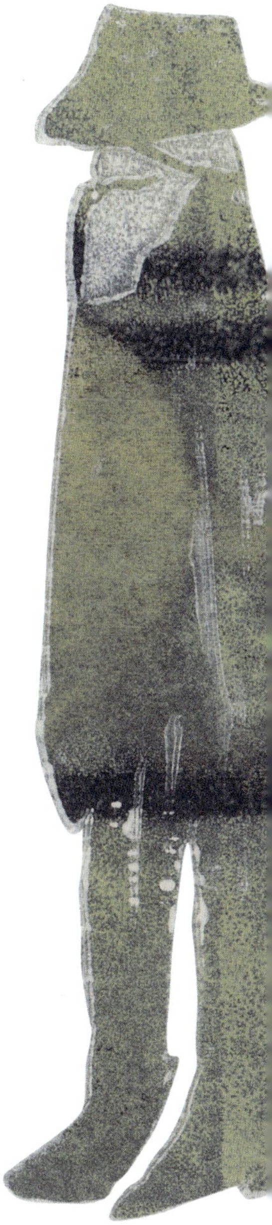

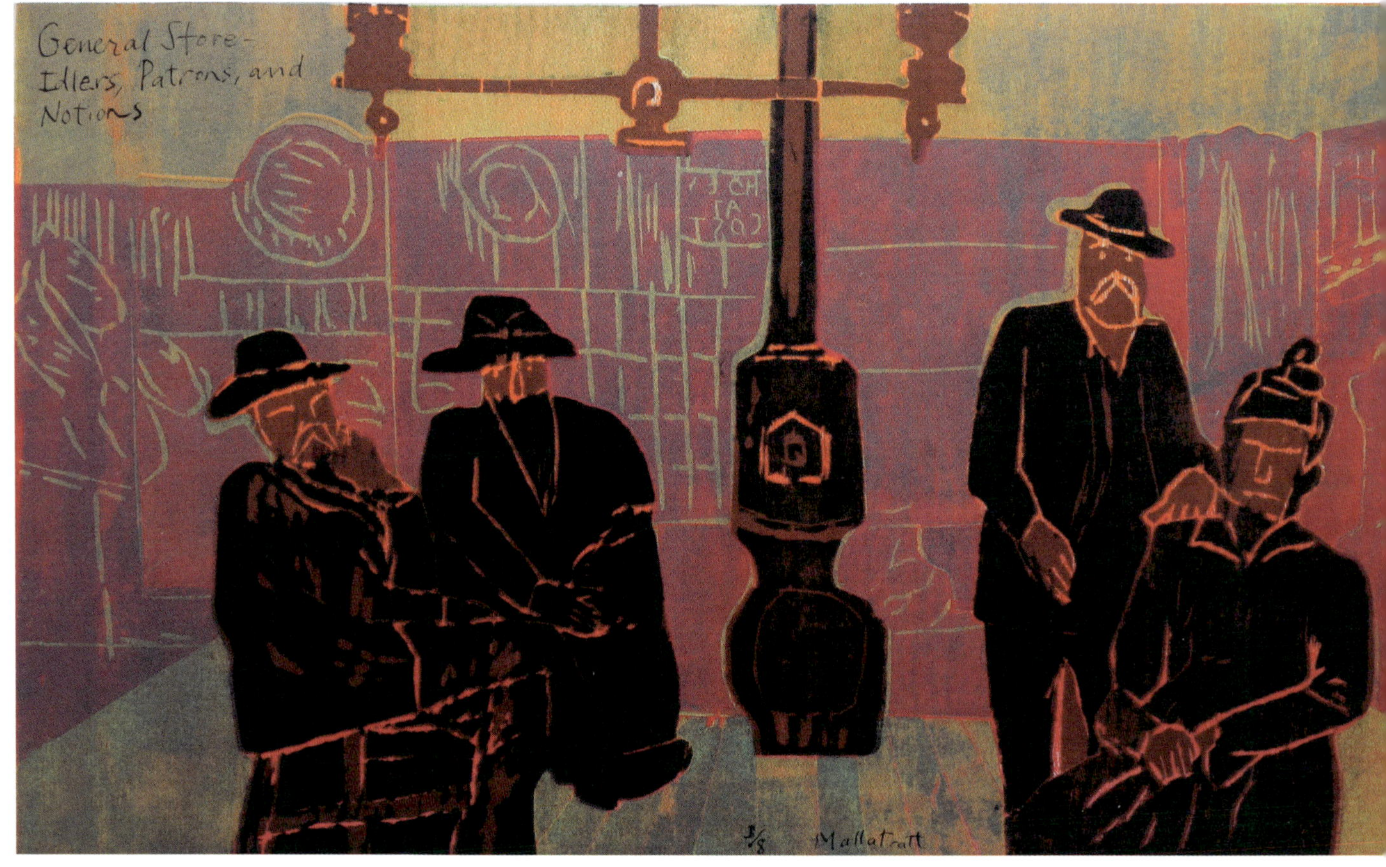

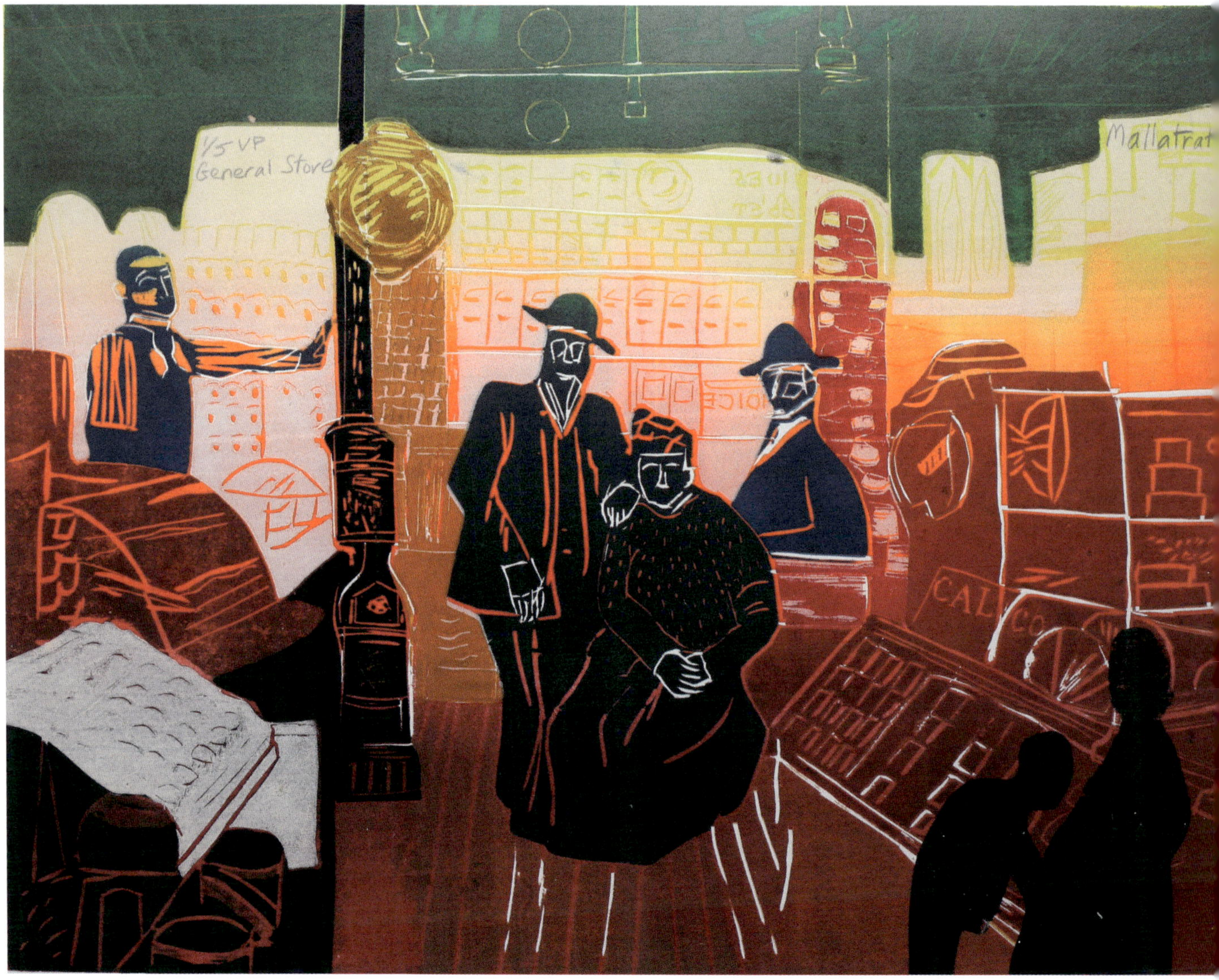

THE STORE #1 & #2

The store keeper was an "all purpose practitioner to the human condition... two of the staple items found on his shelves: whisky to enlarge the spirit and bibles to assuage the soul". He was depended on for everything from wedding clothes to croup medicine, coal oil to opium and snake root.

It was a town centre for gathering around the pot-bellied stove and gossiping: politics, news, the weather…

These Victorian folk are using it as a place to be seen, and wear their best outfits. In these prints I wanted to create an atmosphere of the shop and its folk.

[RWC]

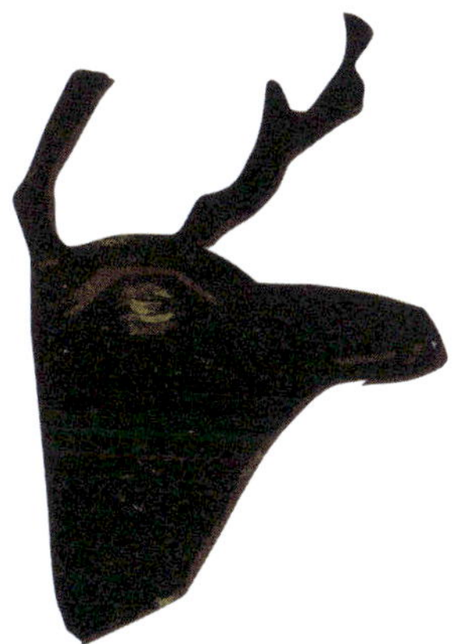

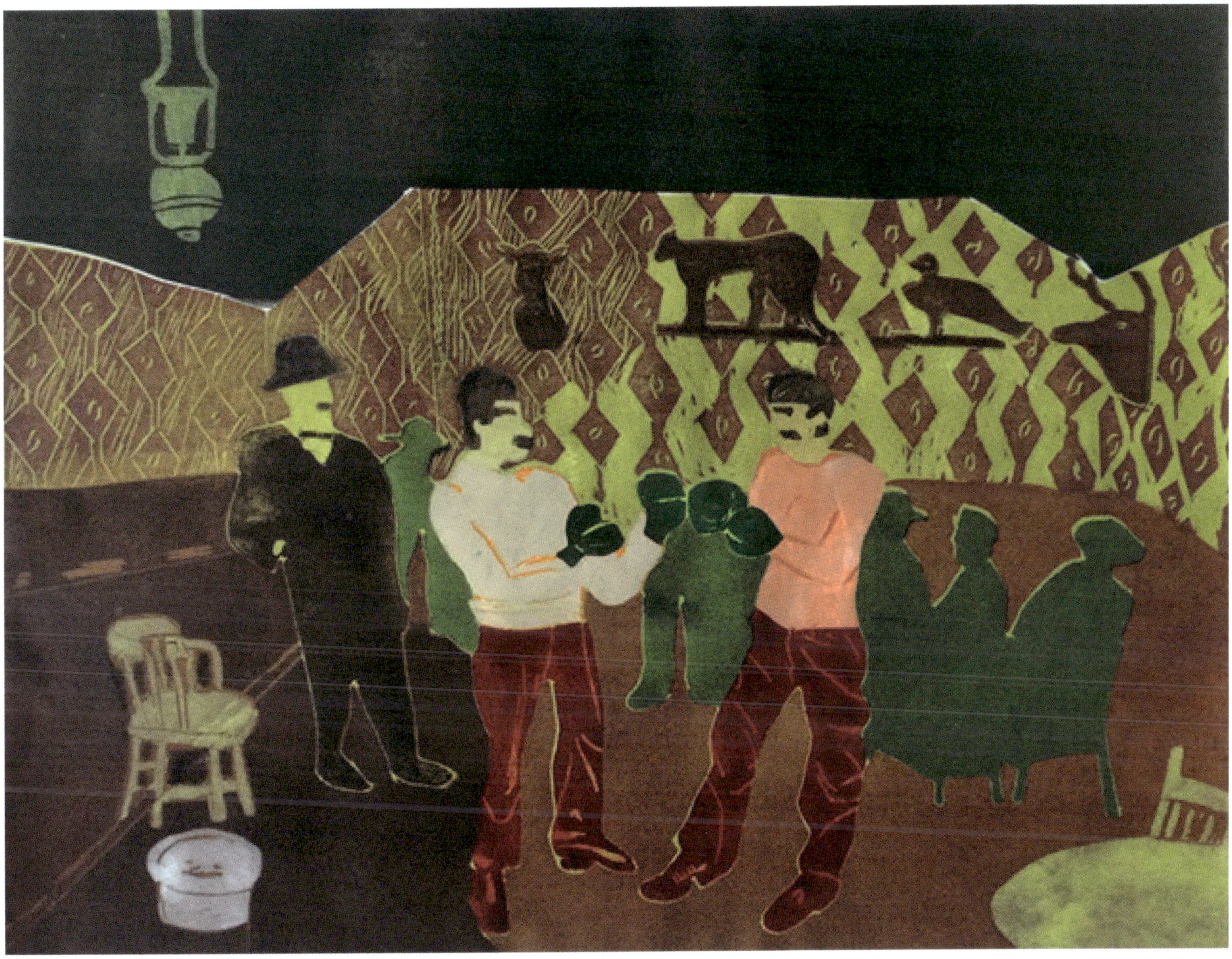

THE SALOON

At a saloon, an audience of drinkers and card players watch a boxing match. The men needed to fight it out. A hat would be passed at the end of the match and "a rousing battle meant a good purse".

I imagined a saloon atmosphere: wallpaper, stuffed dead animals on the wall, the suited man in contrast to the sweaty boxers, the spittoon on the floor. The colours contrasting with the bright light of the west outside; dark and gloomy.

[RWC]

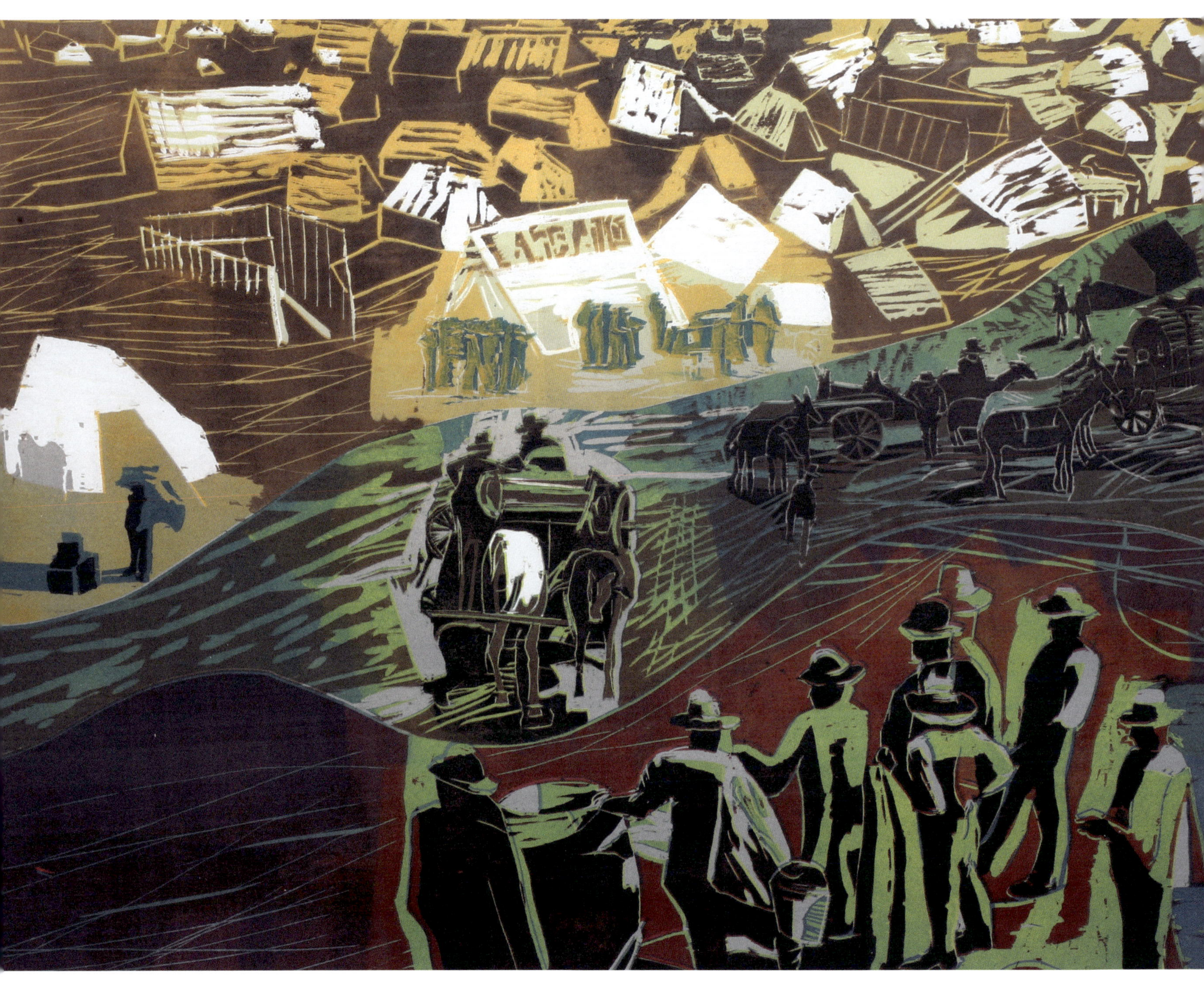

THE TOWN THAT WAS FIVE DAYS OLD

New town settlements were growing like wildfire. As people moved west in crowds, it took just 24 hours to transform a sleepy watering spot for cross-country trains to develop into a city of 10,000 inhabitants. Settlers raced to claim their land.

One such town was to be positioned on the spot where the eastbound train from California and the westbound train from New York were planned to meet, thus putting it in the key position to be the place that literally connected up the country.

After five days the route changed and the town ended up being nowhere near the correct spot. Tents and clapboard houses were taken down in the same rush that they appeared, and the town all but disappeared.

[RWC]

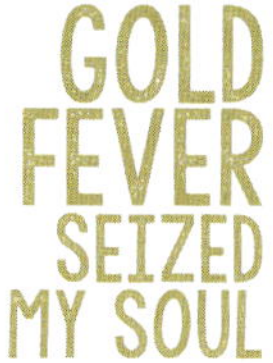

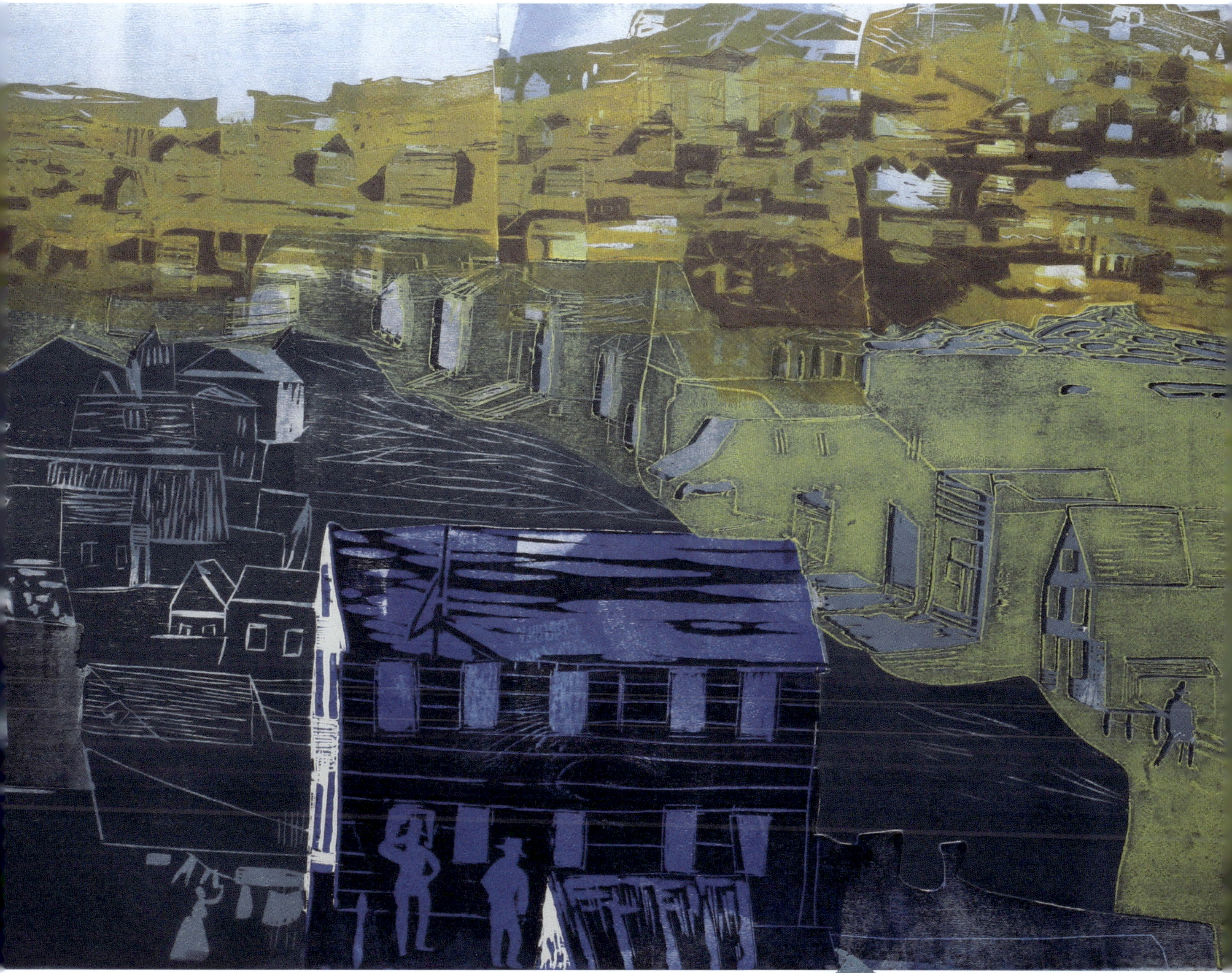

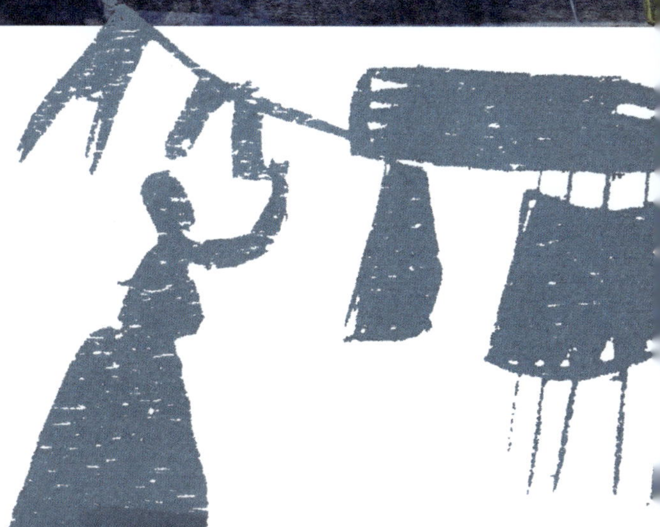

SAN FRANCISCO

Early days. Bright sun and deep shadows as a new country unfolds. This town of new buildings which were prefabricated in the east, was shipped around Cape Horn in South America, and assembled in San Francisco.

[RWC]

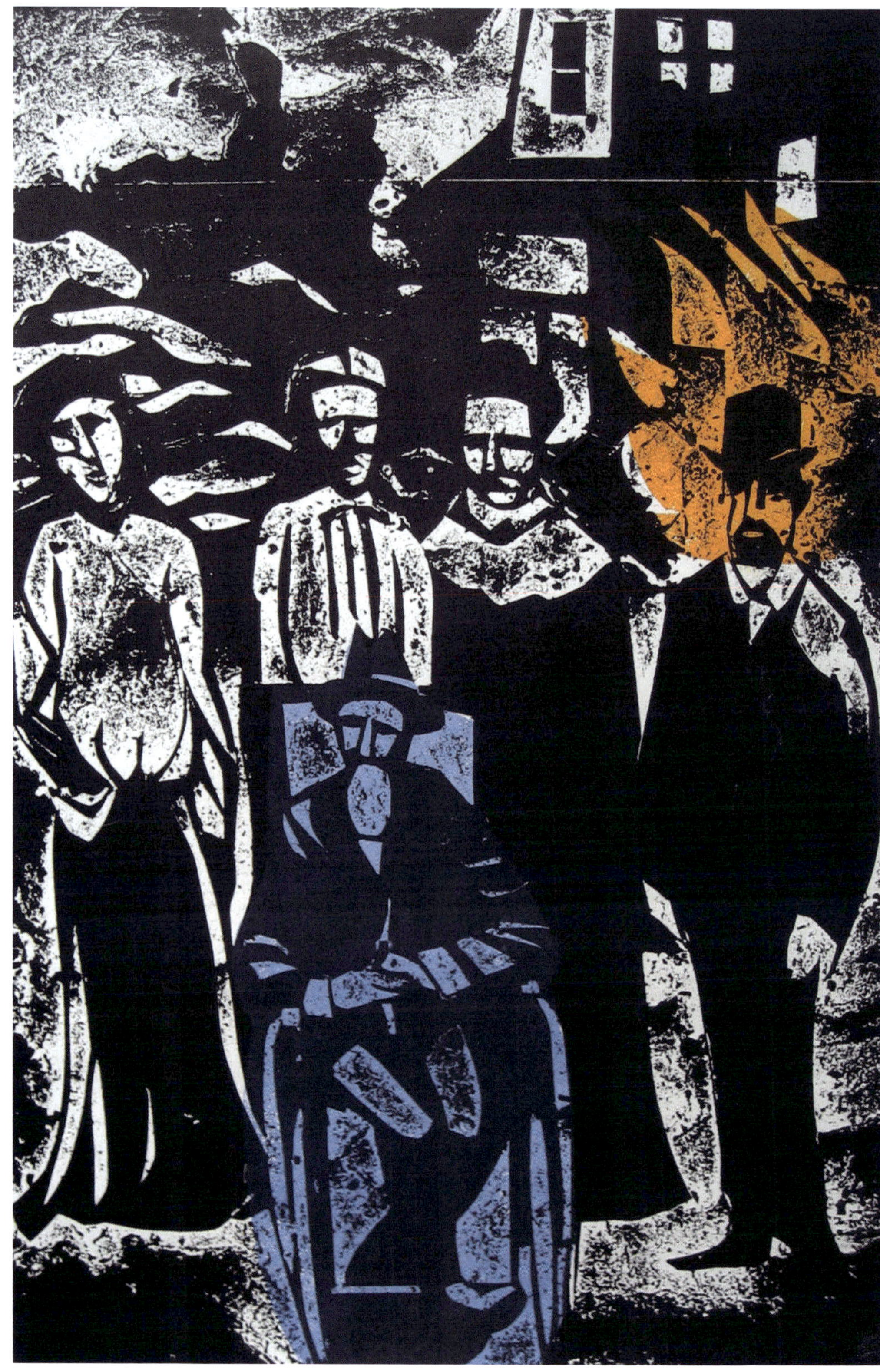

THE FIRST OVERLAND SETTLERS

In my mother's desk, tucked away, was a typed manuscript written in old age by my great-great grandmother Esther Sweasey Axton. That manuscript was the basis of my understanding of our family history.

My maternal grandmother was Esther Jones, a descendant of The Sweasey Axton family: the first overland settlers in Northern California.

This collagraph shows them gathered together. The lighterman is now in a wheelchair, old and frail. Behind him, his wife and offspring have become his carers.

We see the aging effect of hardship and determination. The house on fire suggests their vulnerability as they fought through.

By the early 20th century they had settled comfortably in grand Victorian houses, becoming pillars of the community: state senator, eye doctors and land owners.

[COL]

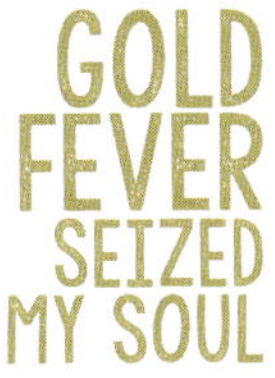

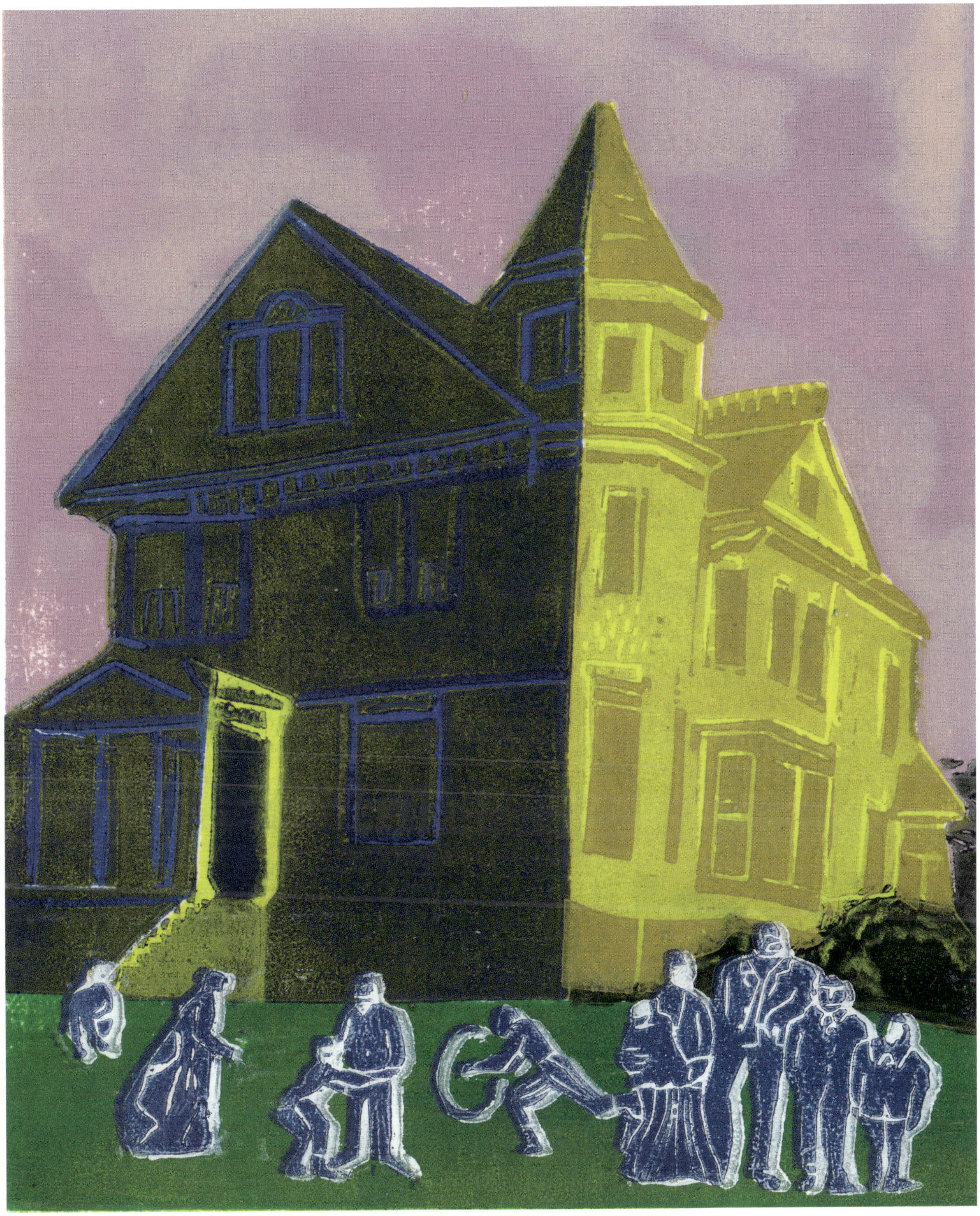

JONES HOUSE
ON CLARK STREET,
EUREKA

*This large wooden
Victorian house built
c. 1900 was a large,
ostentatious and
impressive place for
them to end up.*

*The Joneses had seven
children to fill the house
– one of which was my
grandmother, Esther
Jones Nelson.*

[WC]

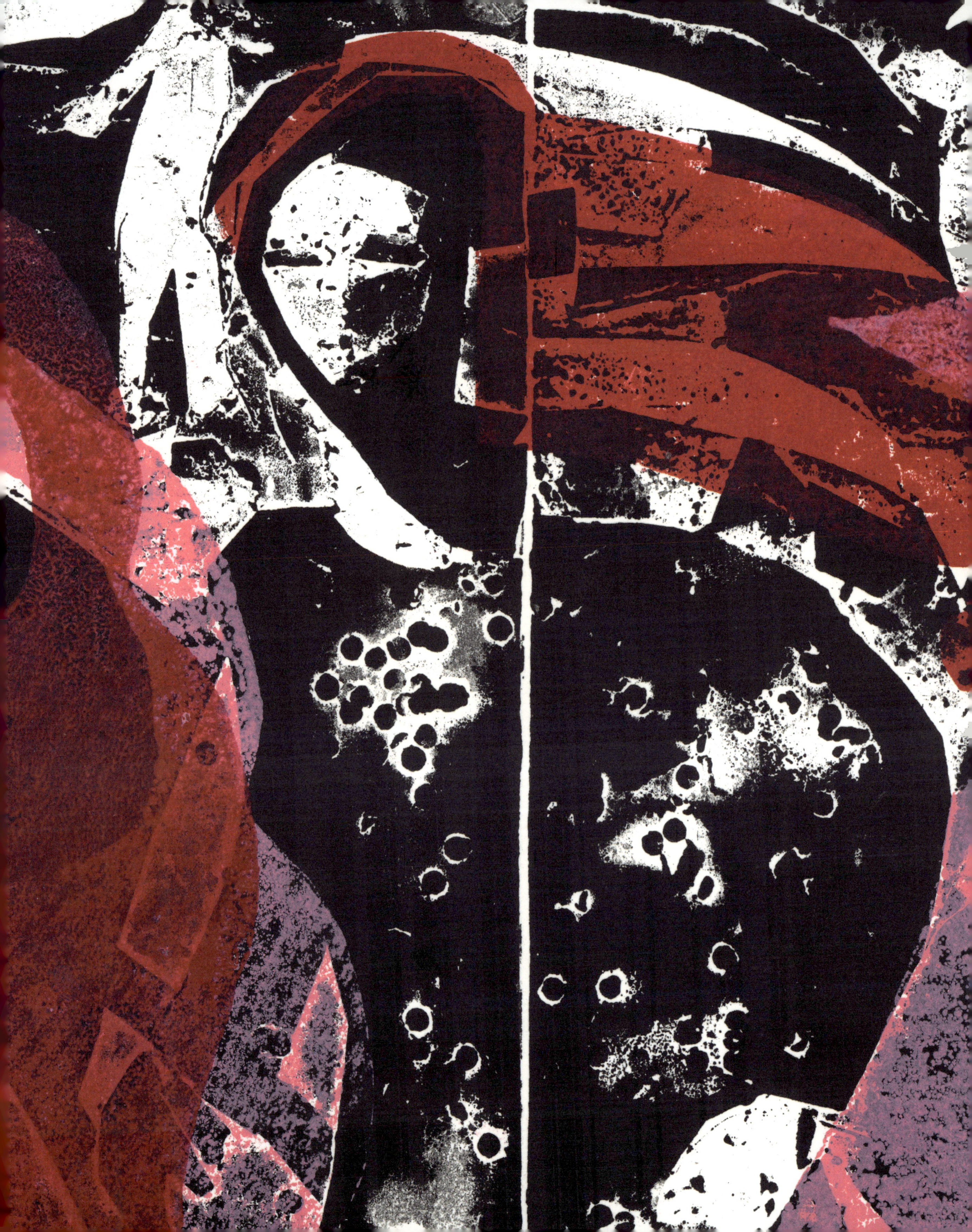

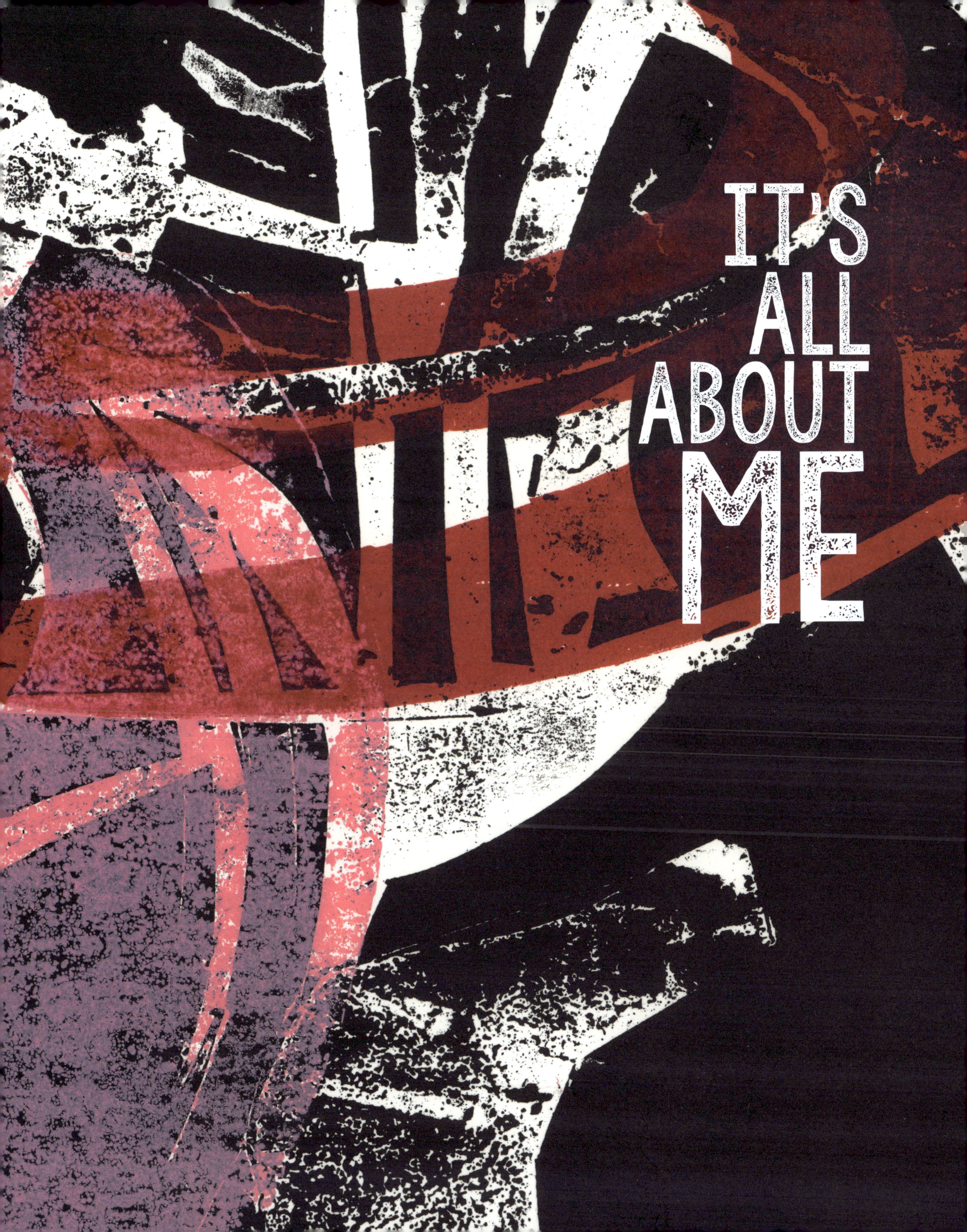
IT'S
ALL
ABOUT
ME

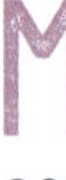

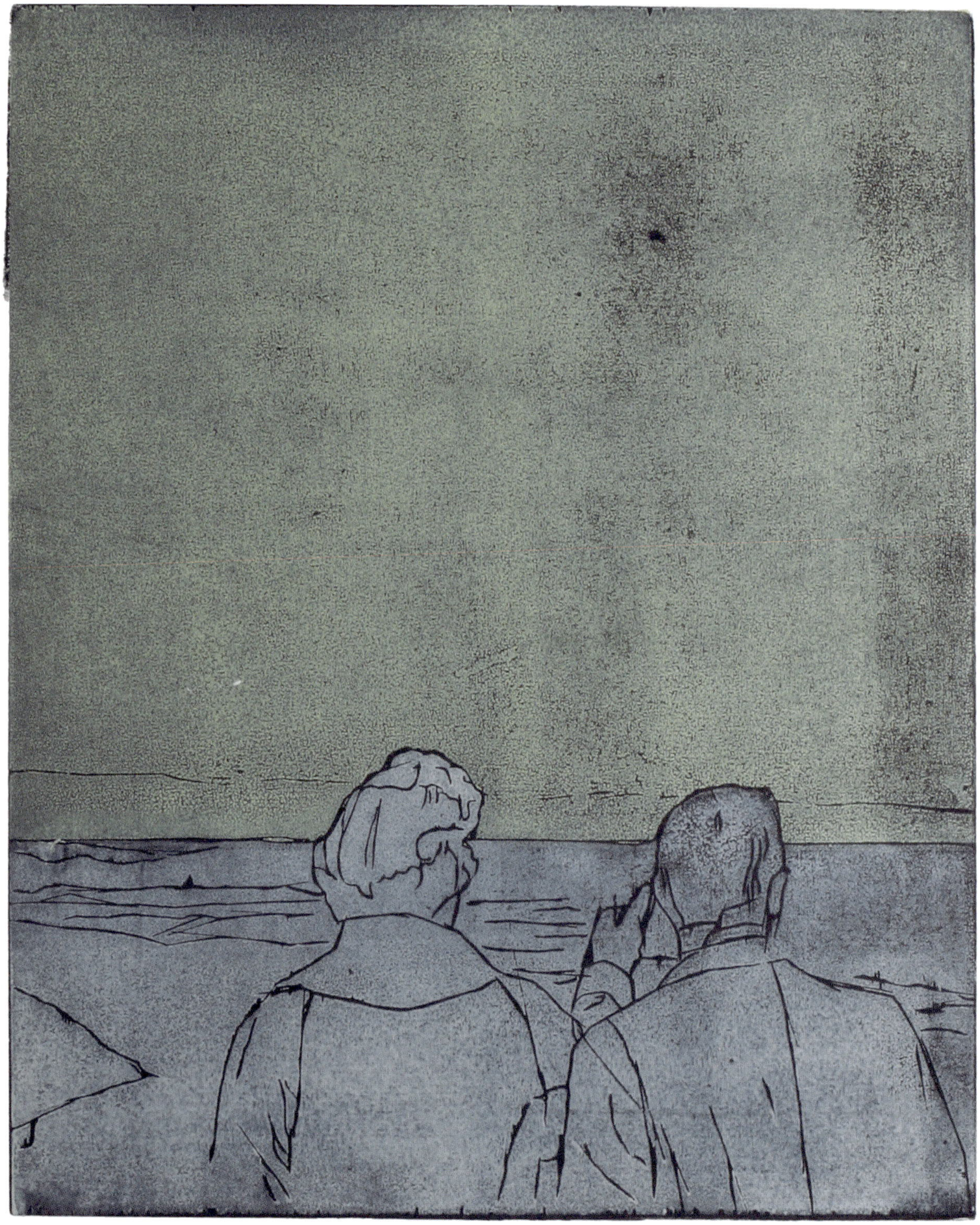

POINTING

This shows my parents conferring. My mother is pointing into the distance. It shows them from the back; an angle I knew well.

[WC]

I WAS BORN IN 1947, and grew up in San Francisco. The aquatint below draws on memories of my early life; playing, bike riding and hanging out on the streets of residential San Francisco. The characteristic telephone pole and Studebaker truck in the background were commonplace on the streets at that time.

As soon as I was able, and had the space in my life (family grown…) I began to take my art seriously. I experimented with painting, but found myself drawn to printmaking.

Through this medium, I was able to reflect on my past and develop a way to express my response to the objects and people around me.

Each print was a surprise. Ink and wood together seemed to have a voice, and as a print progressed, it spoke to me as a person might, suggesting which way to go as it emerged off the press. The photographic source would be the starting point, but the tones, shapes and marks shifted and changed as they were proofed. *"Secrets were being unearthed…"*

Technically, I alternate between collagraph and woodcut. Both seem to work to communicate intense feelings.

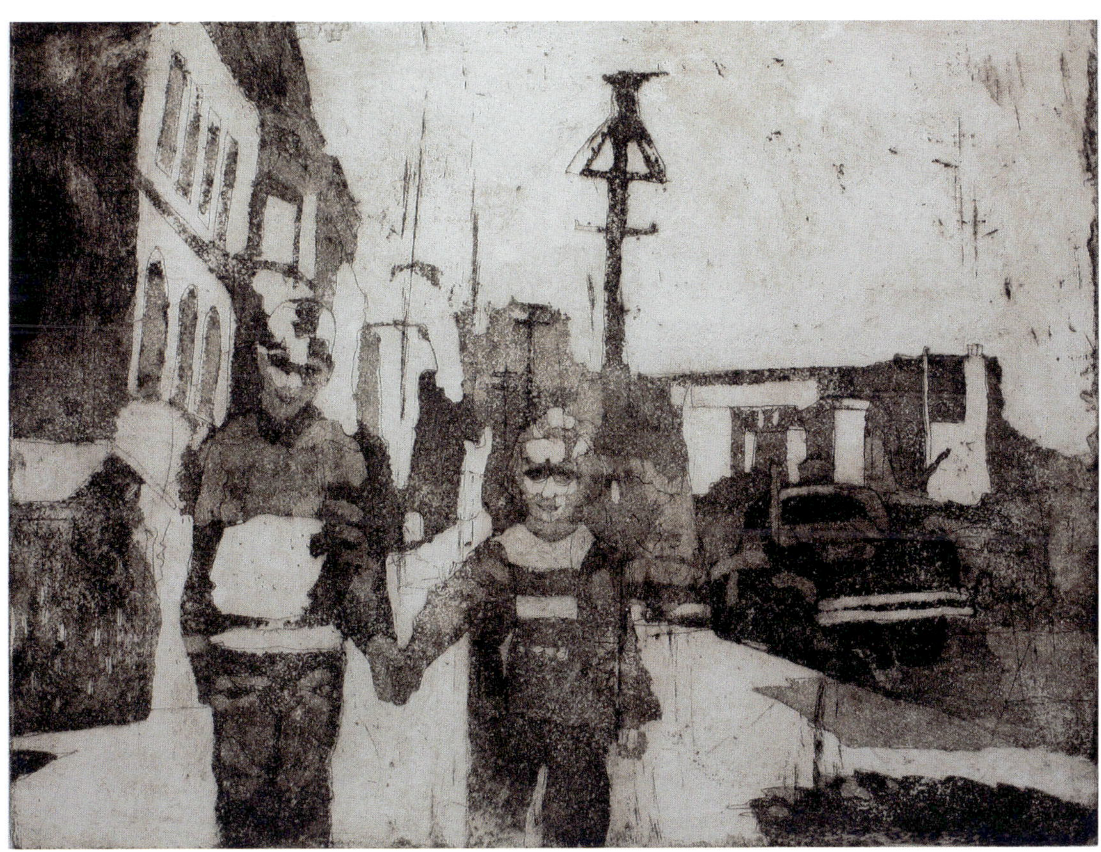

WALNUT STREET
This is printed with sepia ink to enhance the 'old time' feel.
[AQT]

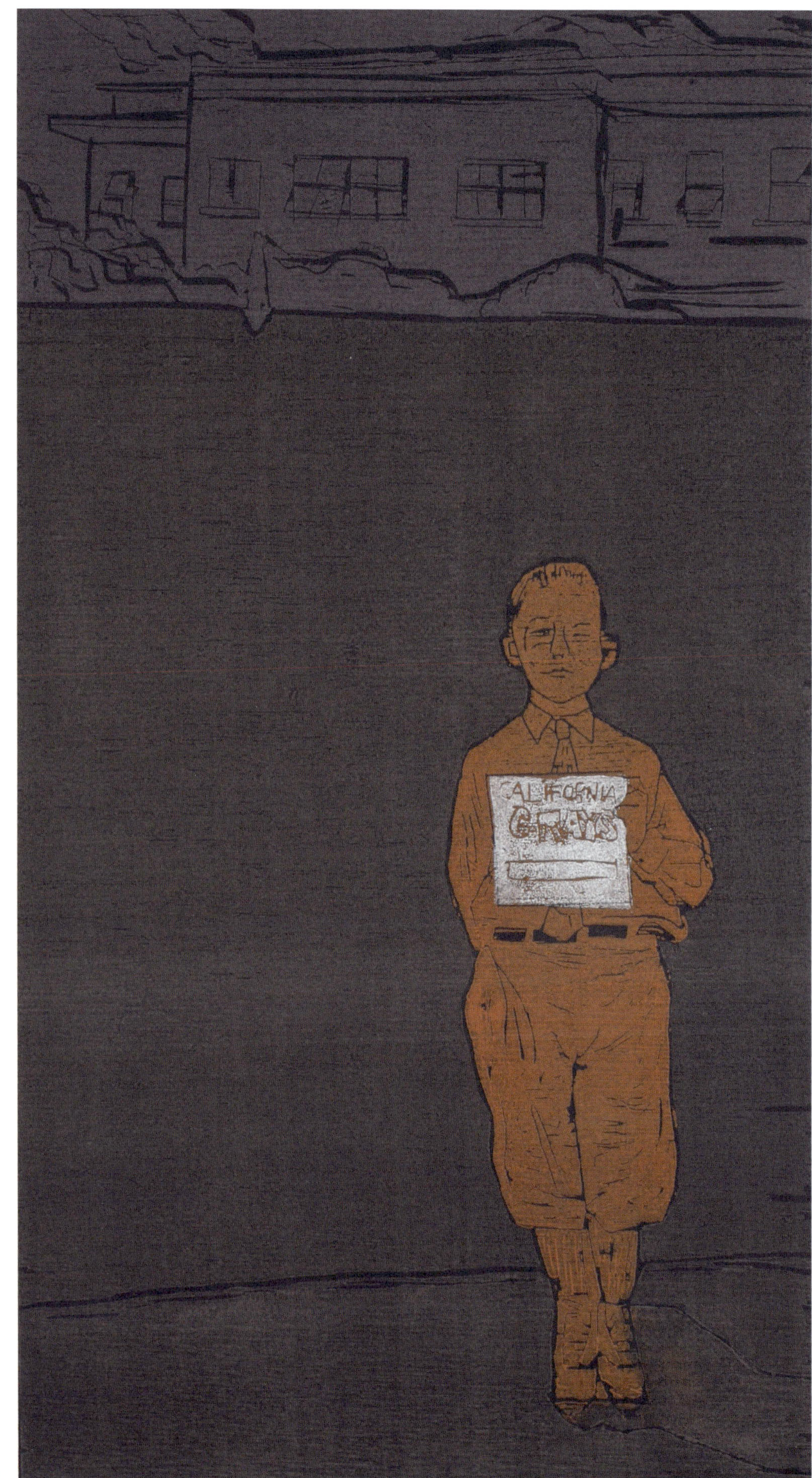

SECOND BASE MAN

A woodcut of my father as a young boy, holding a 'California Grays' baseball team flyer. I feel this is a proud moment for a young boy. The woodcut evokes a sense of the past, of a simpler time, where colour stands out to show excitement.

[WC]

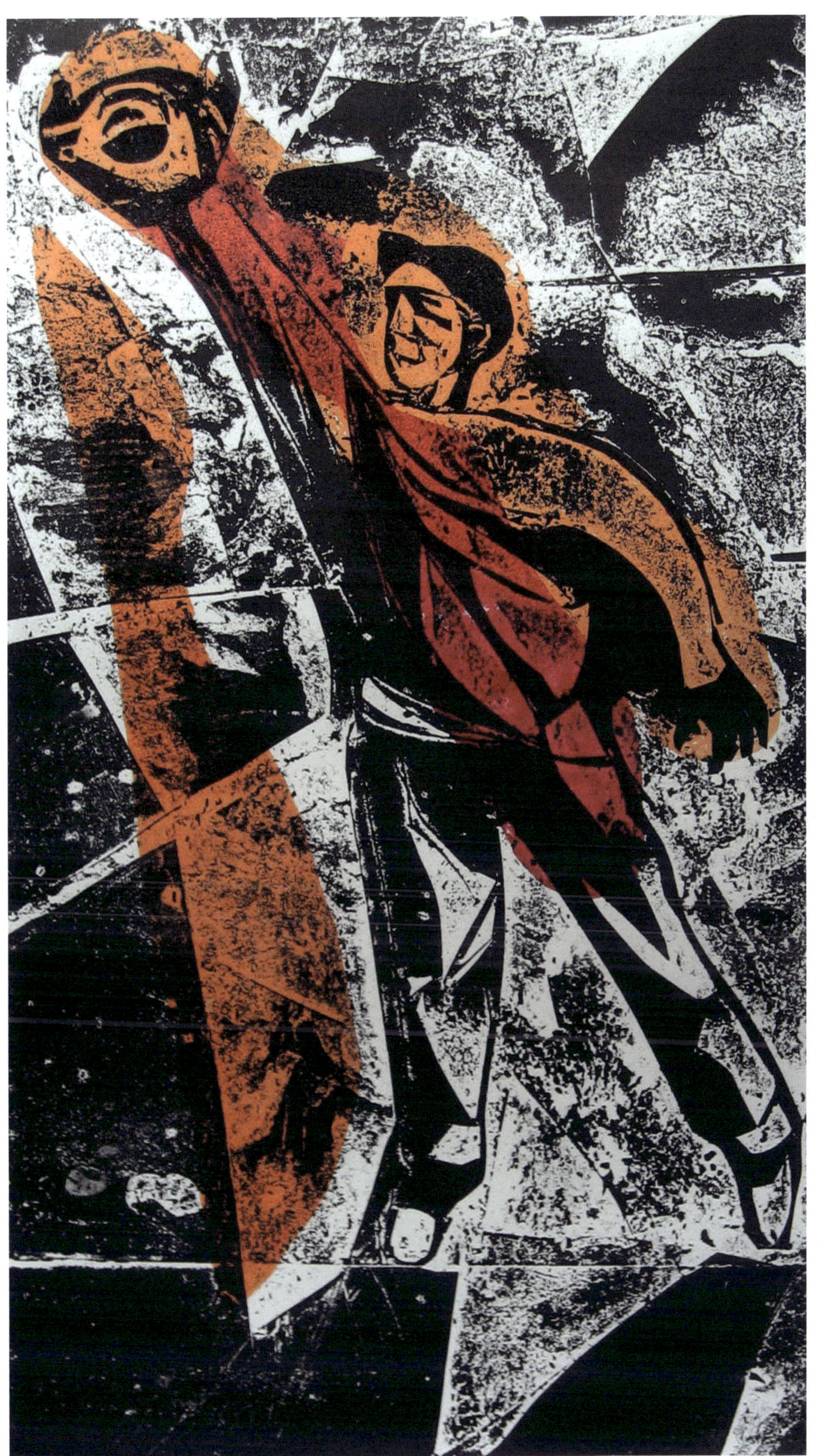

SECOND BASE MAN IN ACTION

My dad was an athlete who played second base for California team The Grays, and later in a demonstration baseball game for Hitler in the 1936 Berlin Olympic Games. One of his teammates was the famous black track and field athlete, Jesse Owens, who won four gold medals at the event.

This collagraph suggests action and movement by using fast, sharp cuts.

[COL]

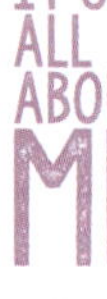

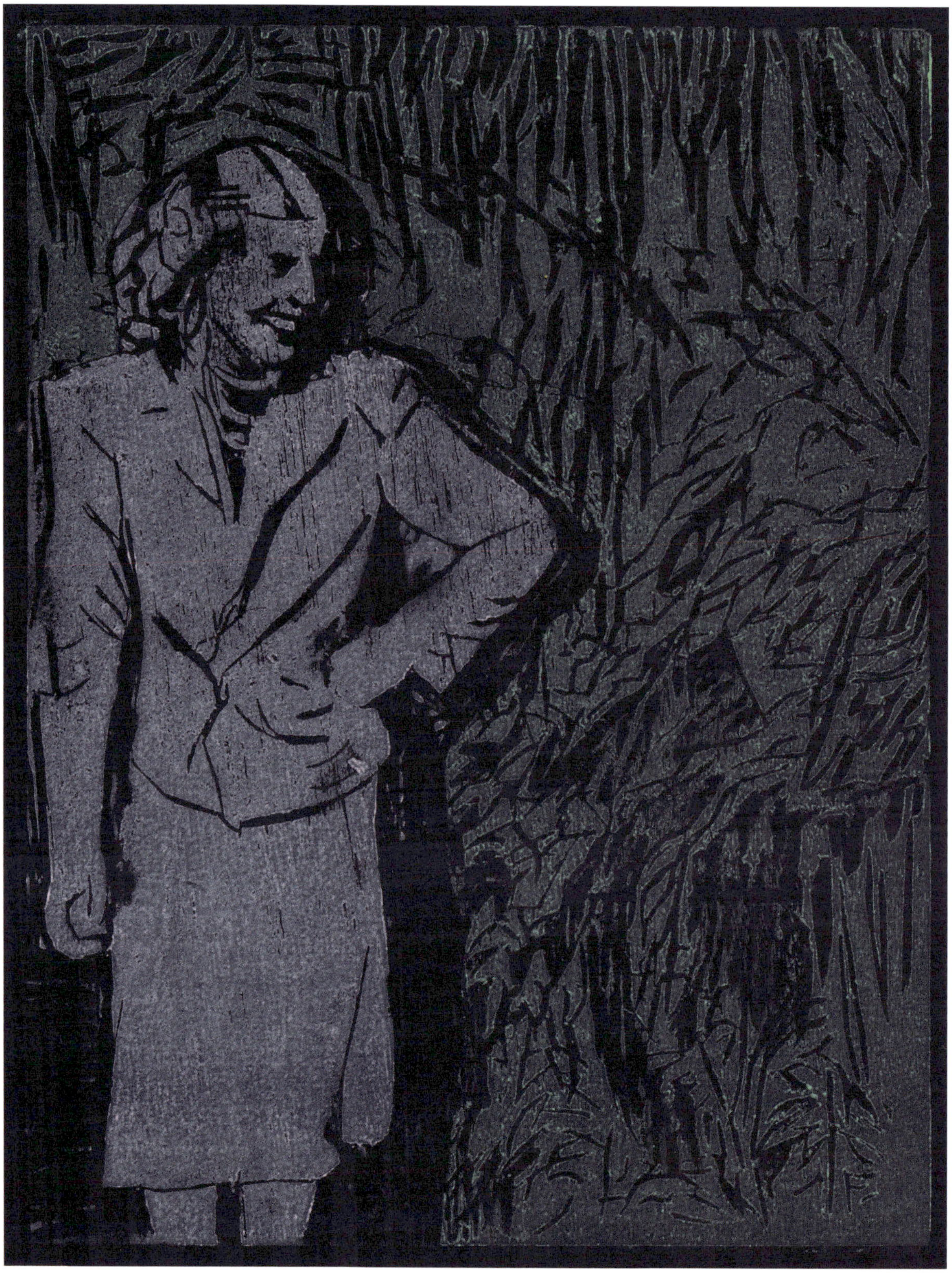

NELLIE

My mother, dressed in her 1930s outfit and hairdo.

The only time she ever smiled, and I caught it in wood for all time.

[WC]

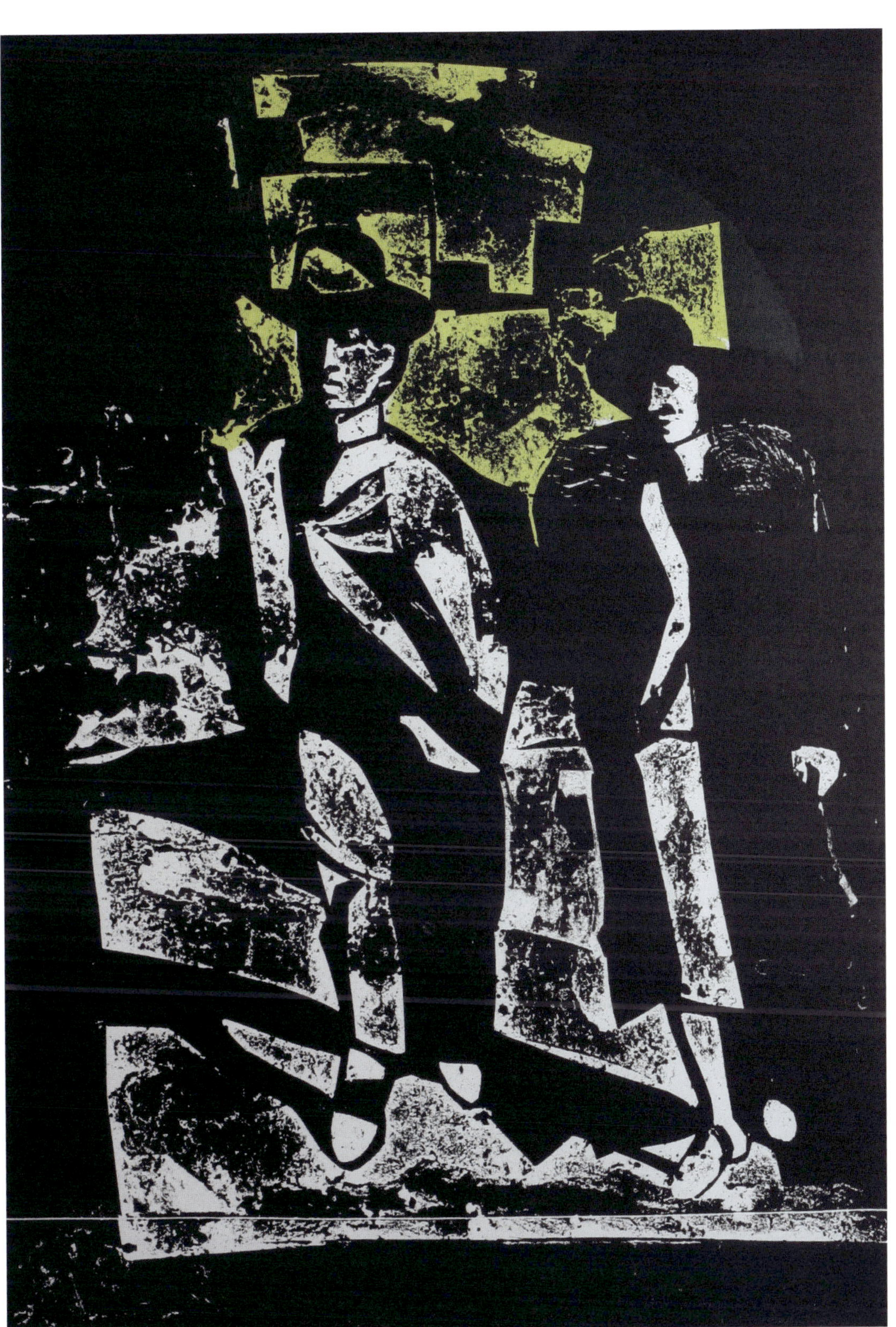

THE COURTSHIP

A collagraph depicting Mom and Dad courting in 1939 with a picnic, dressed in clean saddle shoes, fur collar and ready for a new life together.

Soon WW2 would start. Dad would disappear into the US Navy for five years, and all would be uncertain.

The image uses hard edges and textures merging together. The pale yellow the fading past – time behind them.

[COL]

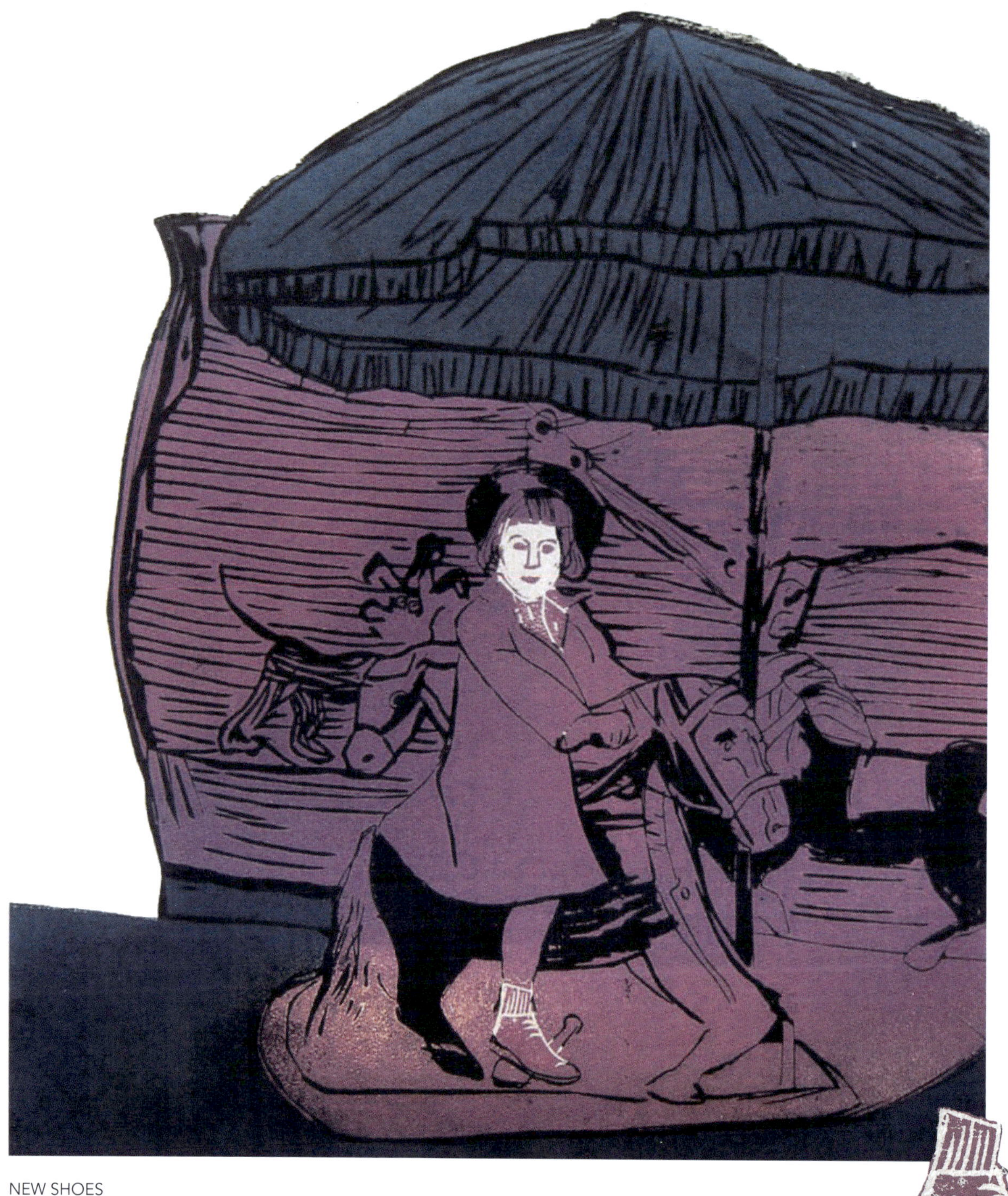

NEW SHOES

*Trussed up, vulnerable yet
excited. What could be better
than new shoes; shiny leather,
the smell of calfskin – and with
the purchase you get to ride on
the creaking merry-go-round.*

[WC]

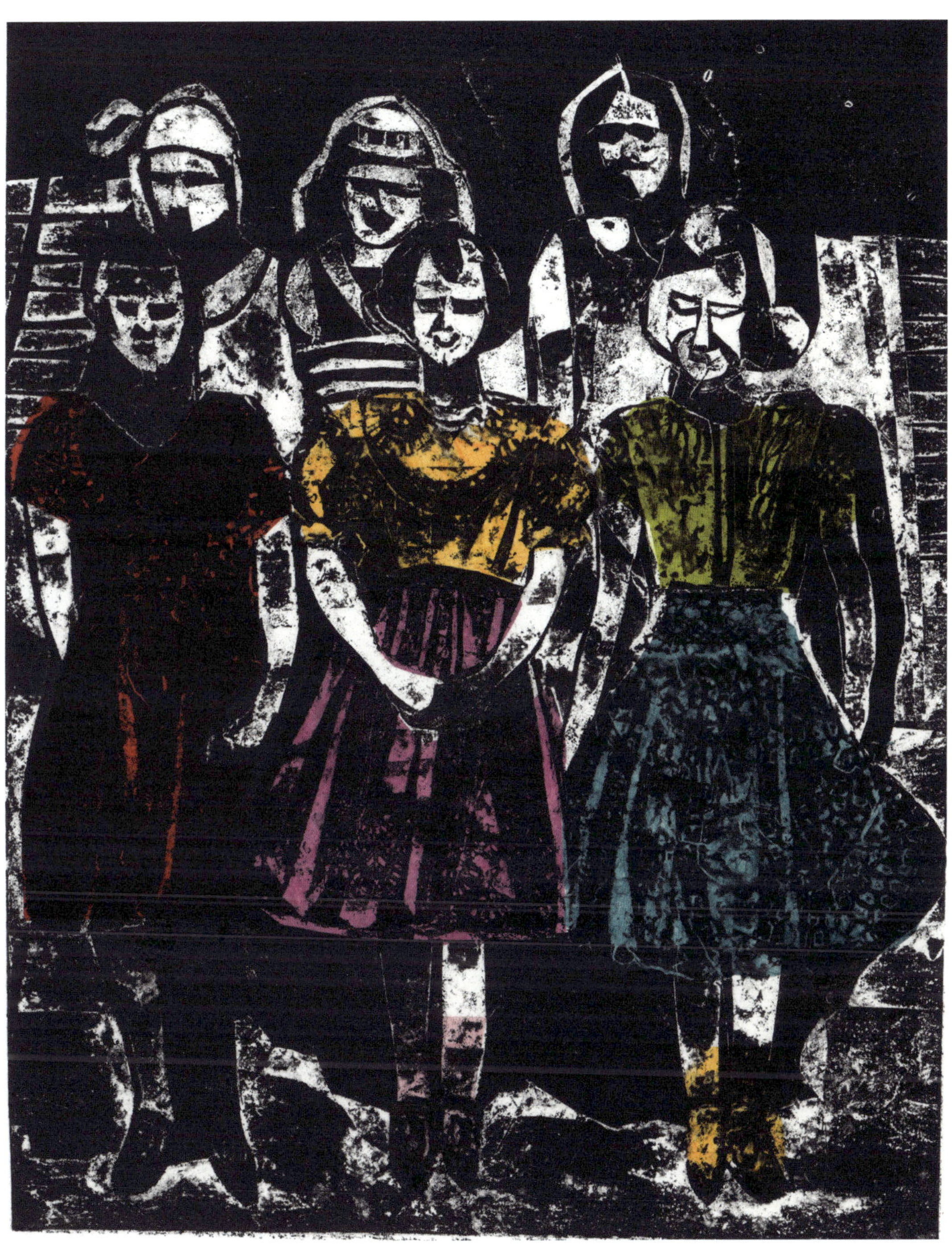

GAIL AT SCHOOL

A collagraph using doilies and tissue for colour and texture, describes the girl group – edgy with its power in numbers but also suggesting the difficulties of growing up…

[COL]

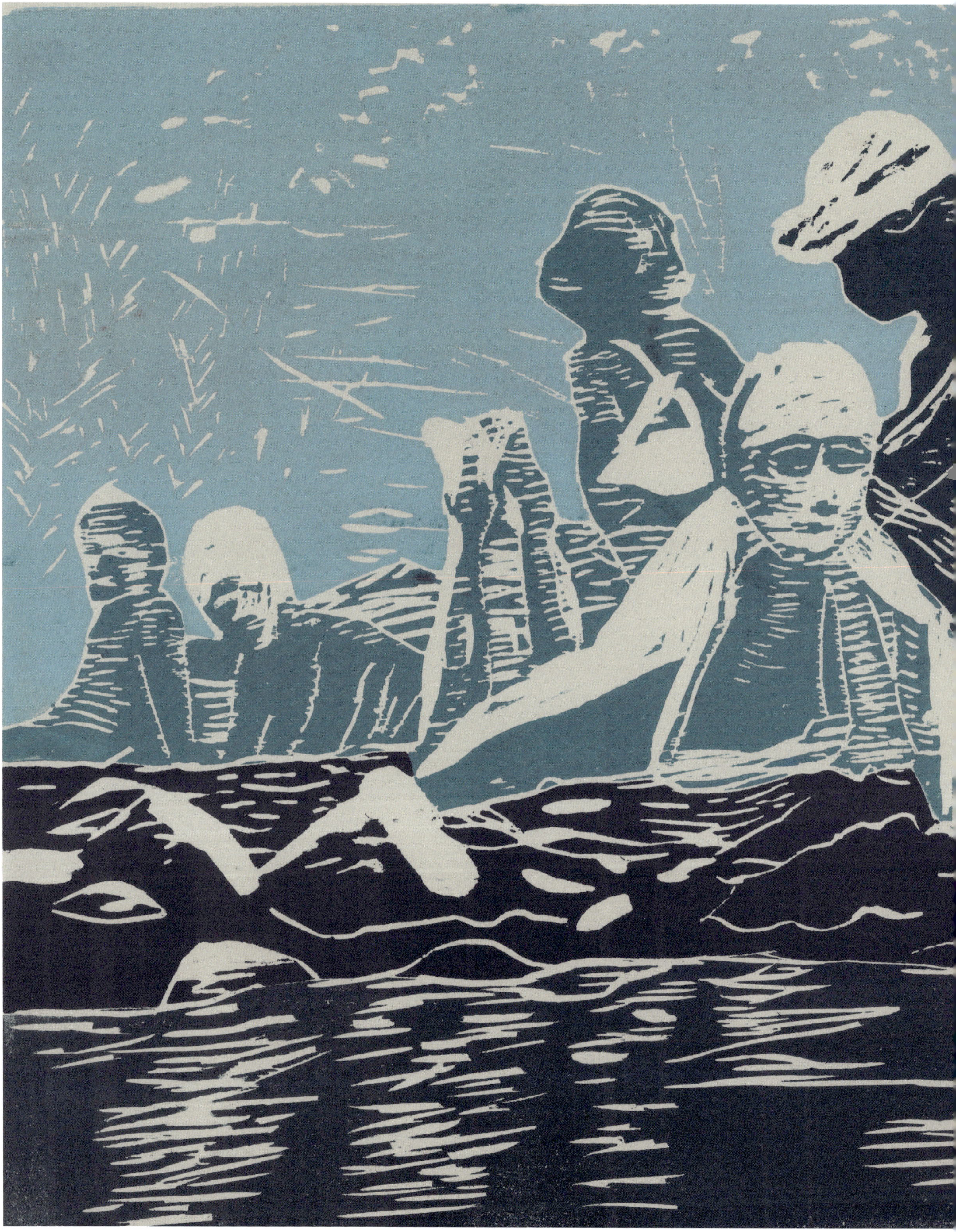

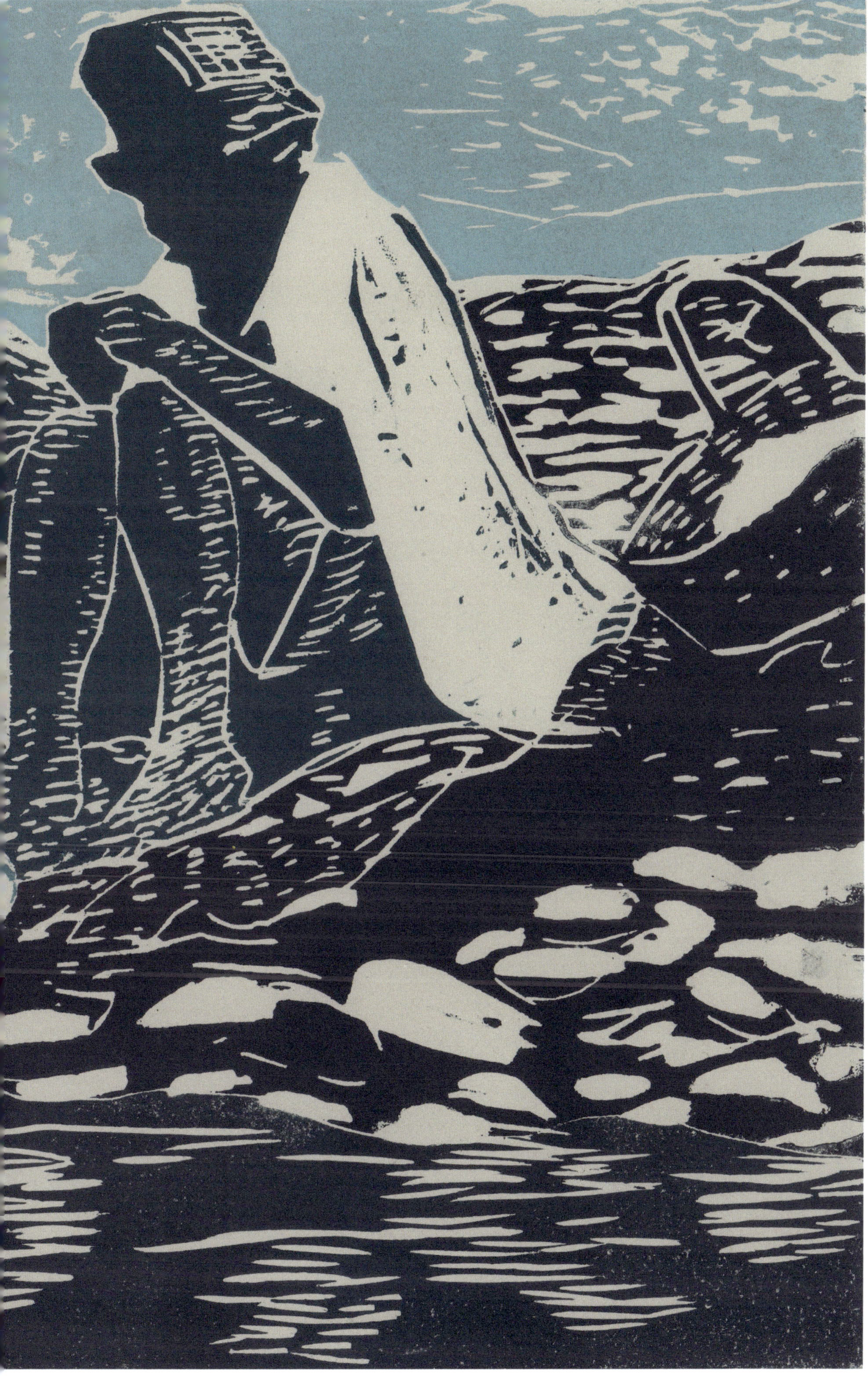

IT DOESN'T LOOK MUCH FUN ON
THE EEL RIVER

*My grandparents built a summer
lodge on the Eel River near the
border with Oregon. In the 1950s
we would take the long seven-hour
drive every summer and spend
two months there. There was a hot
rocky beach that smelt of eels from
the river, where we would have
lunchtime picnics.*

*That's me in the front in a watertight
bathing cap, and wrapped in a
towel. The rocks were treacherous
and the eels in the water scared me.
But I remember swimming with my
Dad and even with those swimming
snakes I felt happy and safe because
he was there.*

*I used different cutting shapes to
differentiate the movement in the
water and the static rocks.*

[WC]

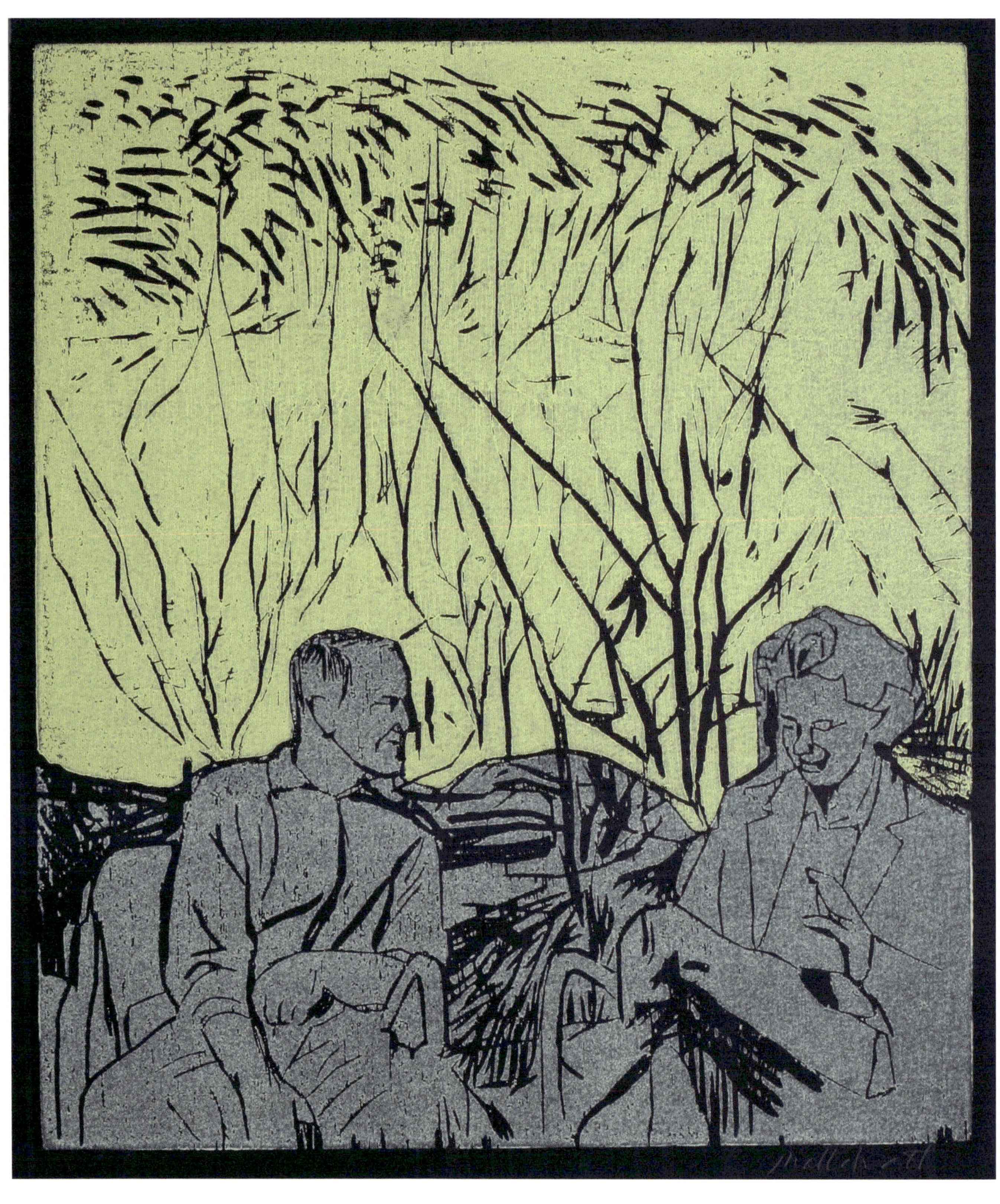

NEEDLEPOINTING *(opposite)*

A peaceful evening together: she with her needlepoint and he watching adoringly. With these woodcuts of my parents I was printing light colours on black Somerset paper, to evoke the past and referencing photographs with simple shapes.

[WC]

THE CUDDLE

Grown-up me with my own little baby. A cut-out figure shape emphasises intimacy and separateness from the world around.

[COL]

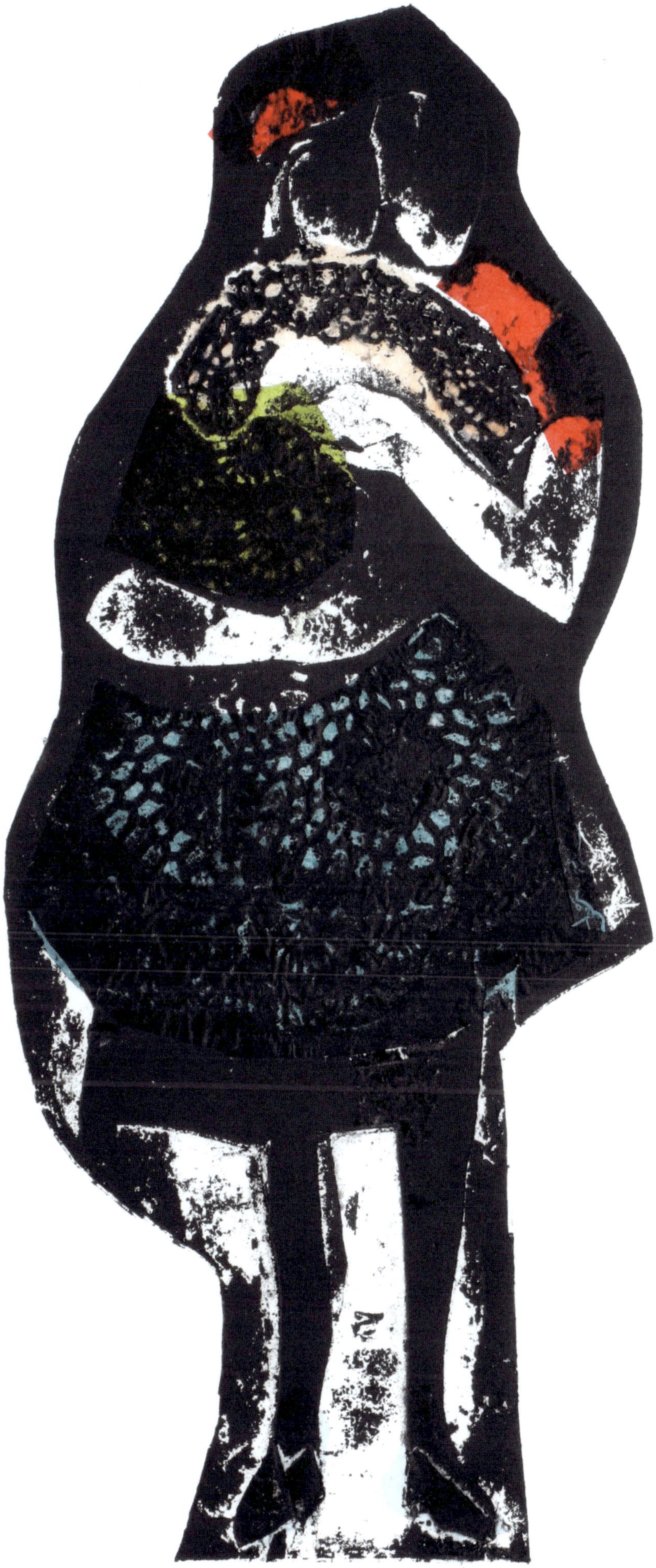

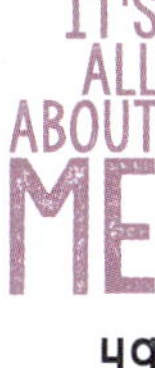

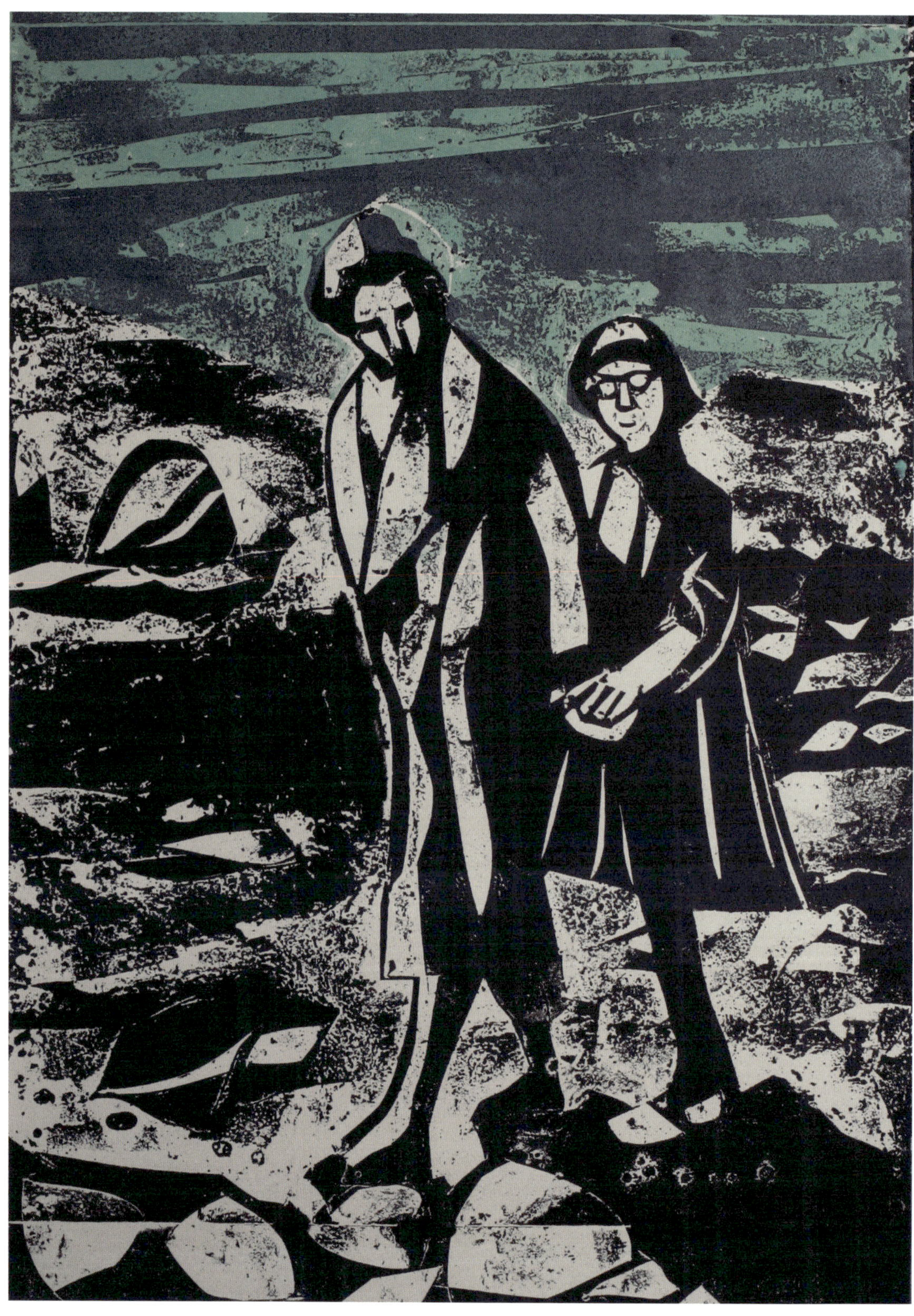

PROUT'S NECK, MAINE

Walking on the rocky beach in Maine behind my mother. It was treacherous going.

This collagraph expresses the precariousness of growing up.

[COL]

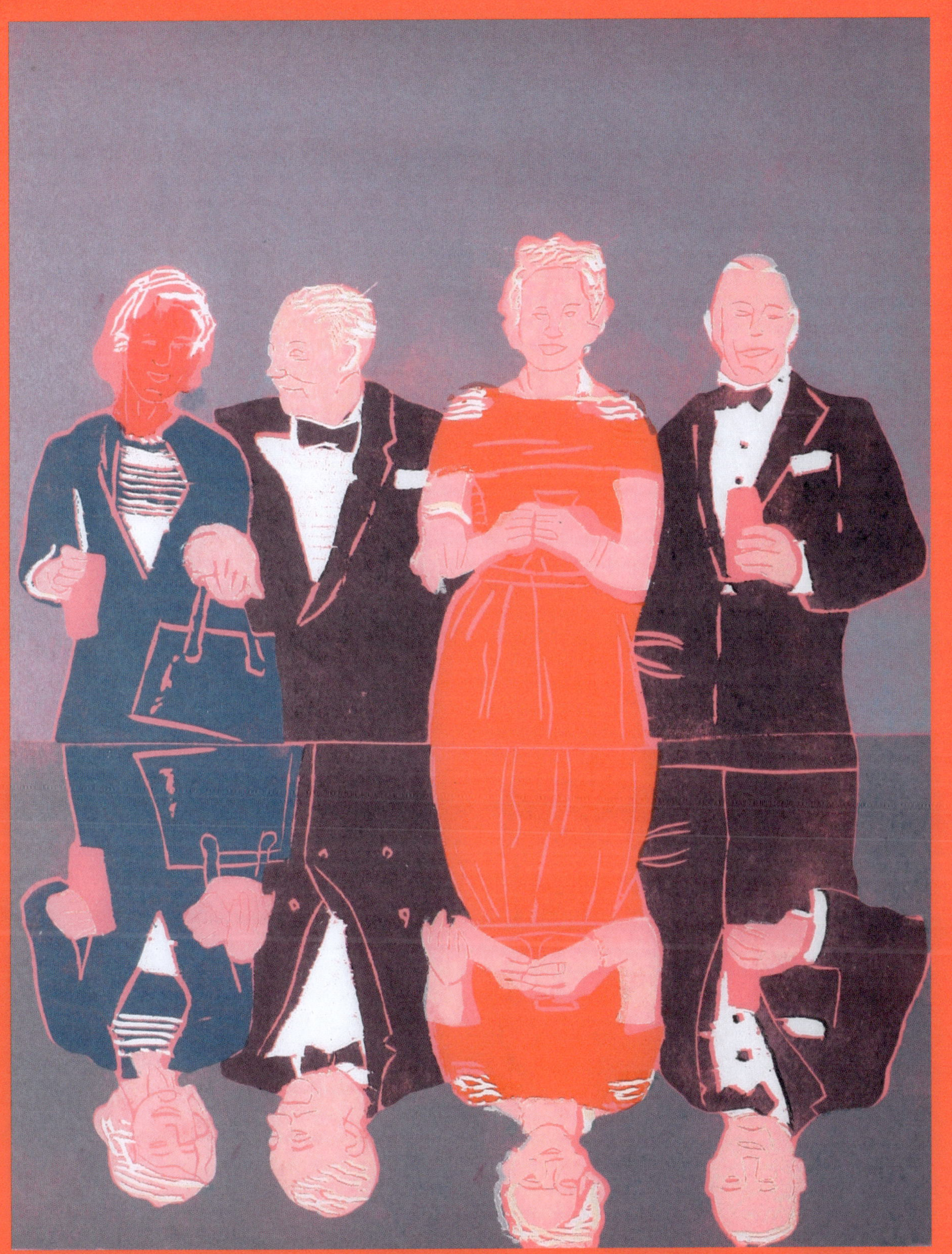

ME TOO

When the Harvey Weinstein court case opened up public debate, I reflected on my own experience with older men being 'forward'.

This print is a memory of one such occasion, on a Gala trip to Lake Como – when I was on my best behaviour.

I drew my parents looking detached and unaware while some old man came on to me.

Why the mirror image? Nobody saw anything.

[WC]

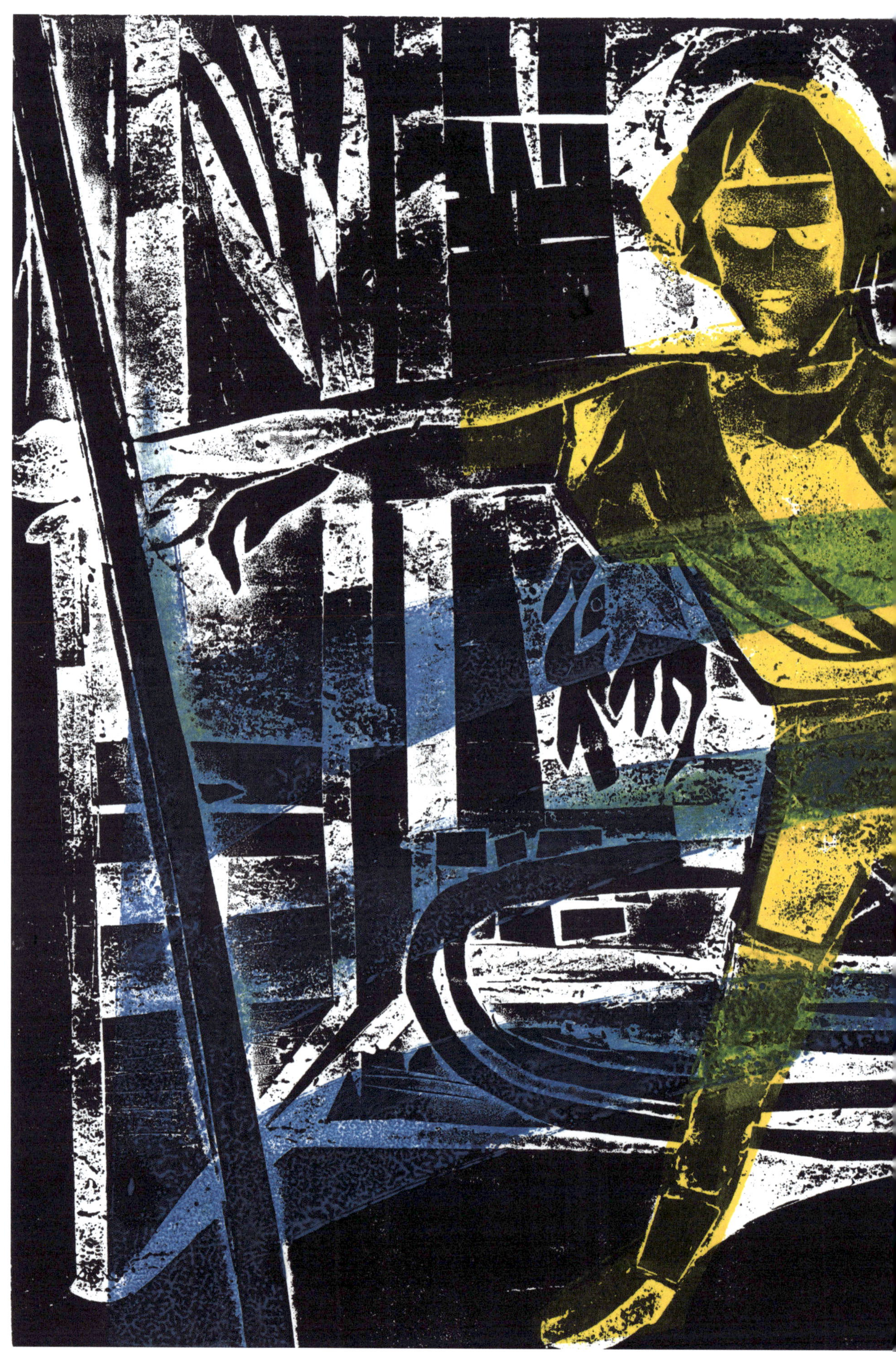

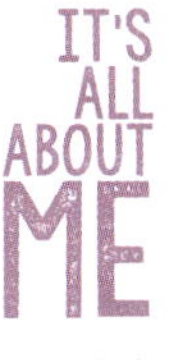

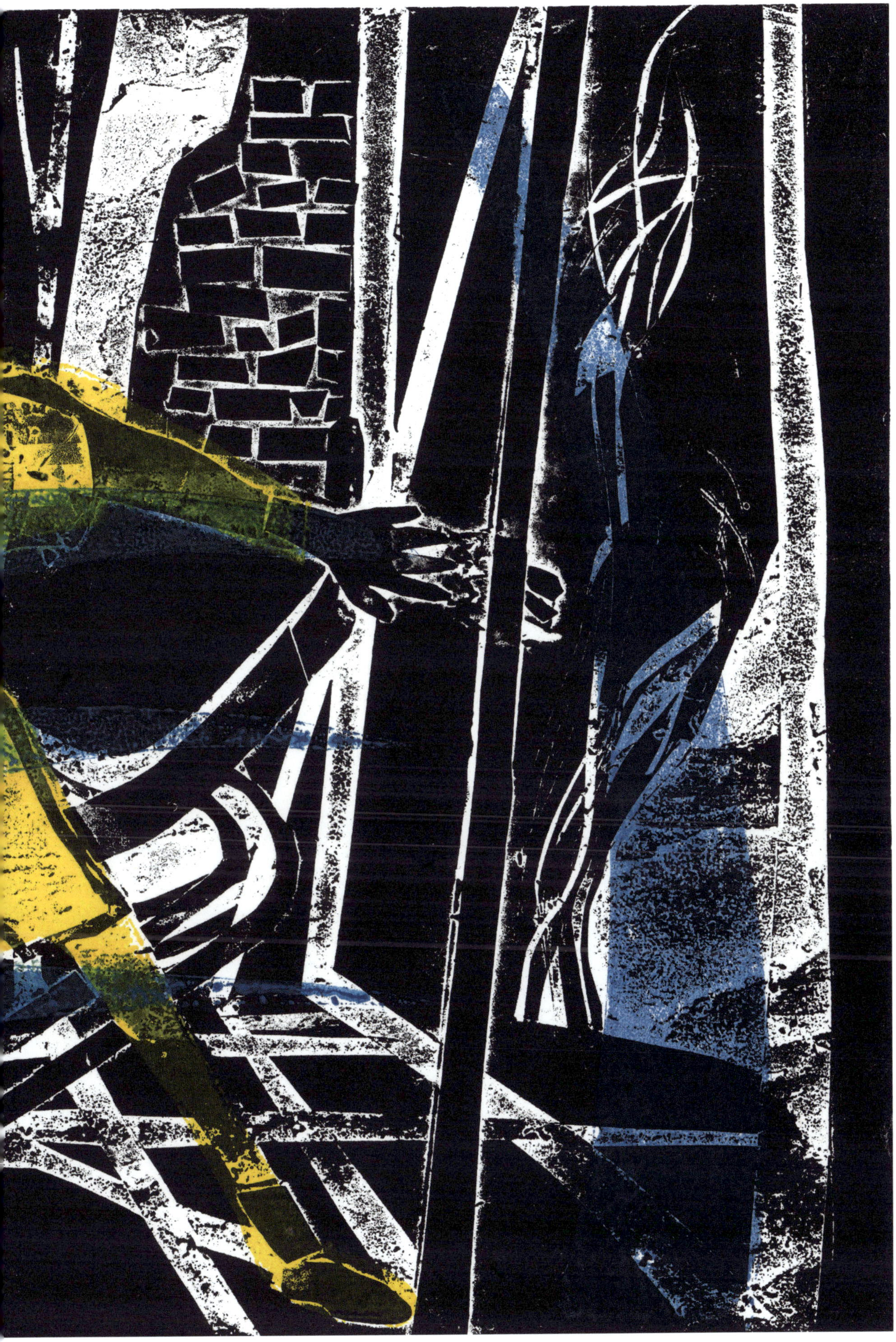

GARDEN GAMES

Jumping between poles in our walled garden in San Francisco.

[COL]

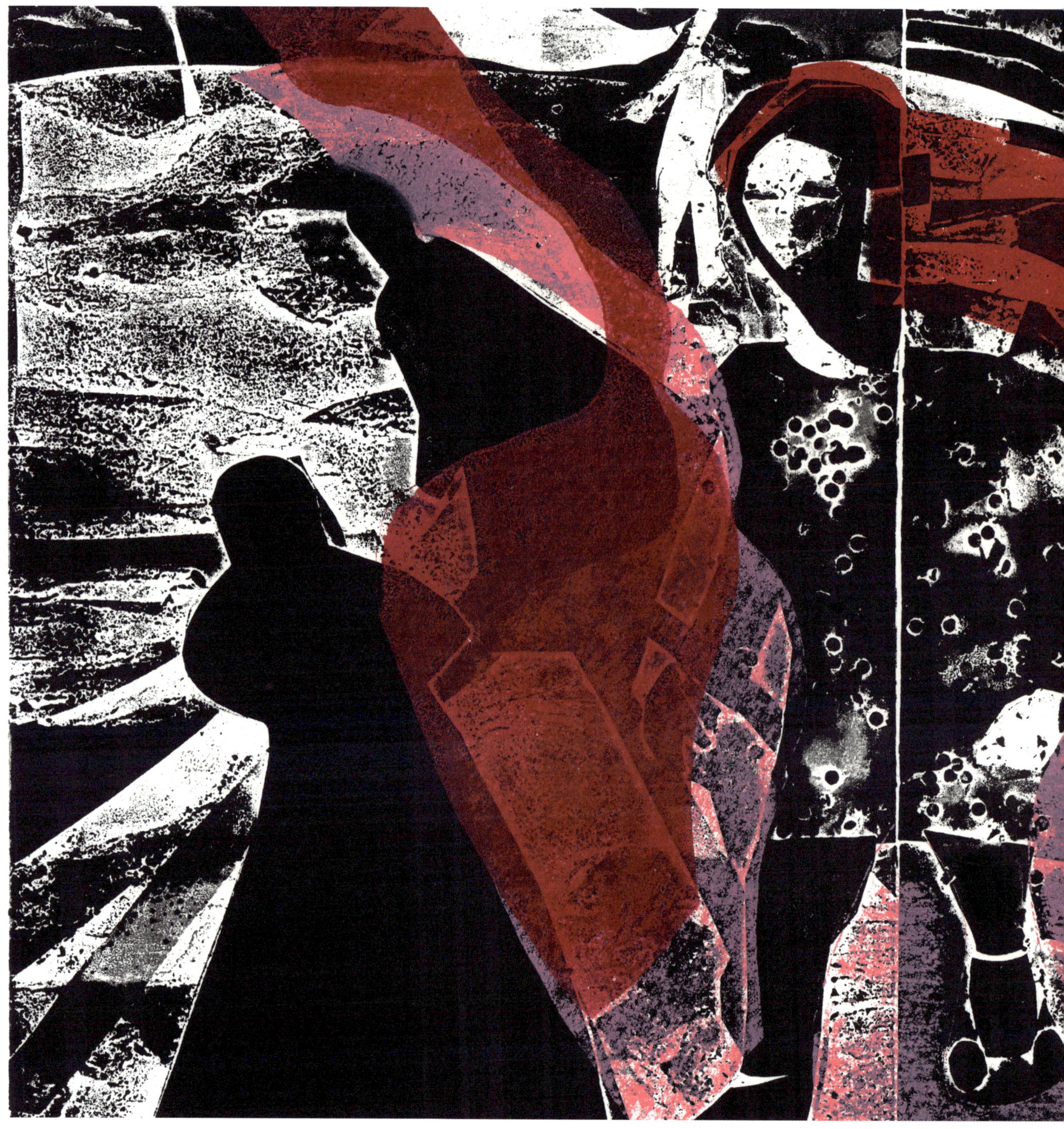

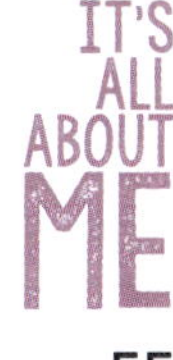

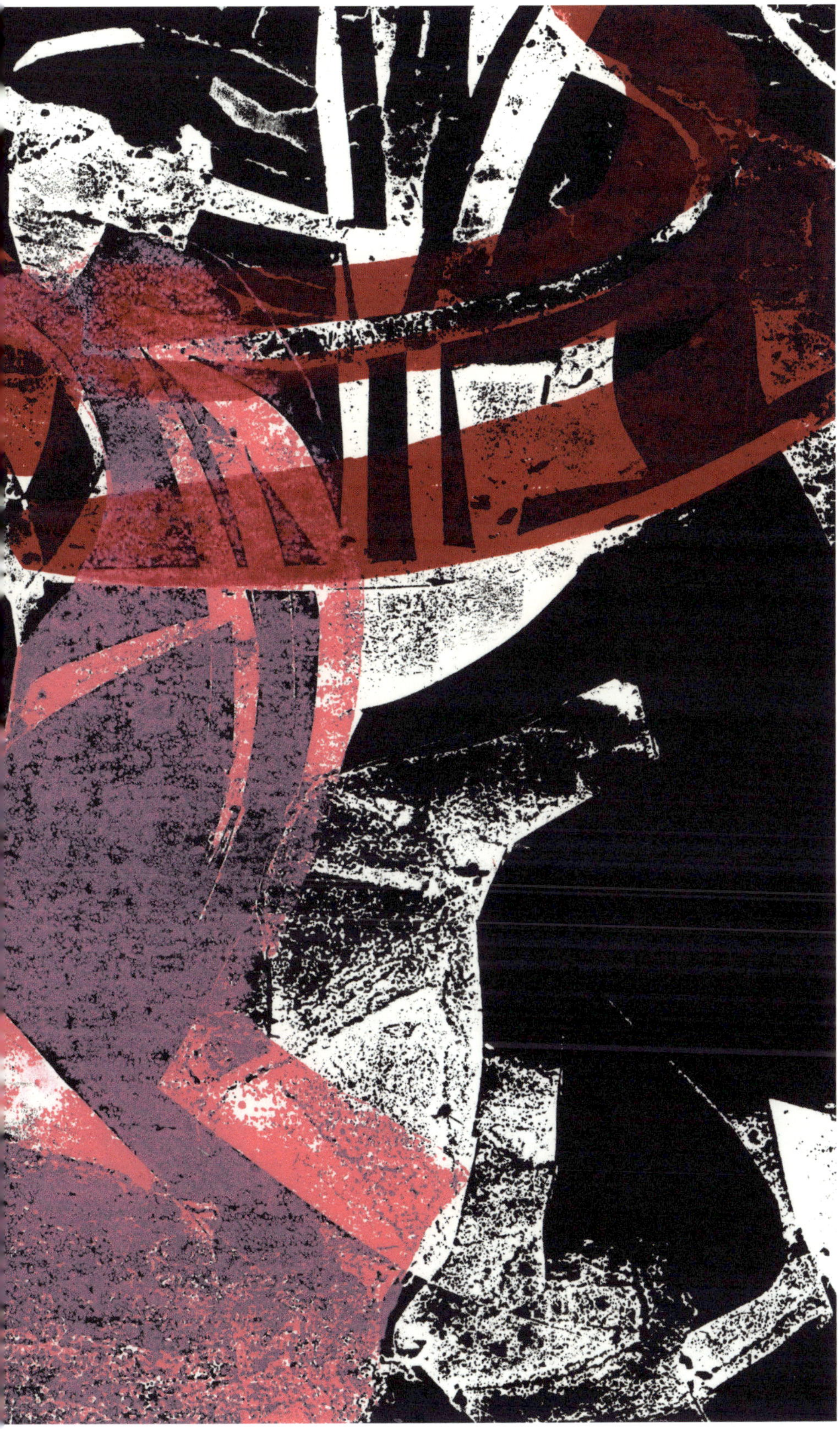

SHE'S LOST A BUTTON ALREADY

Roller skating in Central Park, N.Y.C, on a winter's day. My mother's shadow with a camera and me trying to stay vertical. My Christmas coat which was fuzzy and scratchy was my proud new possession – but mother commented: **"She's lost a button already."**

[COL]

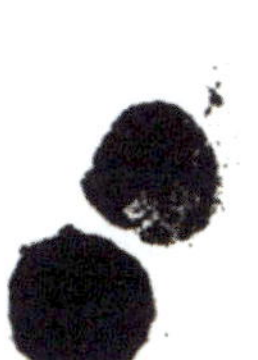

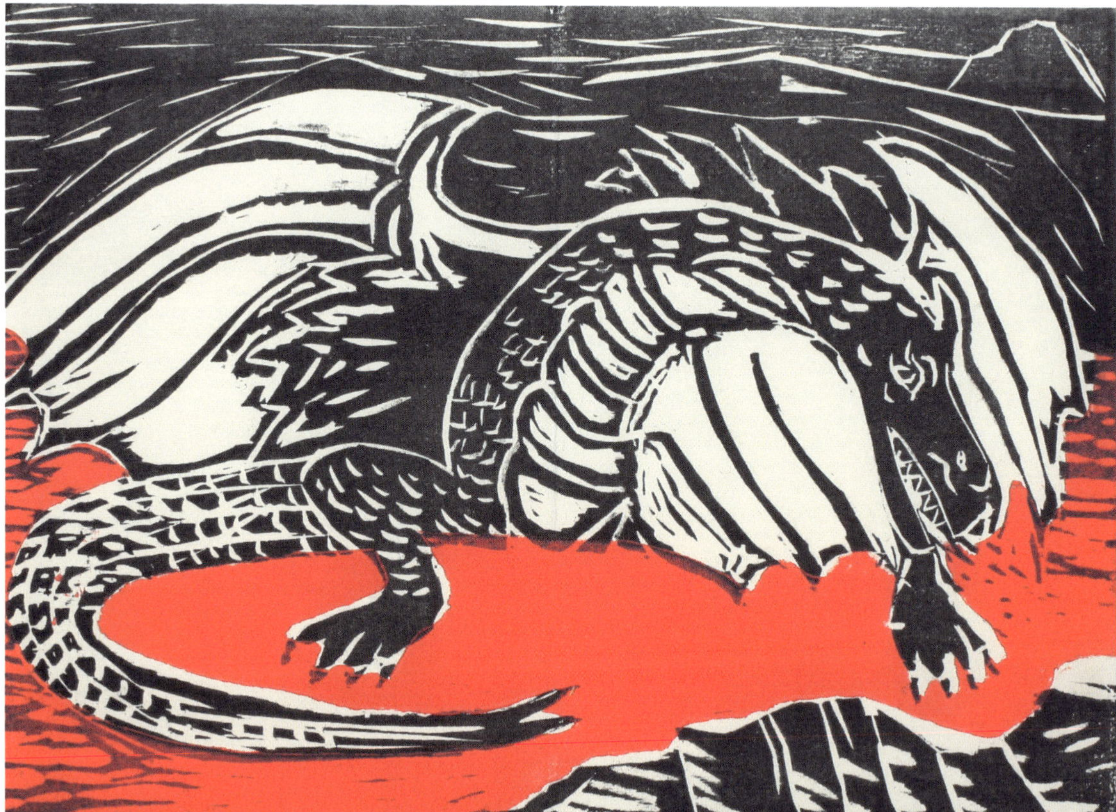

DRAGON

Dragons to me are the mythical embodiment of fear. In order to survive, one needs to be conscious of their powers and let the fear pass out of one's life. I have used them on Christmas cards as a wish for friends to be strong.

[MWC]

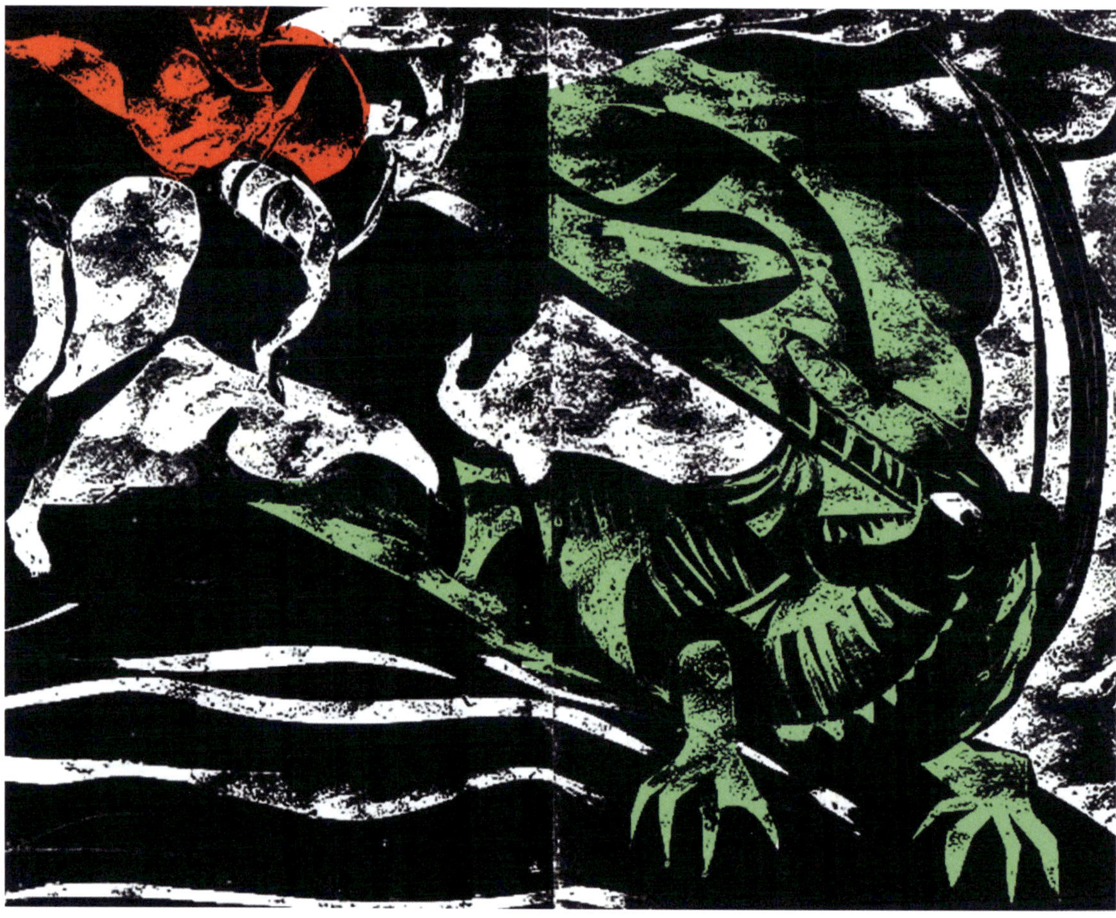

AFTER TINTORETTO:
ST. GEORGE AND
THE DRAGON

Based on Tintoretto's painting as spotted in the National Gallery.

[MWC]

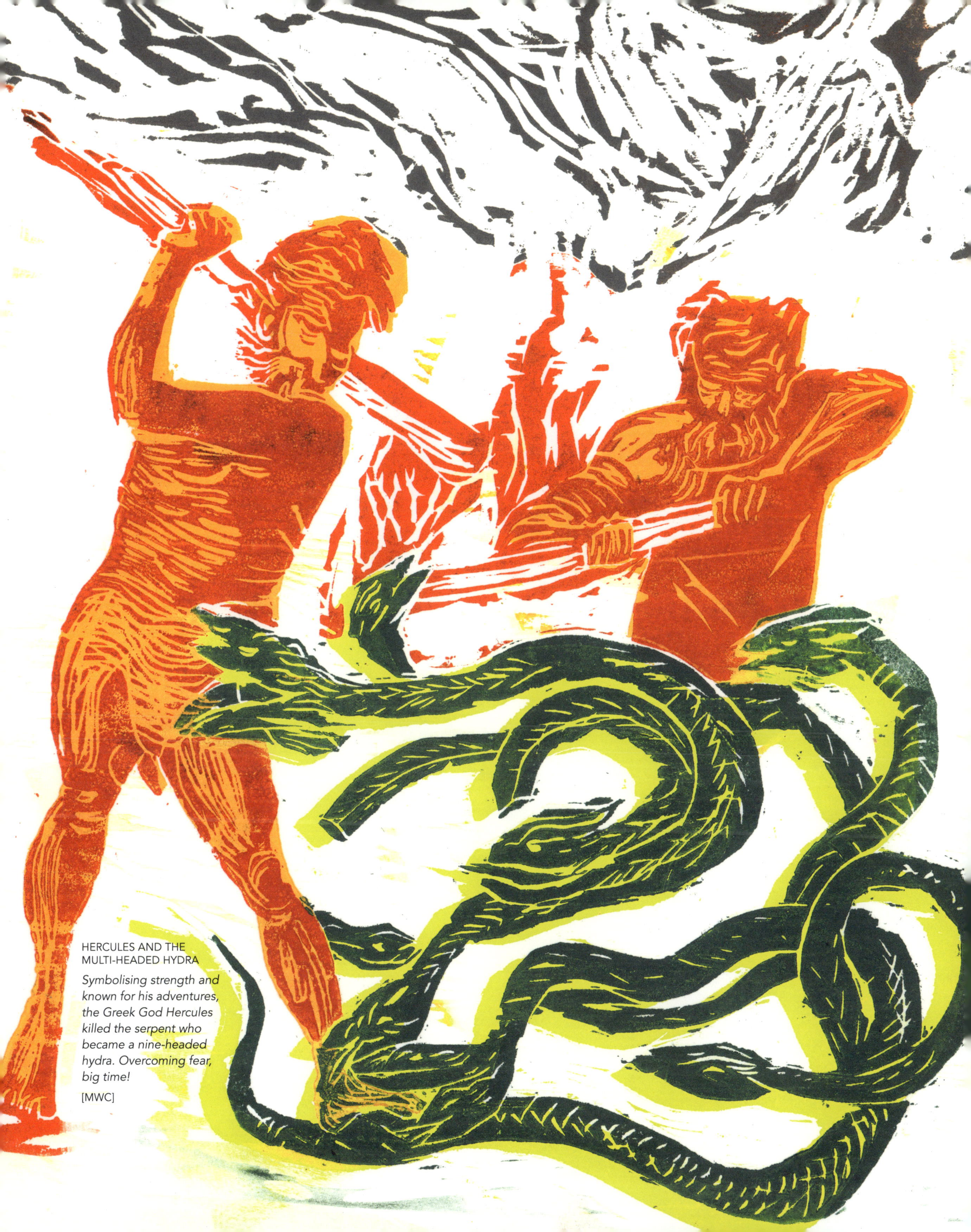

HERCULES AND THE
MULTI-HEADED HYDRA

*Symbolising strength and
known for his adventures,
the Greek God Hercules
killed the serpent who
became a nine-headed
hydra. Overcoming fear,
big time!*

[MWC]

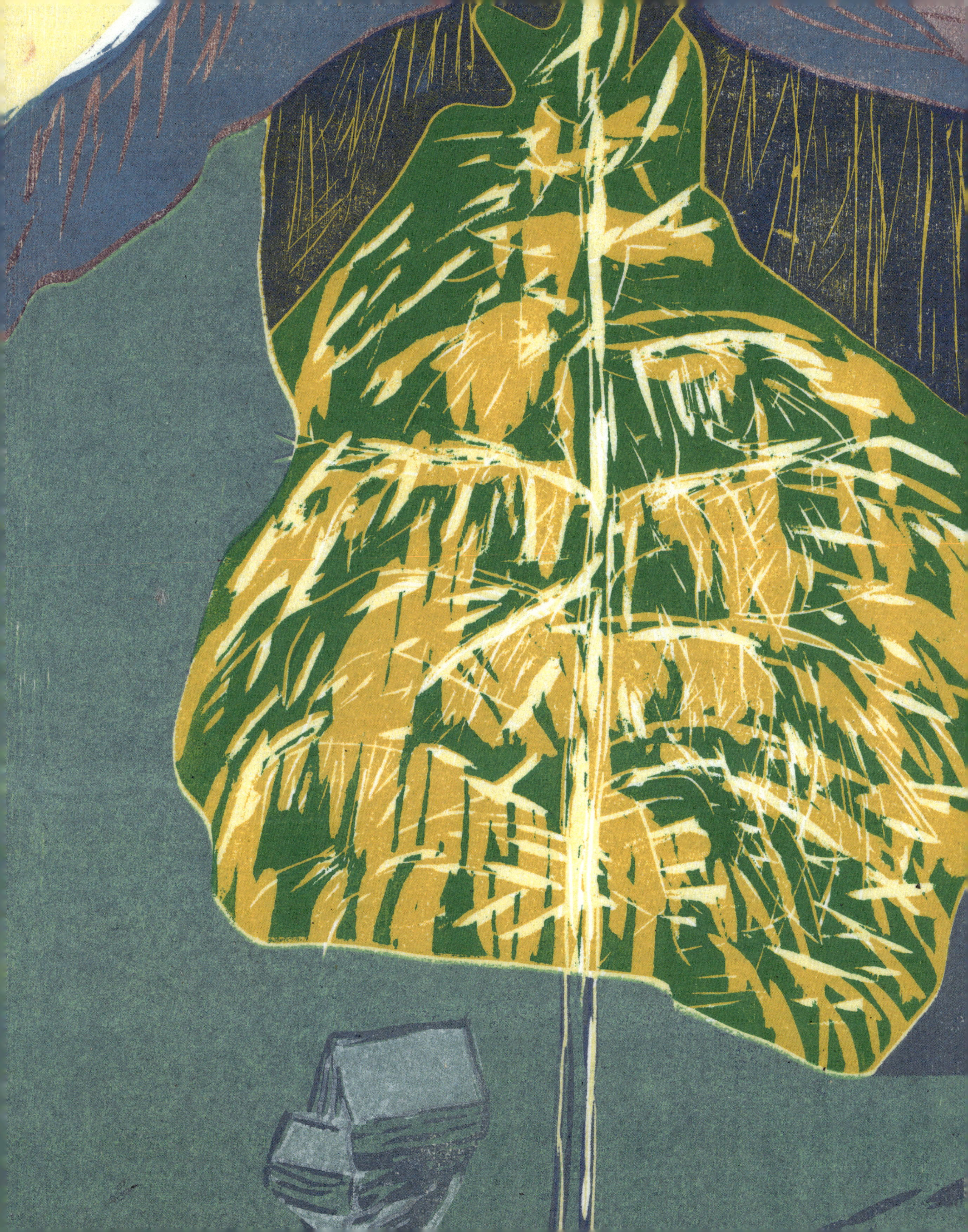

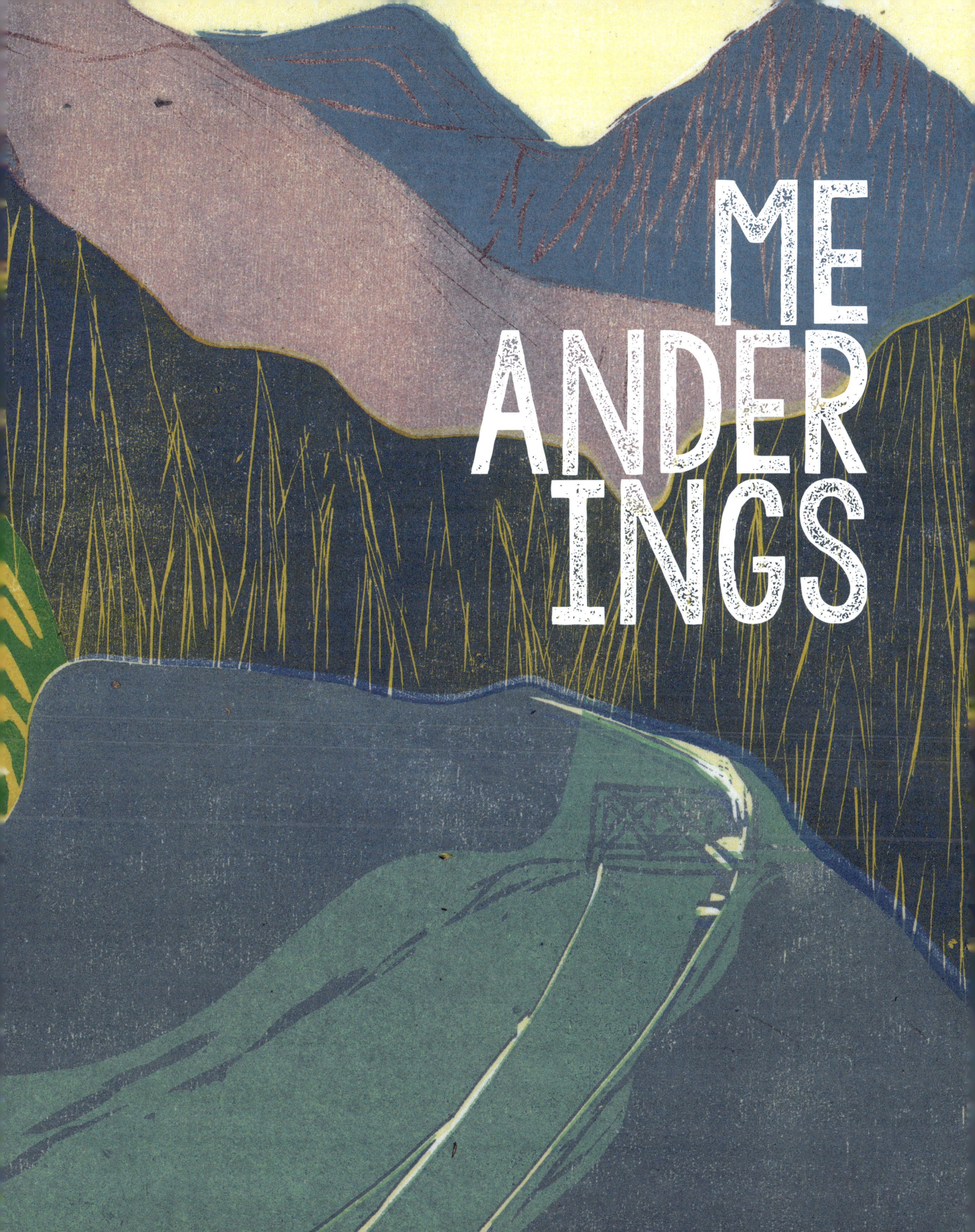

ME
ANDER
INGS

 I have been fortunate enough to travel. The images that follow are recordings of the many impressions made on me during those trips. I learned so much and saw so many things I could never have imagined: from the jungle and shack houses in Tobago, to the magnificent Terracotta Warriors in China; the spiritual entities of Kachinas of the Hopi Tribe in Arizona, USA, to the compulsive bag lady on her bench in Lima, Peru and the Gloucester Old Spot pigs who frequented Sussex in the UK.

I always returned home with sketches and ideas. When I was studying for a Masters Degree in Printmaking at Camberwell, I was able to show and discuss these sketches, and was allowed the space and encouragement to work on them in a well-equipped studio environment.

One of my heroes is Ernst Ludwig Kirchner, a free-thinking German Expressionist from the 1920s and 30s, who produced paintings, drawings and prints that go straight to the heart. Many of his works were destroyed by the Nazis, who claimed they were degenerate. An eccentric bohemian and heroin addict from the pain of his injuries in WW1, Kirchner was sent to a sanitarium near Davos. He eventually settled with his wife in a house in the valley nearby, where he shot himself on the eve of WW2. I was so enthralled with Kirchner and I wanted to find his house. In 2008 I set off on a pilgrimage to look for it. I found the house and the valley, and the prints opposite and below are my reflections on what I saw. Outside his house were traces of wood chippings which Kirchner had cut from his sculptures.

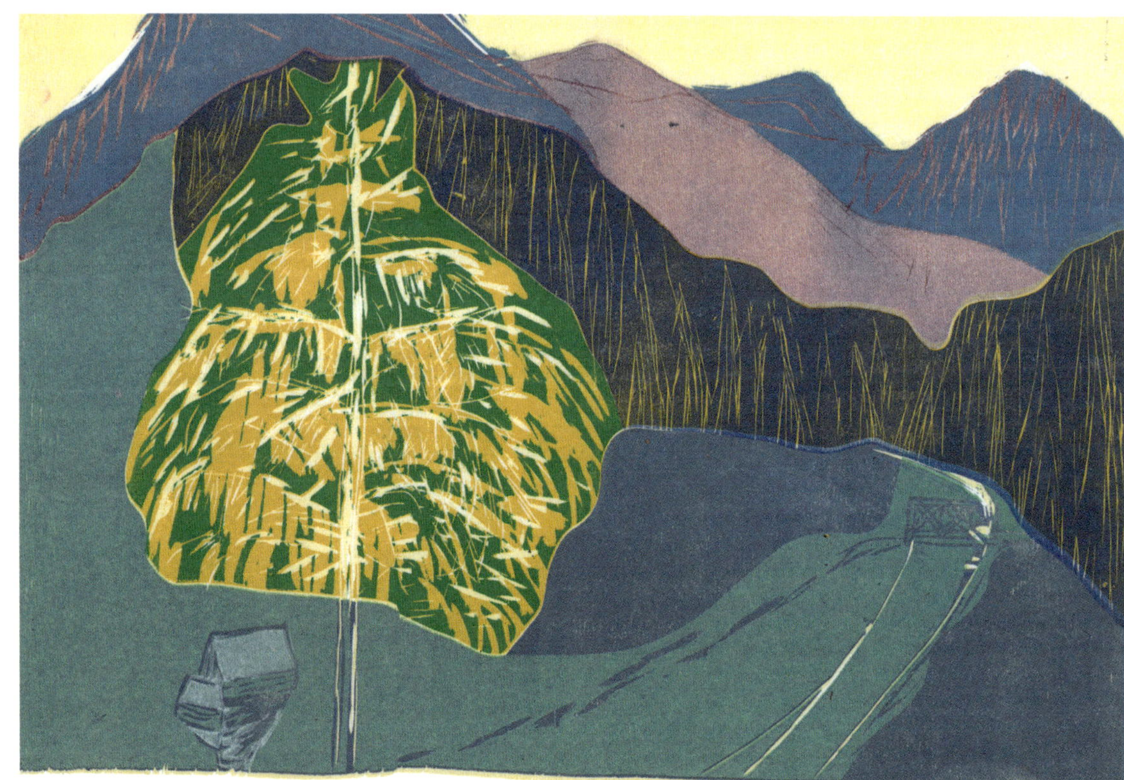

DAVOS VALLEY,
SWITZERLAND

Serene and still, with cool mountain air and Kirchner's house tucked in below.

[RWC]

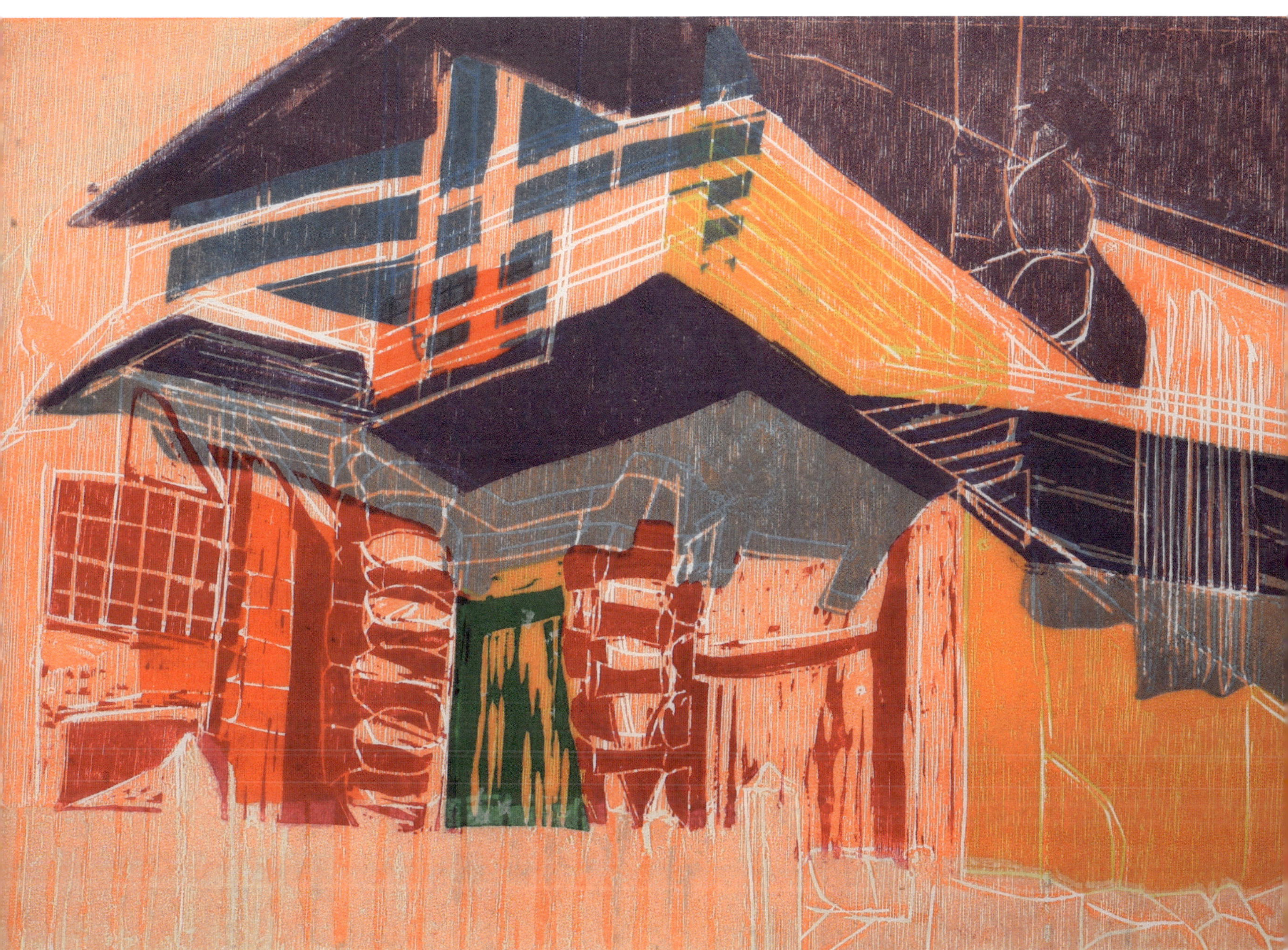

KIRCHNER'S HOUSE, SWITZERLAND

I tried to work with uninhibited exuberance to show Kirchner's house. It was so exciting to find it and match his paintings to the views of the valley from the upstairs balcony. It filled me with energy.

[RWC]

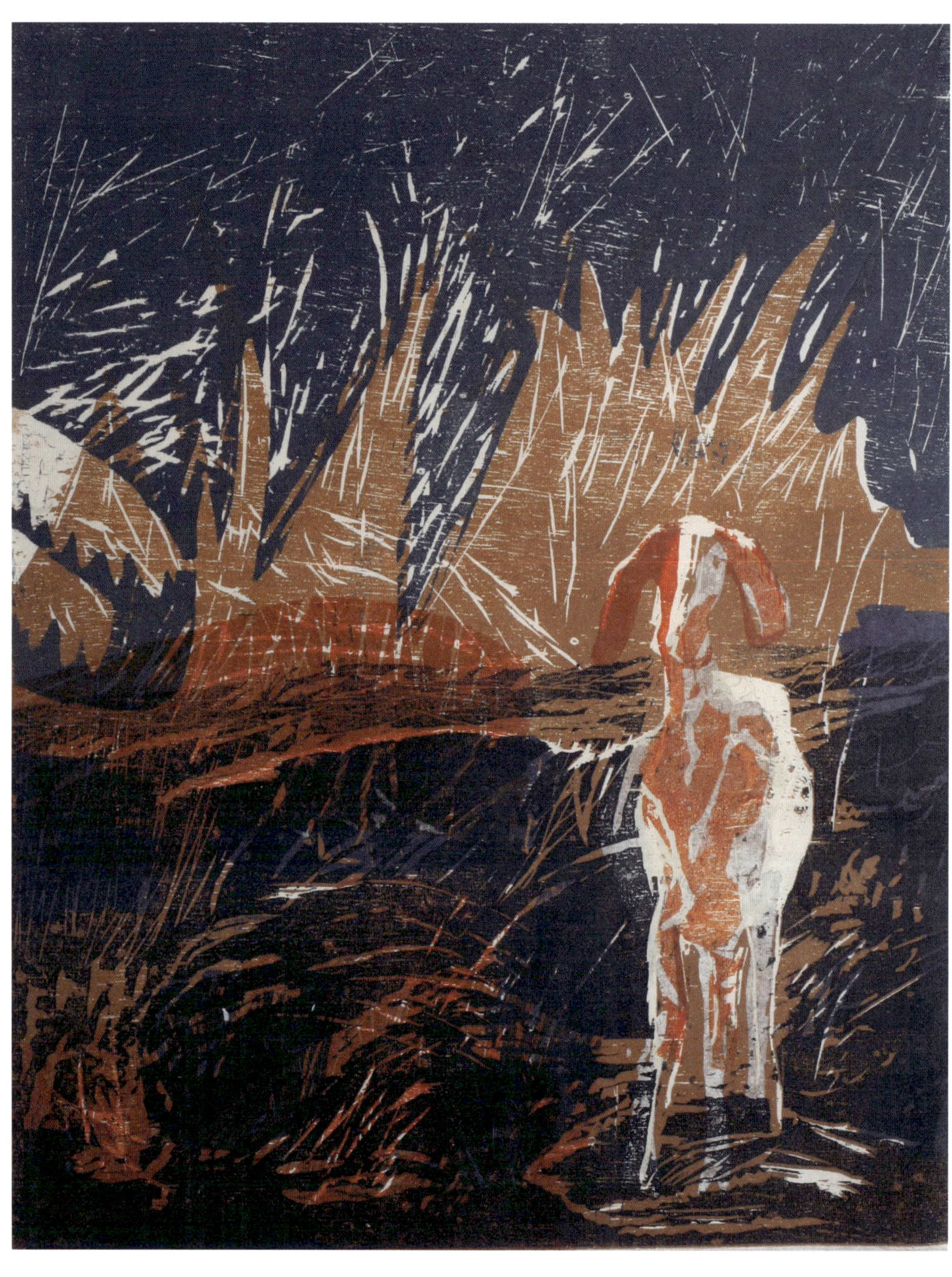

GOAT, TOBAGO

*He blended naturally
into the grasses around
him, but with a cool,
distinct penetrating eye.*

[RWC]

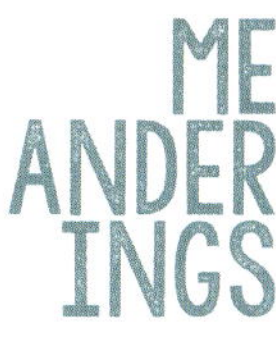

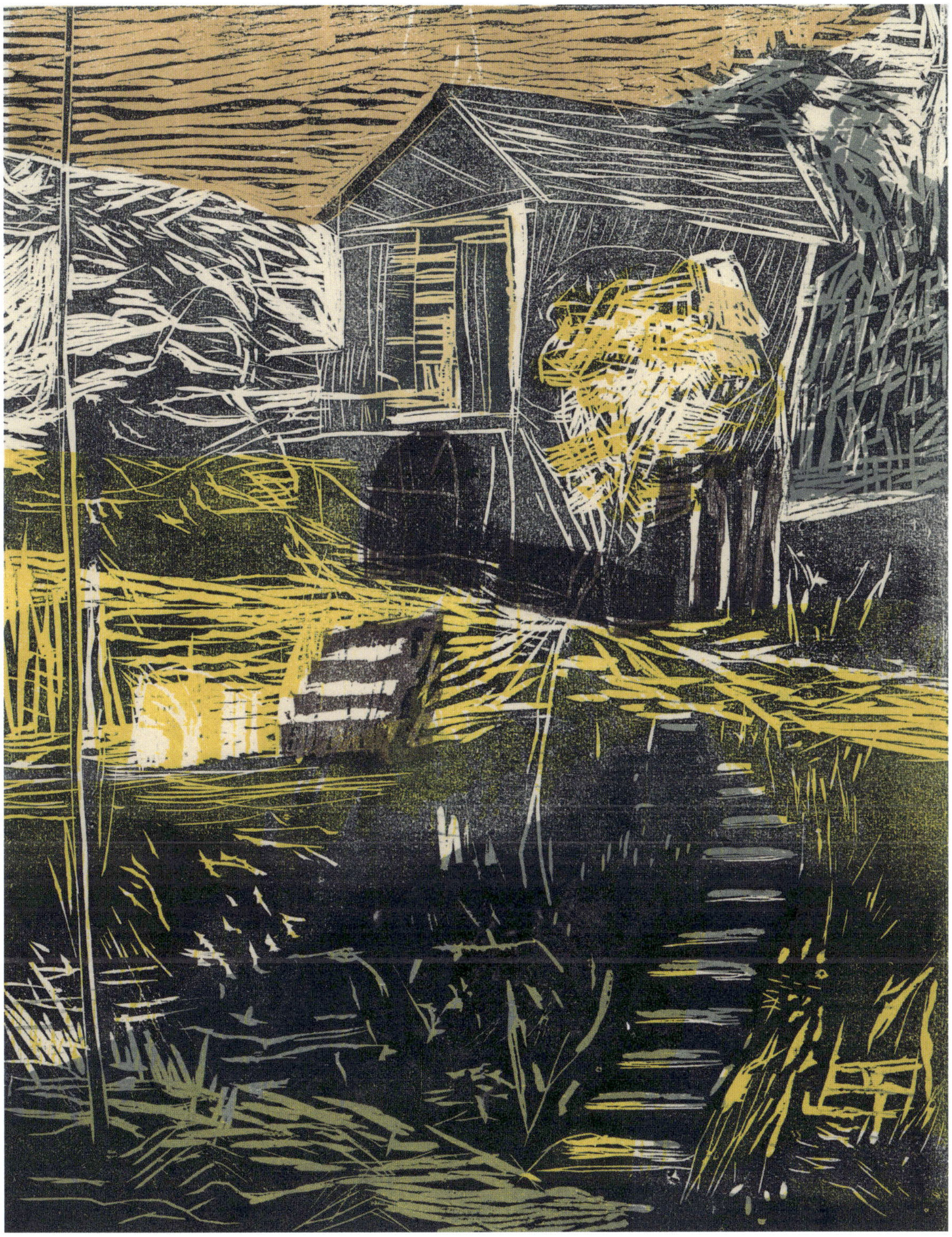

DWELLING, TOBAGO

The jungle rainforest is dense with vegetation, tangled vines, trees with parasites and a unique atmosphere of moisture and heat.

The overall chaos of the jungle and the little settlements nestled into them was a thrilling sight and inspiration. Well camouflaged, this stilt house was nevertheless quite an eerie presence. Man and nature as one.

[MWC]

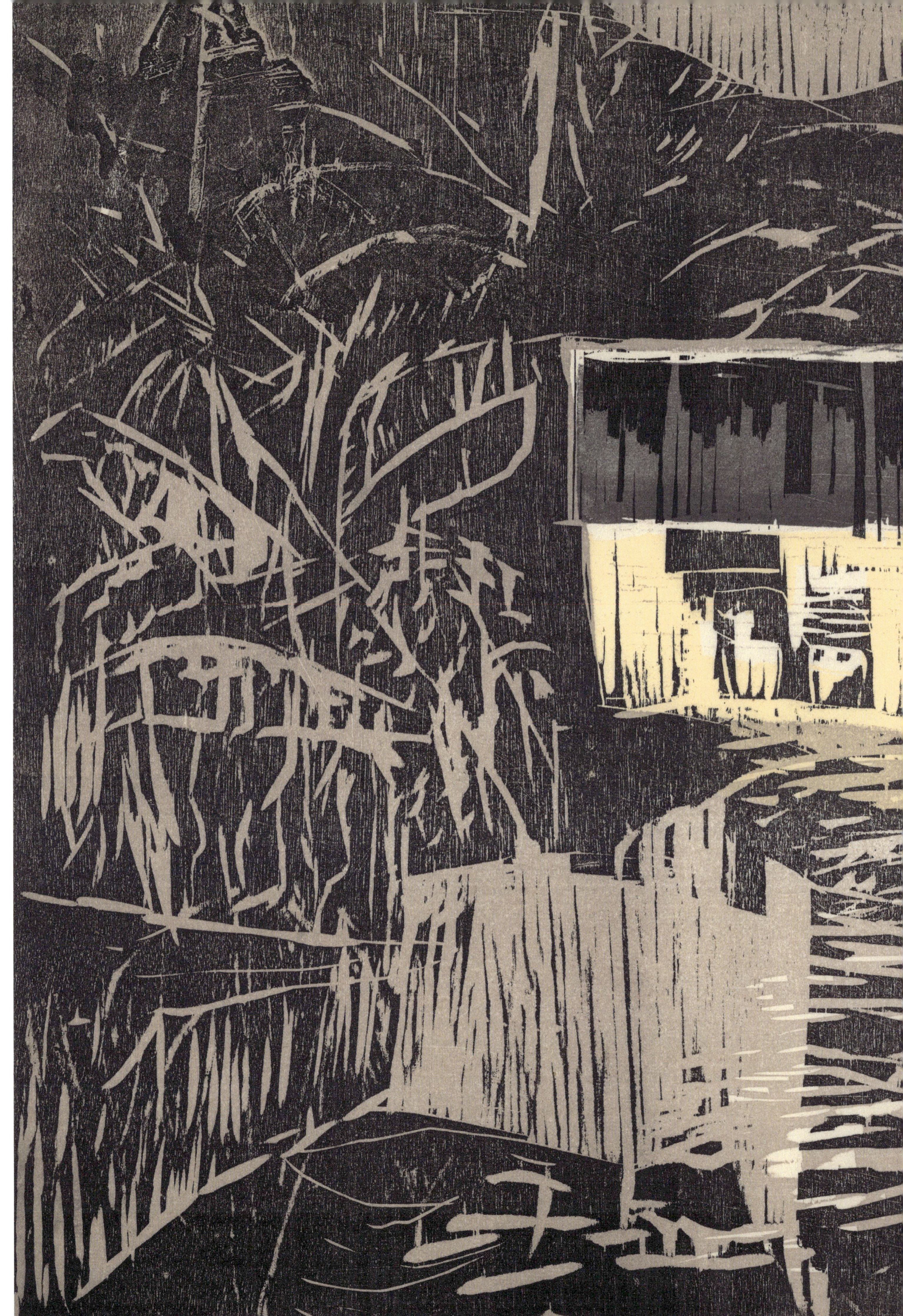

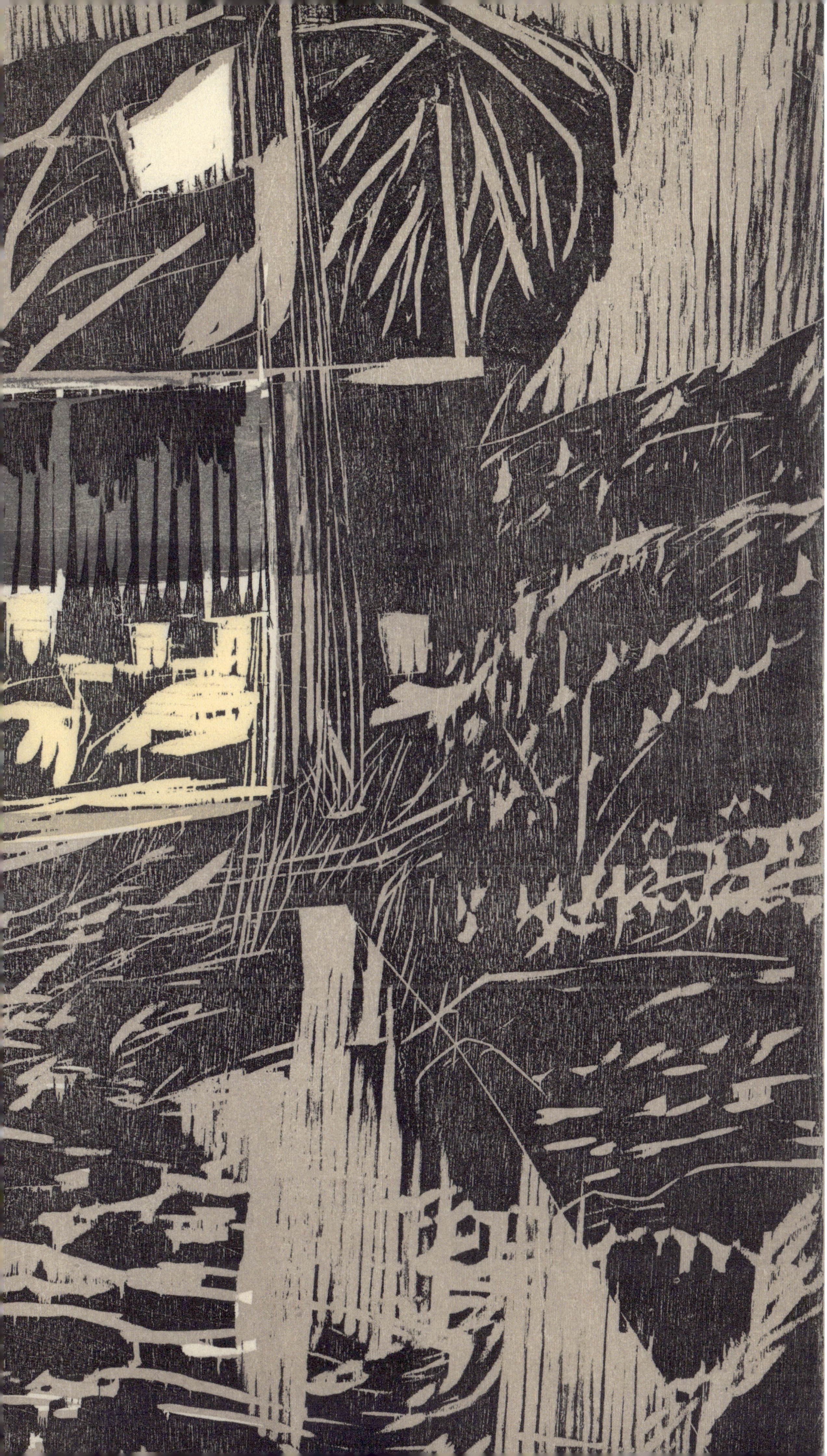

COME CLOSER, TOBAGO

We walked into the jungle. I took photographs of the shanty shacks. Suddenly a loud male voice boomed out "Come Closer".

It was sudden and it was alarming. It startled me.

[MWC]

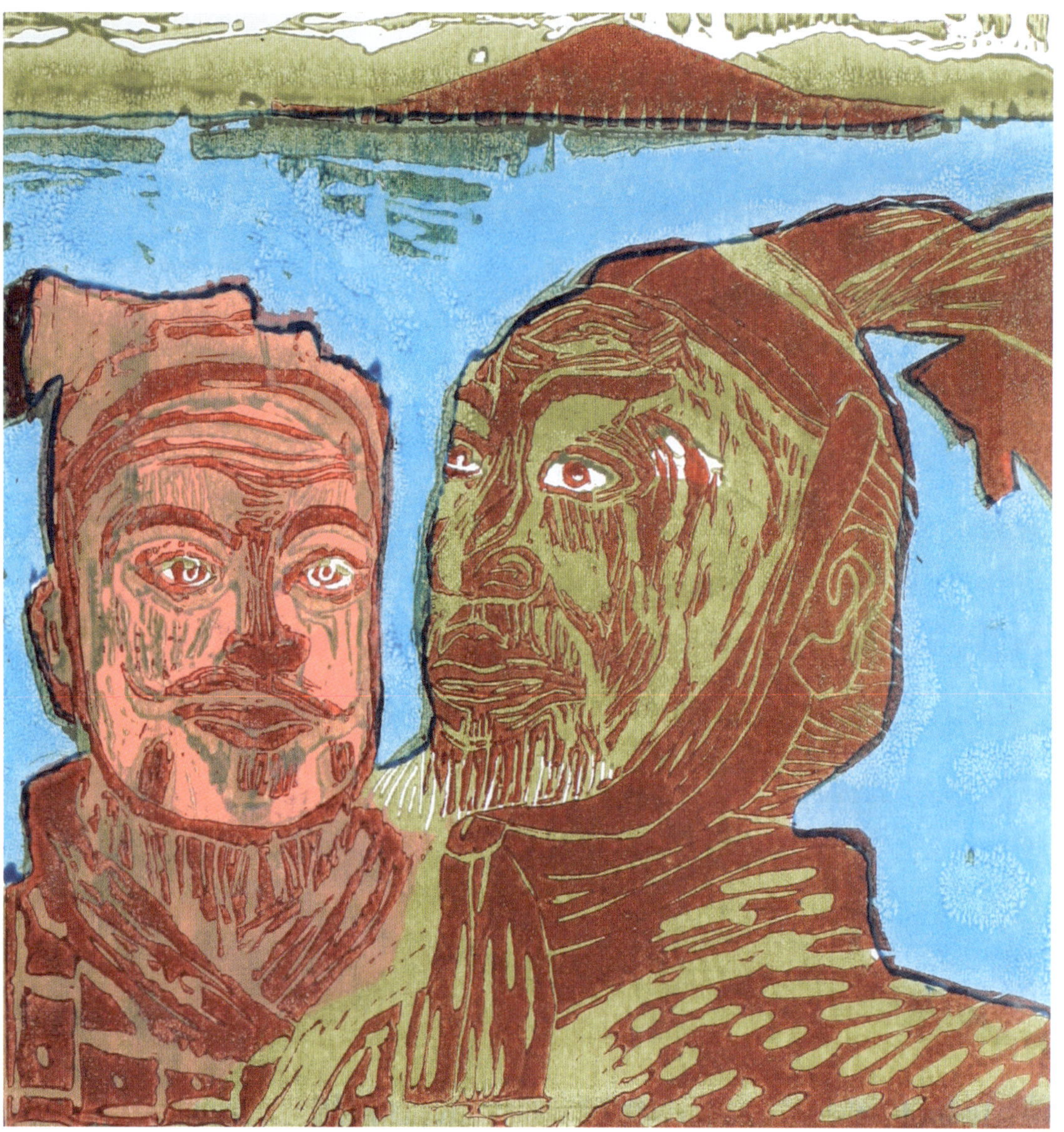

TERRACOTTA WARRIORS, CHINA
#1 AND #2 (opposite)

Completely awe-inspiring were the Xian Terracotta Warriors – buried in their hundreds – full size, each with individual faces and varying military uniforms; buried to guard the Emperor's grave and scare off the enemies.

I made these multi-plate woodcuts to emphasise their power and excellence.

[MWC]

EMPEROR'S CARRIAGE, CHINA

One intriguing sculpture was the emperor's carriage in which one could only see the driver at the front. The Emperor himself sat in the rear carriage, hidden so none of his subjects could see him. He sat behind a small sliding screen so he could look out secretly when he chose. His hidden presence seemed somewhat bigger and more important for not being seen.

[MWC]

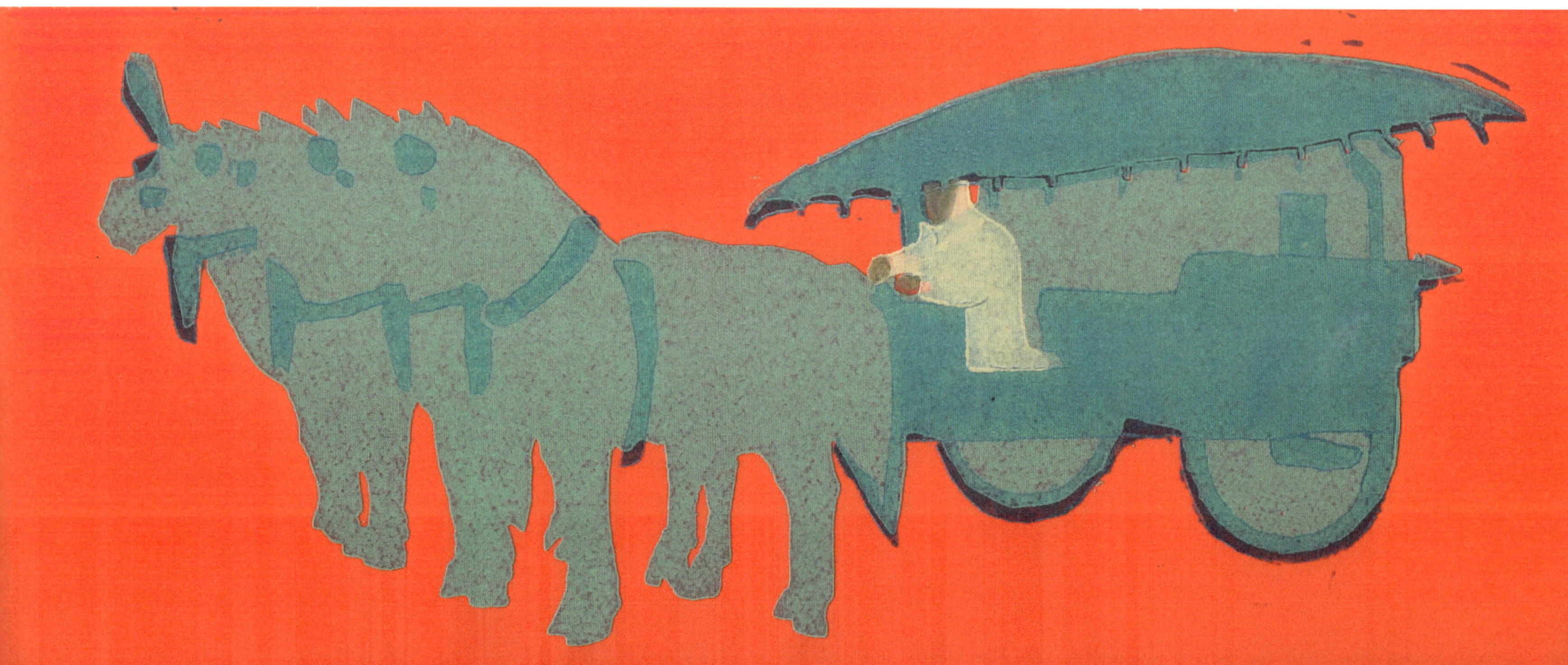

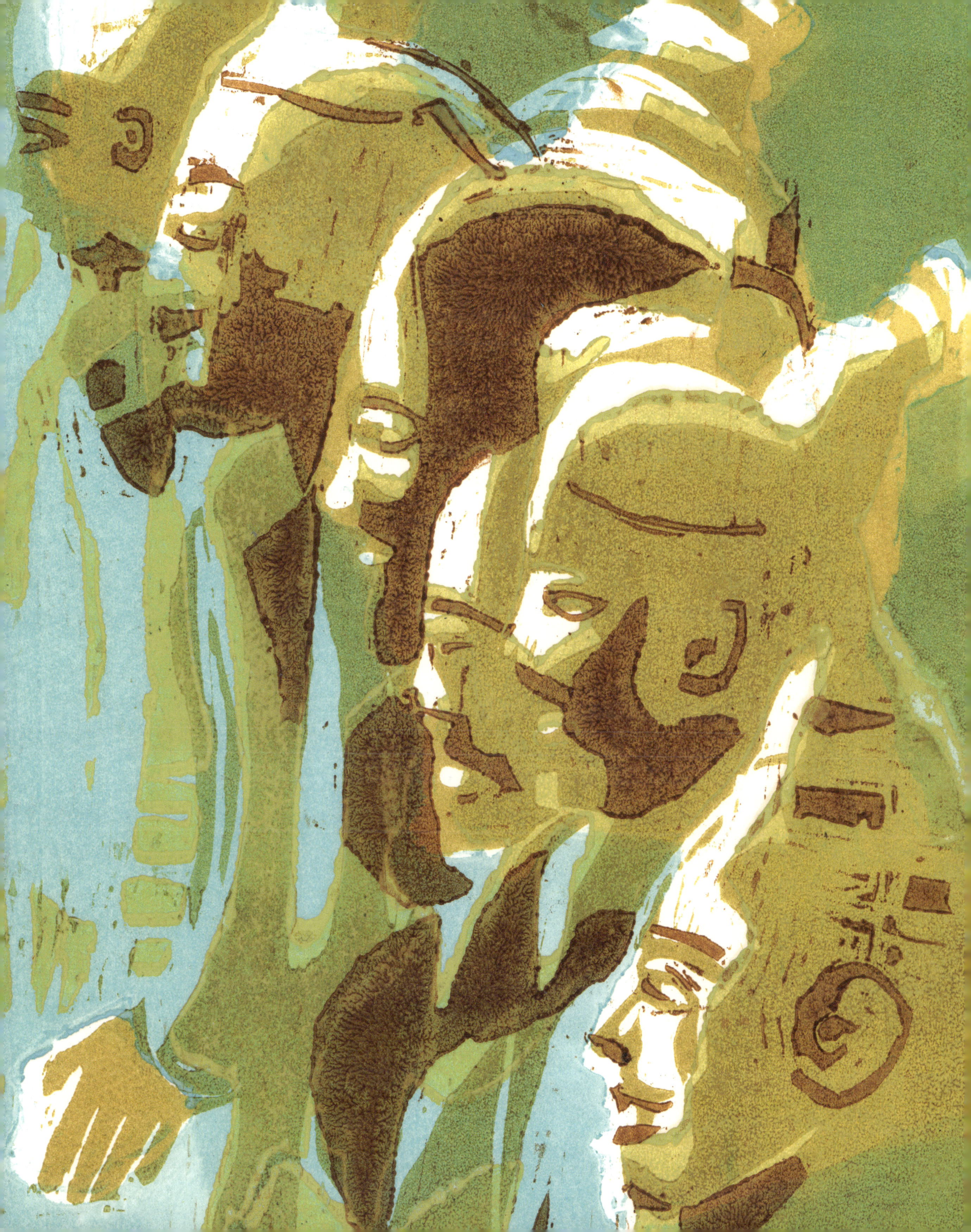

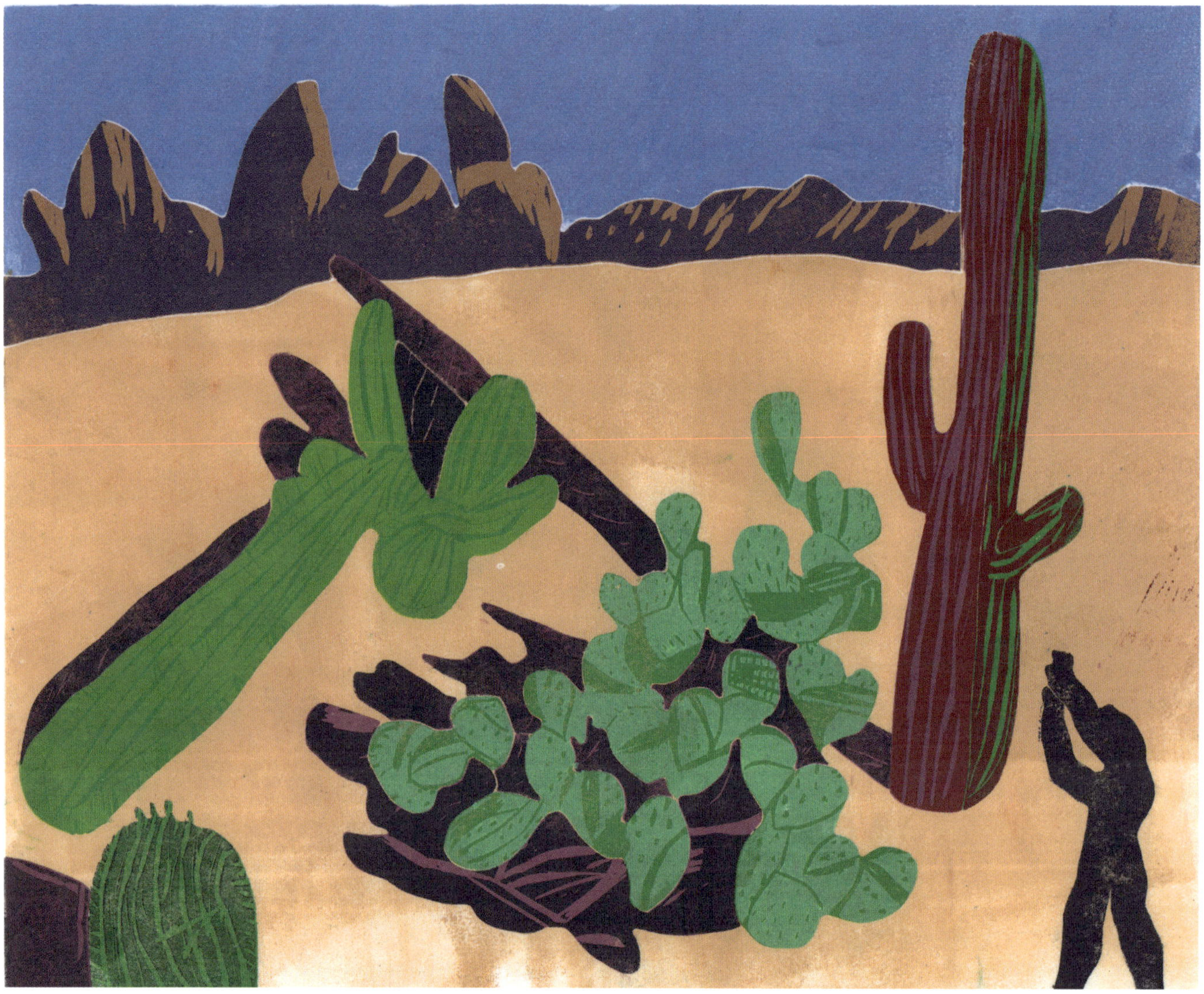

CACTI WITH IPHONE,
ARIZONA

*The rocks and cacti of the
Arizona desert are bizarre
and other-worldly. The
shapes are intriguing and
weird. The human presence
holding an iphone to
photograph them adds
another quirk.*

[RWC]

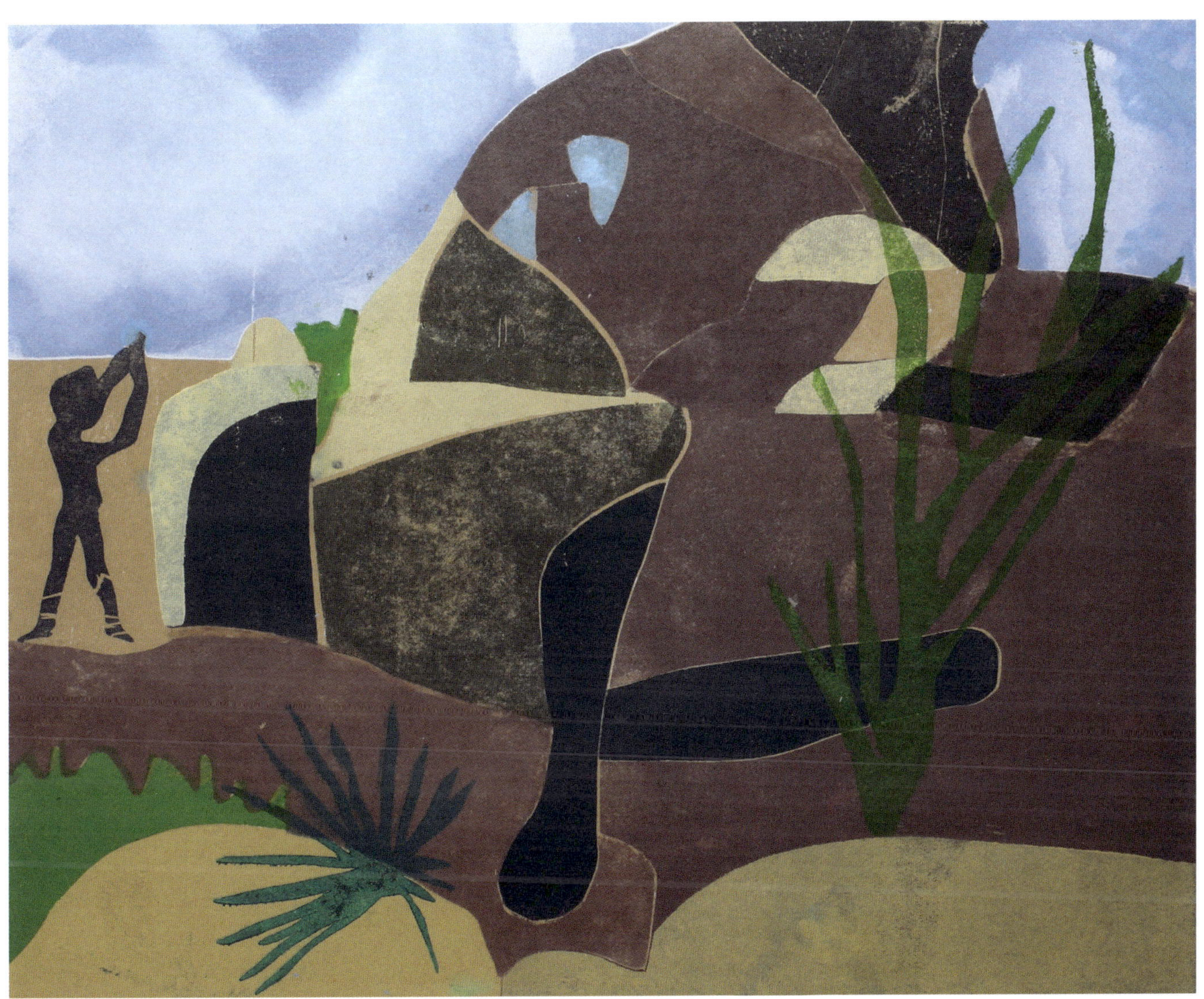

ZACHARY ON THE ROCKS,
ARIZONA

*The desert rocks seem to
take on a life of their own.
I love the menacing quality
of the rocks and cacti
presenting themselves
in the desert.*

[RWC]

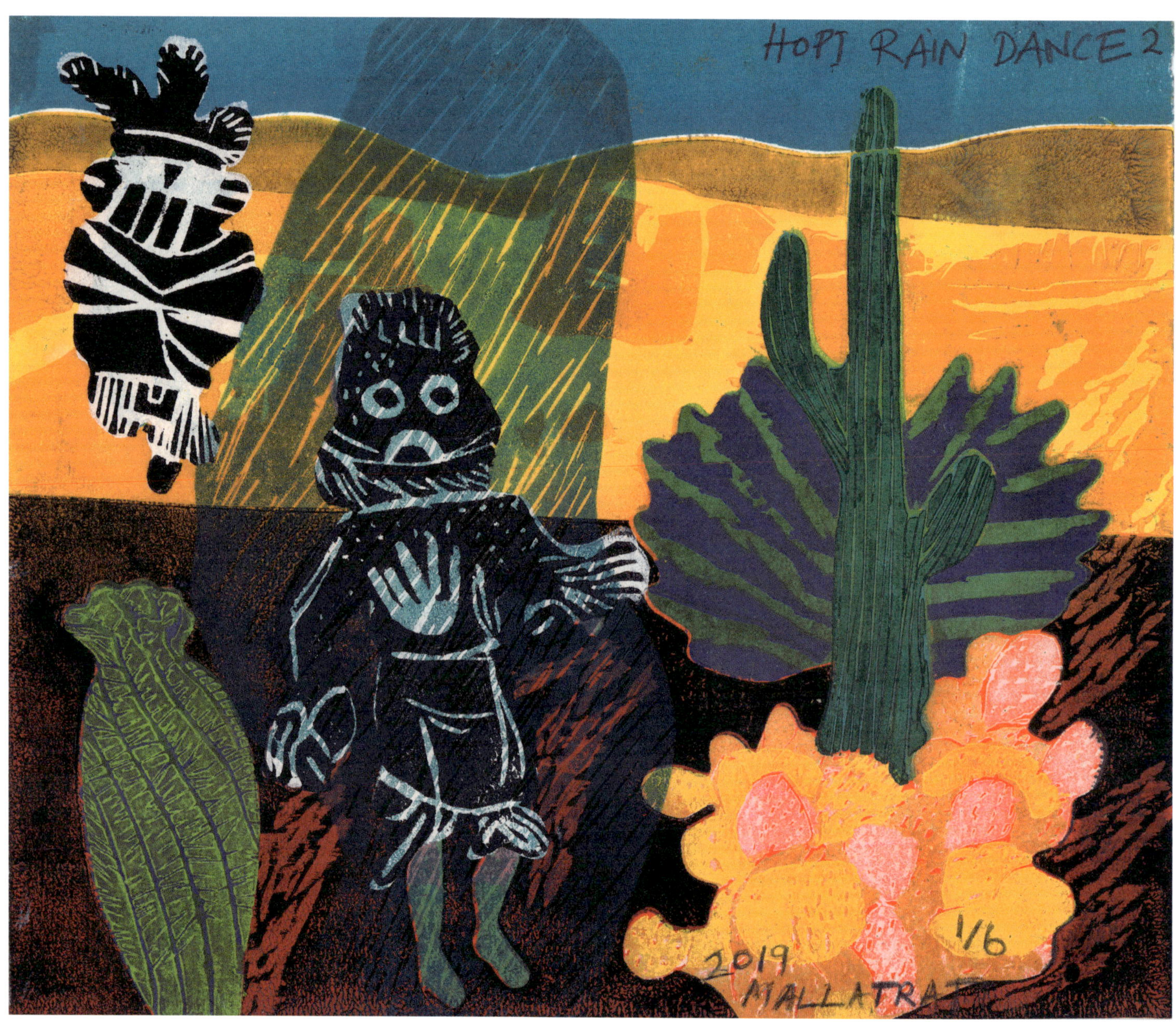

KACHINAS, ARIZONA #1 AND #2

The spirit of the Kachina still lives among the Hopi Indians of Arizona. They are worshipped as the bringers of rain water for crops. The Hopi make Kachina dolls which sell exclusively in shops in Sedona.

A tourist attraction originally generated by Max Ernst who bought up the entire shop when he discovered them on his exile from Germany during WW2. Hopi men also dress up in Kachina costumes and perform dances and rituals.

I was enchanted by the cactus, the sand and mountain colours and produced these prints to conjure up the Kachinas. The darker one is more structured into light and dark areas. Darker to suggest the tinge of the sinister they carry.
[RWC]

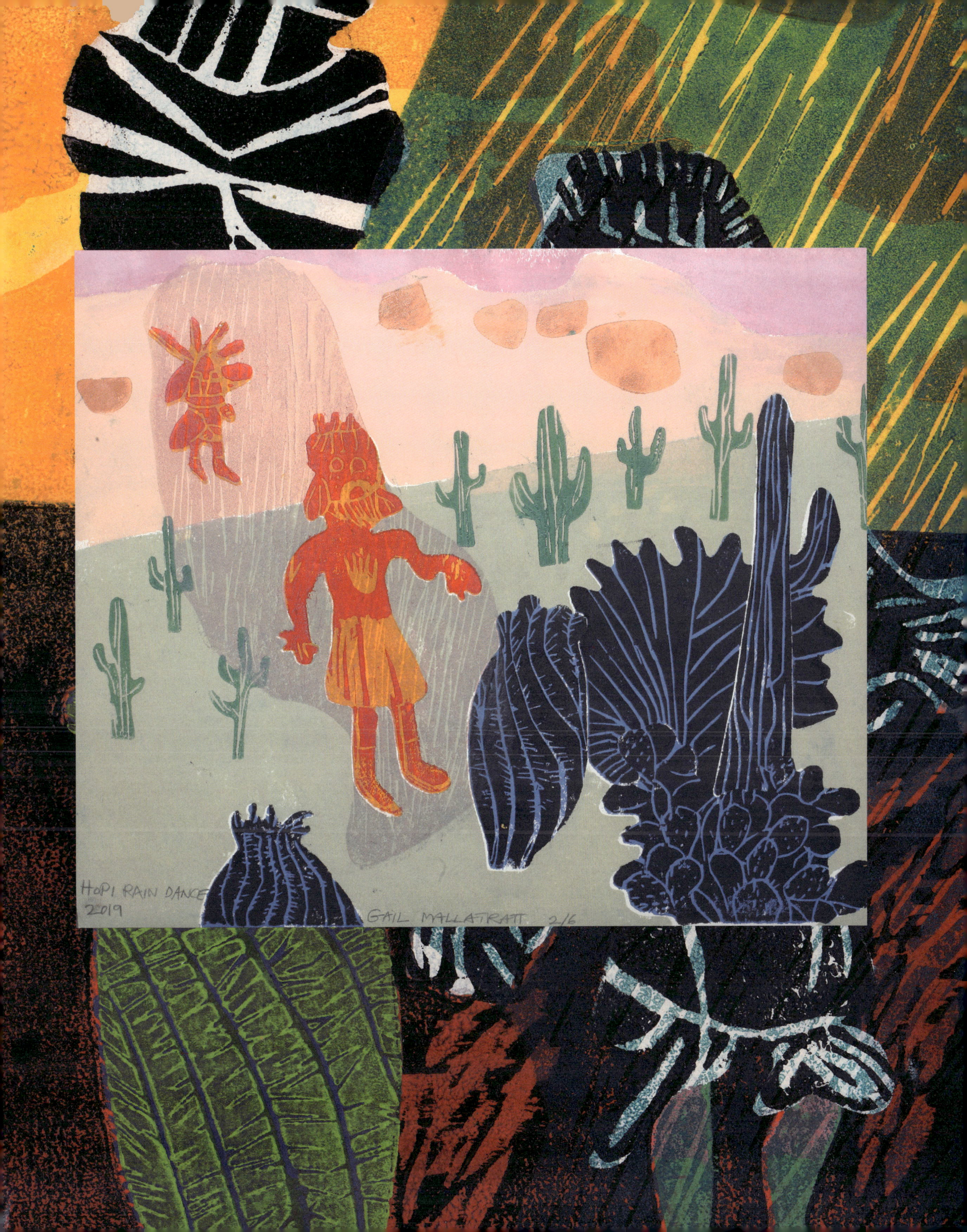

HOPI RAIN DANCE
2019
GAIL MALLATRATT   2/6

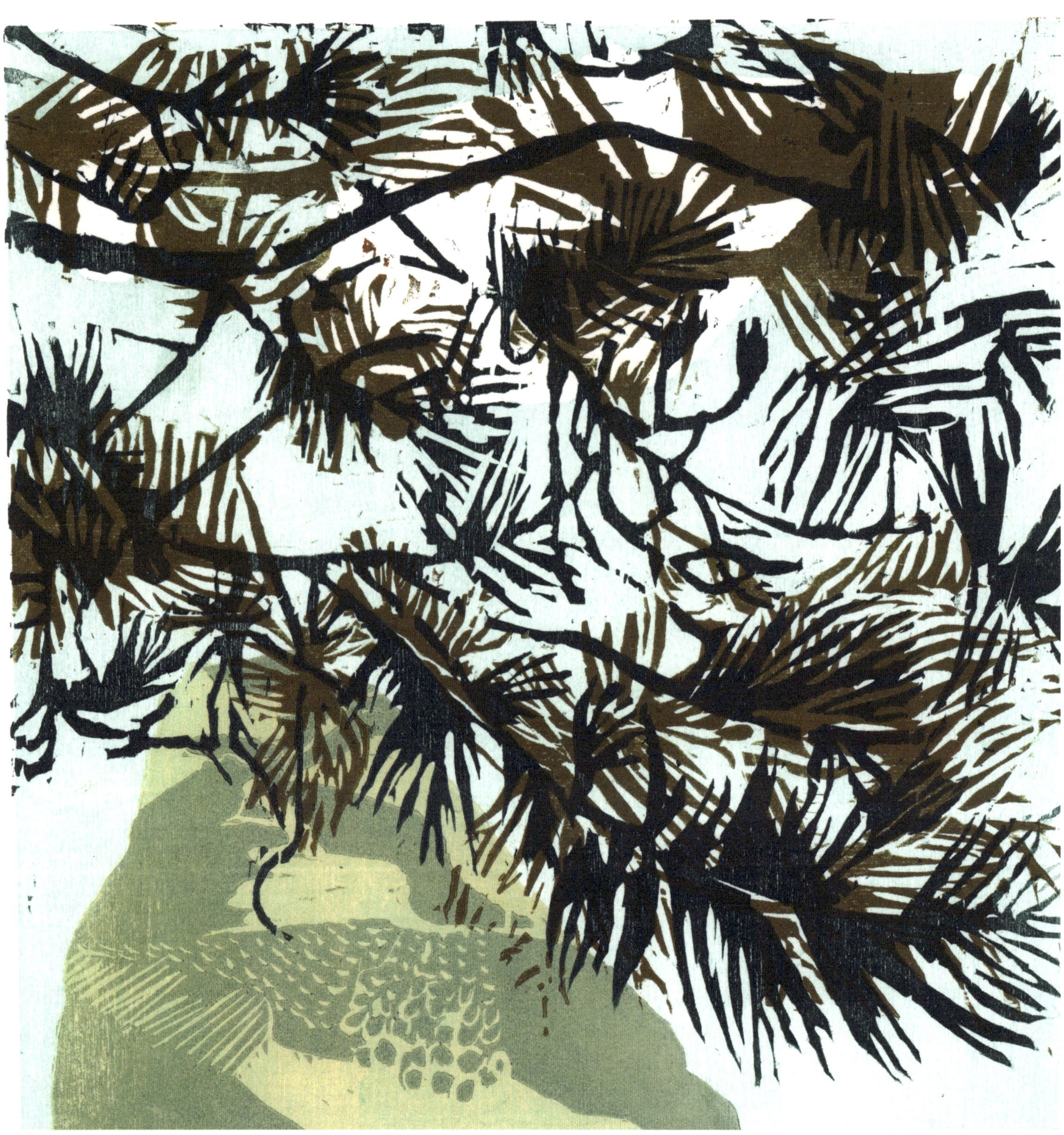

TUSCANY PINES, ITALY

Pines gently waving in the breeze. I cut two separate un-registered pieces of wood, drew the pine branches slightly differently as though they had moved, rolled up with different tones of green on each of the plates and printed them together. It was an experiment to defy registration. [MWC]

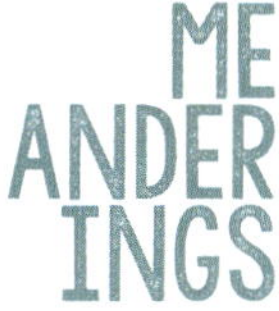

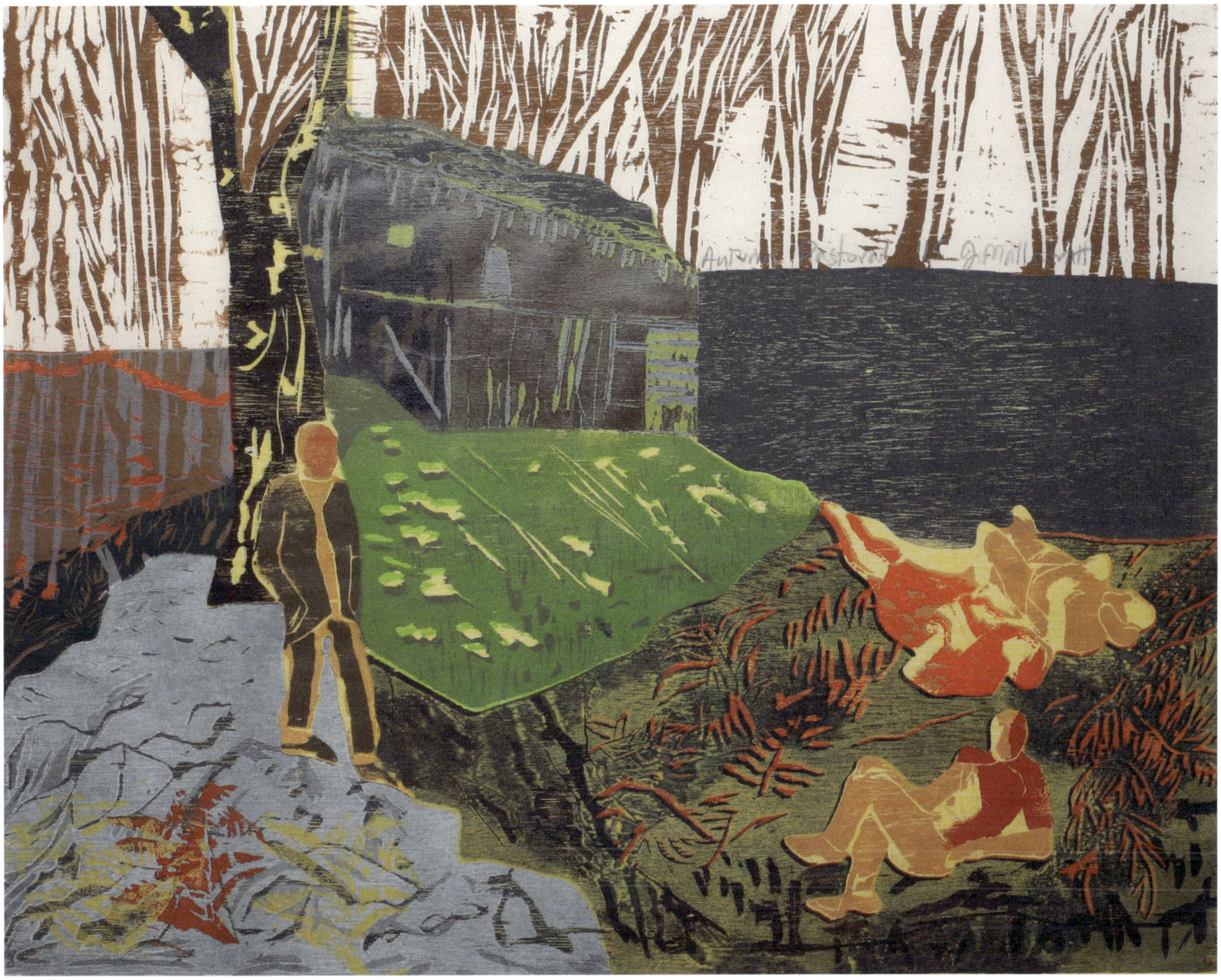

SOCIAL MEDIA, CONNECTICUT

This is set in a lush Connecticut summer. There is a forest, a run-down old barn and some chatty figures having a picnic. I called it 'did he sleep with her…?' as a suggestion of the gossipy trashy magazine social media conversation, in contrast to the rich and beautiful natural world around them.

[RWC]

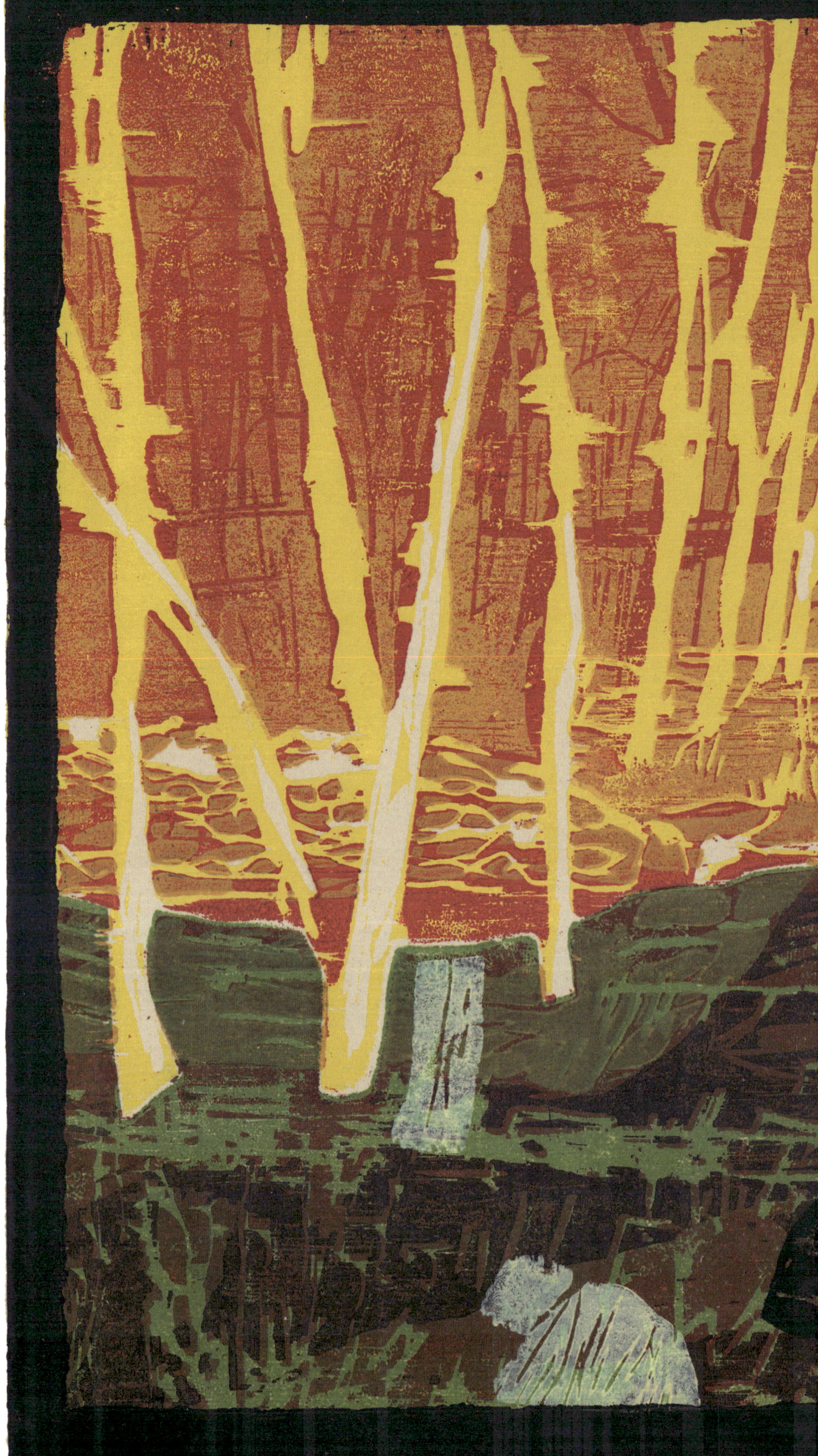

WILTON WOODS,
CONNECTICUT

*As a schoolgirl growing up
in New York City, we would
spend weekends in retreat
in Wilton, Connecticut. This
picture is my memory of being
caught in a winter landscape –
a teenager without any friends
or social life.*

*I used jagged cutting tools
to evoke the sharpness of my
anxieties, with the colours
of red and yellow being
counter-intuitive for winter
woods – but expressing the
desperation I felt.*

[RWC]

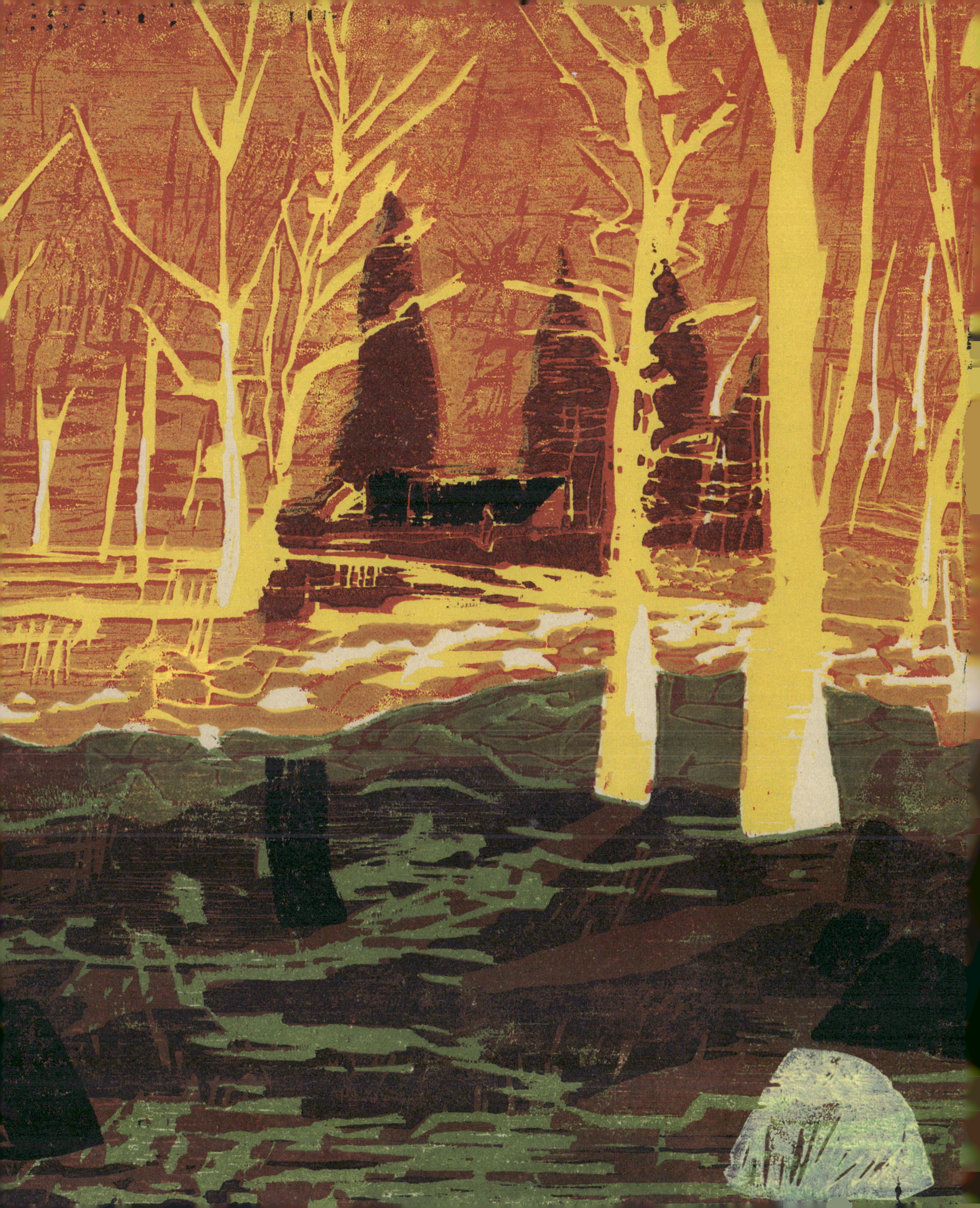

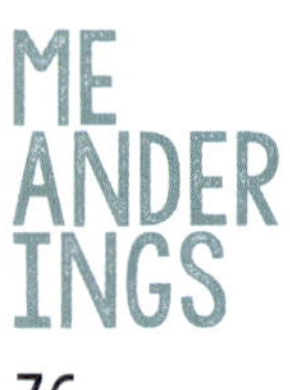

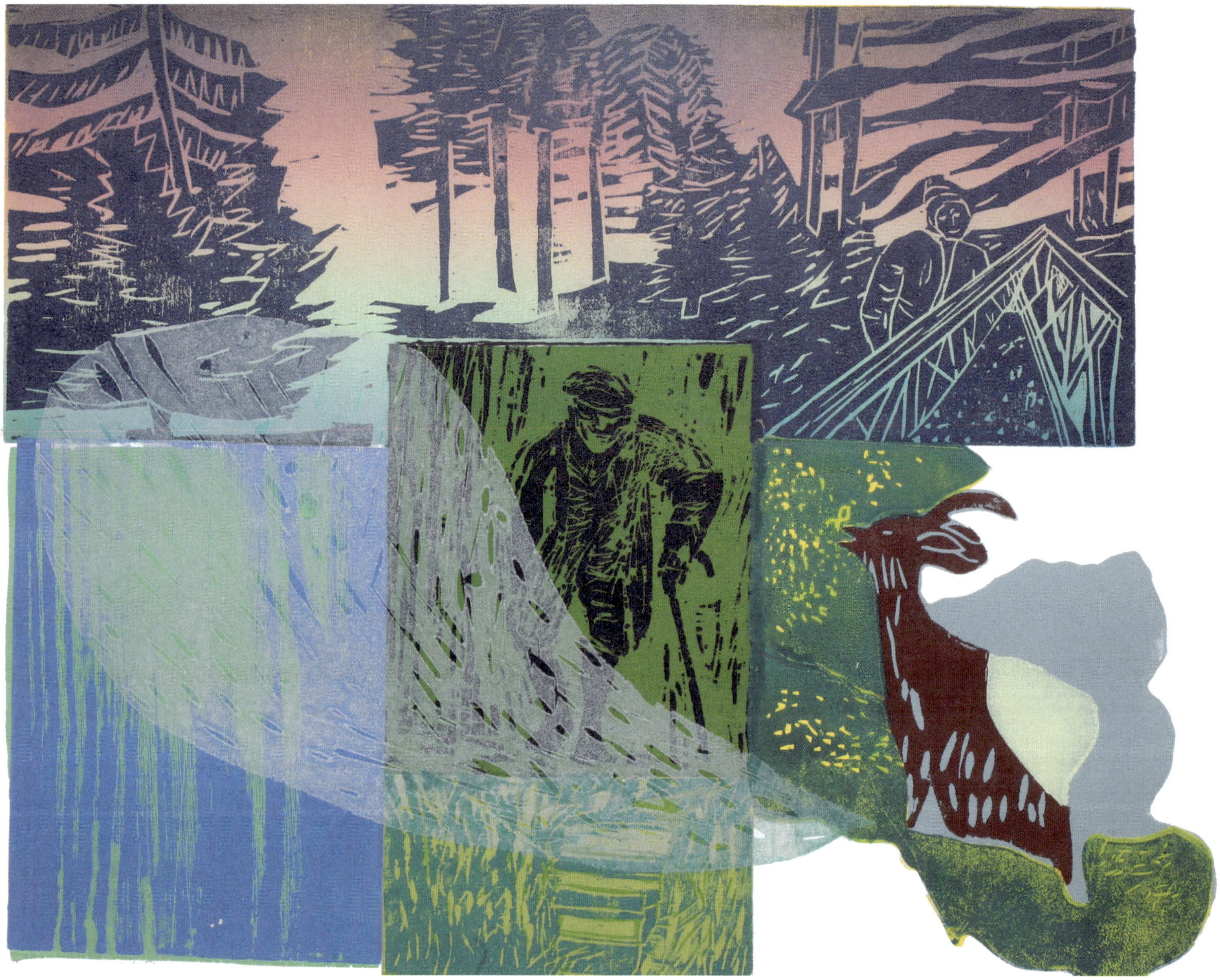

MEMORY OF DEVON

Devon, with all its richness of weather, trees, has become a precious memory.

This chap – old man Ridd – used to walk unsteadily up the road in front of our house in Devon every day. He became a symbol of the place for me. Timeless, ancient, and fixed in his habits.

[VP]

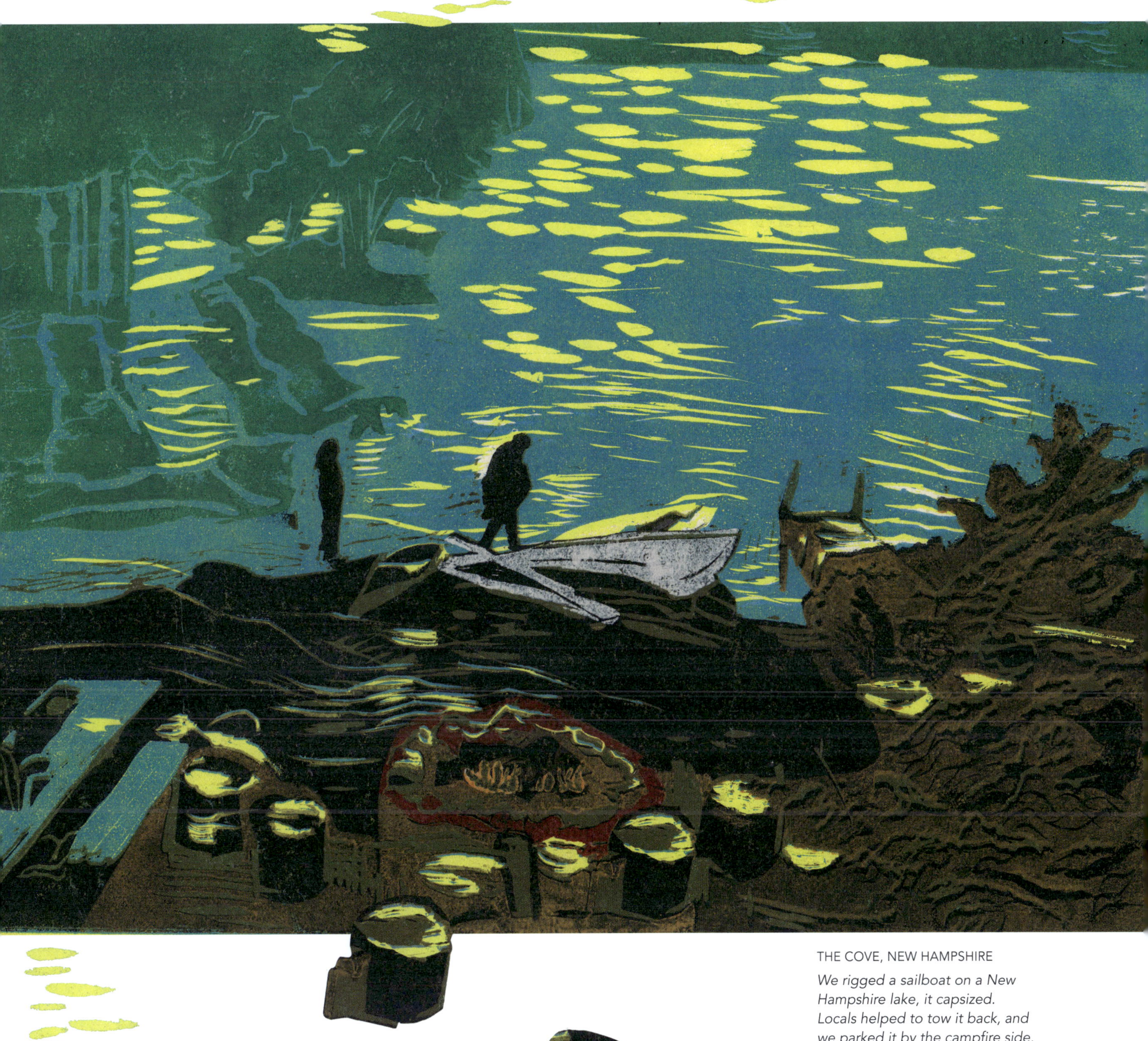

THE COVE, NEW HAMPSHIRE

*We rigged a sailboat on a New
Hampshire lake, it capsized.
Locals helped to tow it back, and
we parked it by the campfire side.*

[RWC]

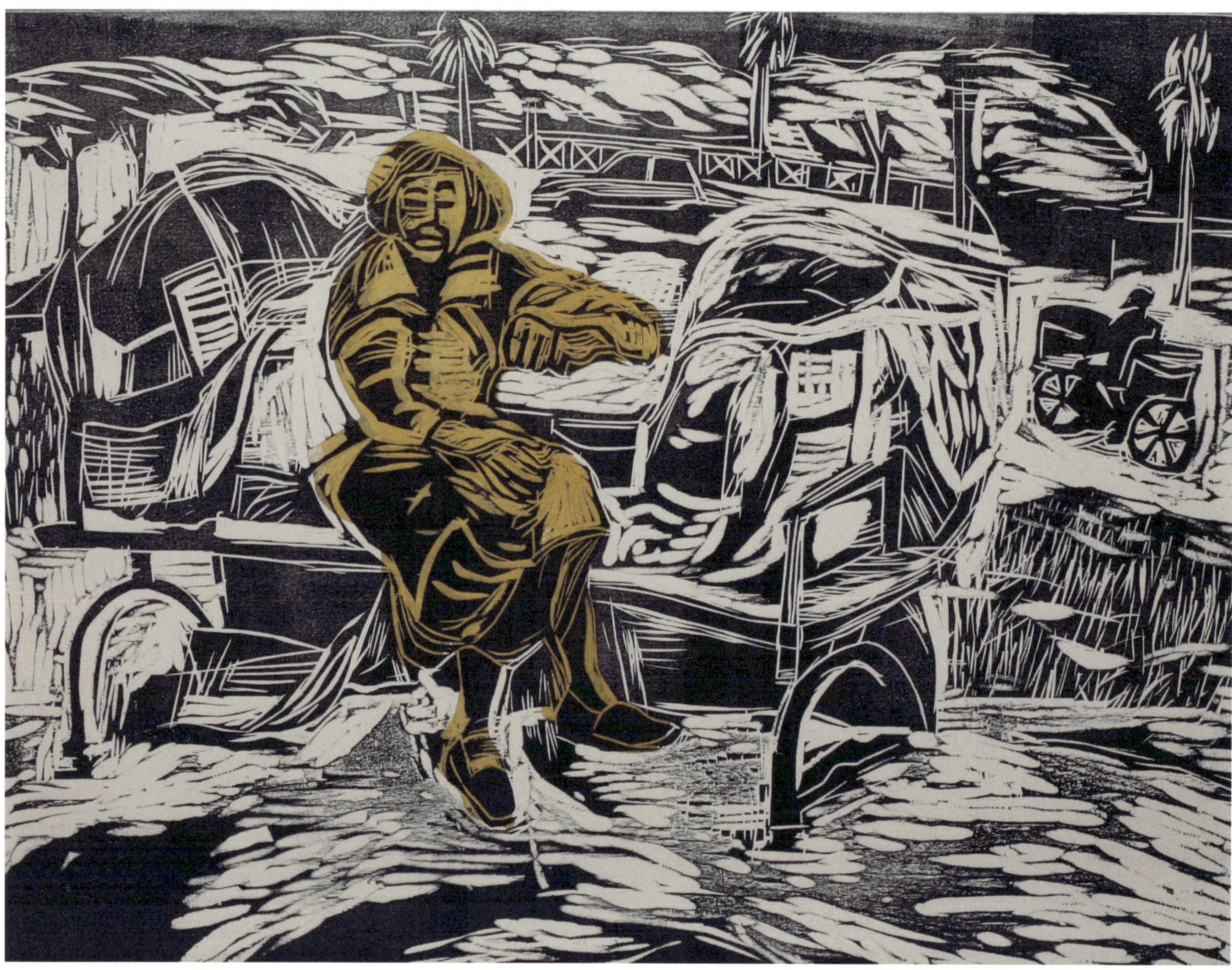

BAG LADY, PERU

*This lady arrived at the bench,
unpacked her numerous bags and
laid out the contents around her.
Then she sat there all day. When
the sun dropped down she began
packing them up again, loaded
her trolley and walked away. What
a life! What is she getting from all
that? Did she need those things?
Or was she empty without them?
It seemed like an exercise in
futility. Or was it a metaphor for
our endless consumerism?*

[WC]

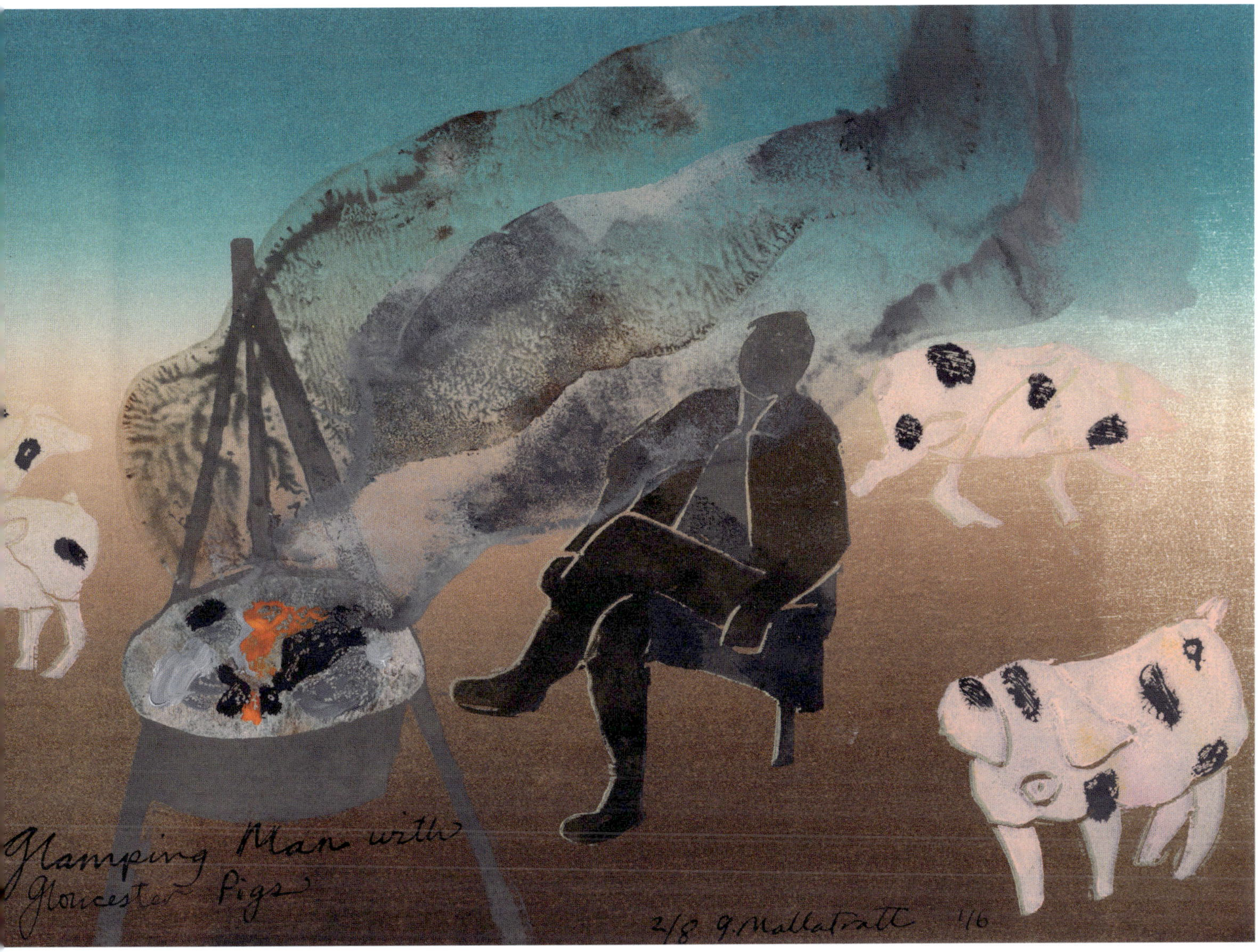

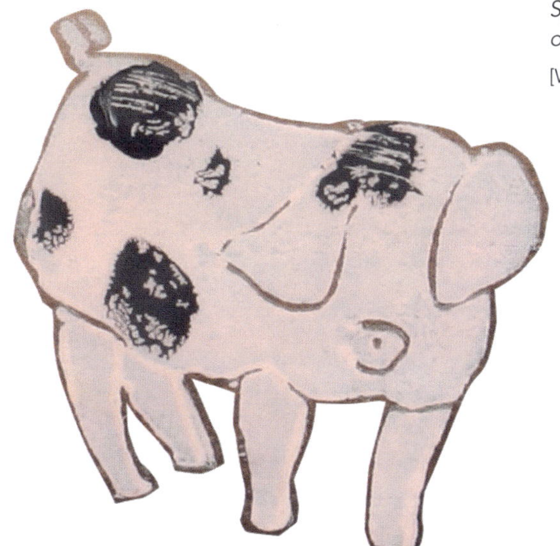

GLAMPING MAN, SUSSEX, UK

My son and his family went glamping with us in Sussex one summer. It was perilously cold and rainy so we sat close to the fire and were visited by Gloucester Old Spot pigs – the fire smoke blew in our faces, wherever we sat.

[WC]

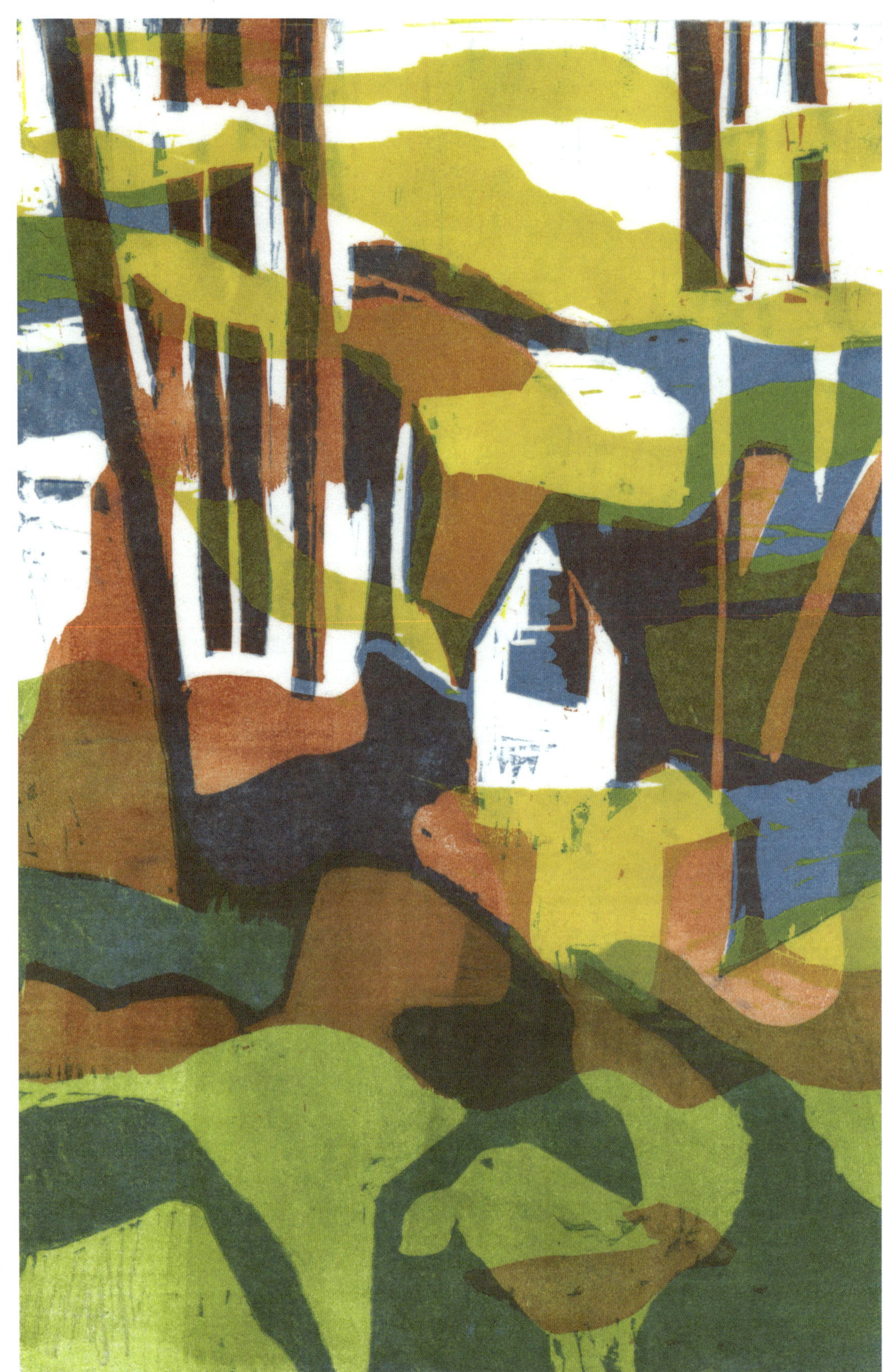

HOUSE IN THE WOODS,
NEW HAMPSHIRE

*I wanted to capture
the sunlight filtering
down through the trees
to this isolated house.
I used transparency
medium and over-
lapping colours to
build the scene.*

[MWC]

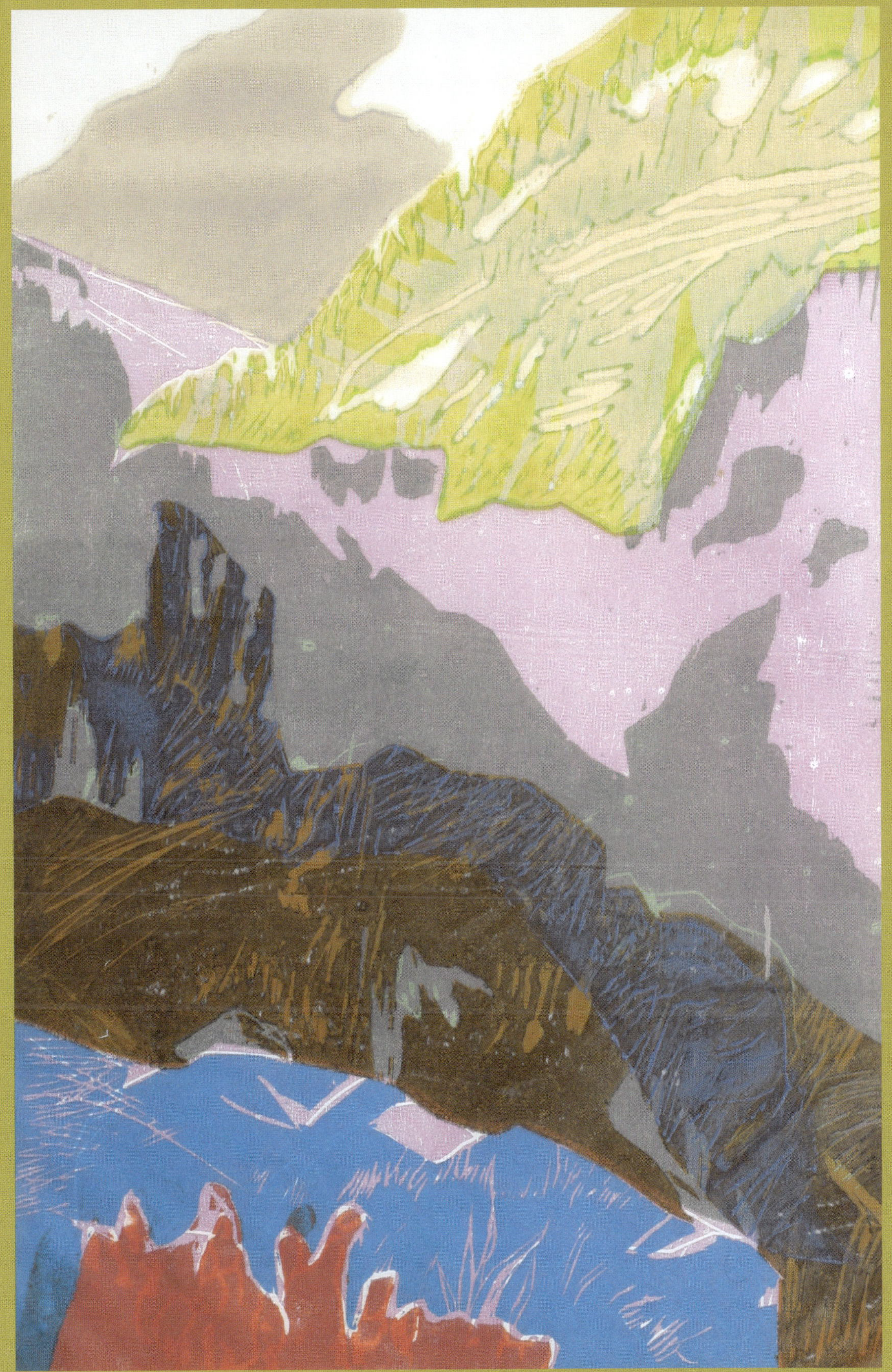

ALPINE MOUNTAINS
*This was further
abstracting the
mountain image.*

[MWC]

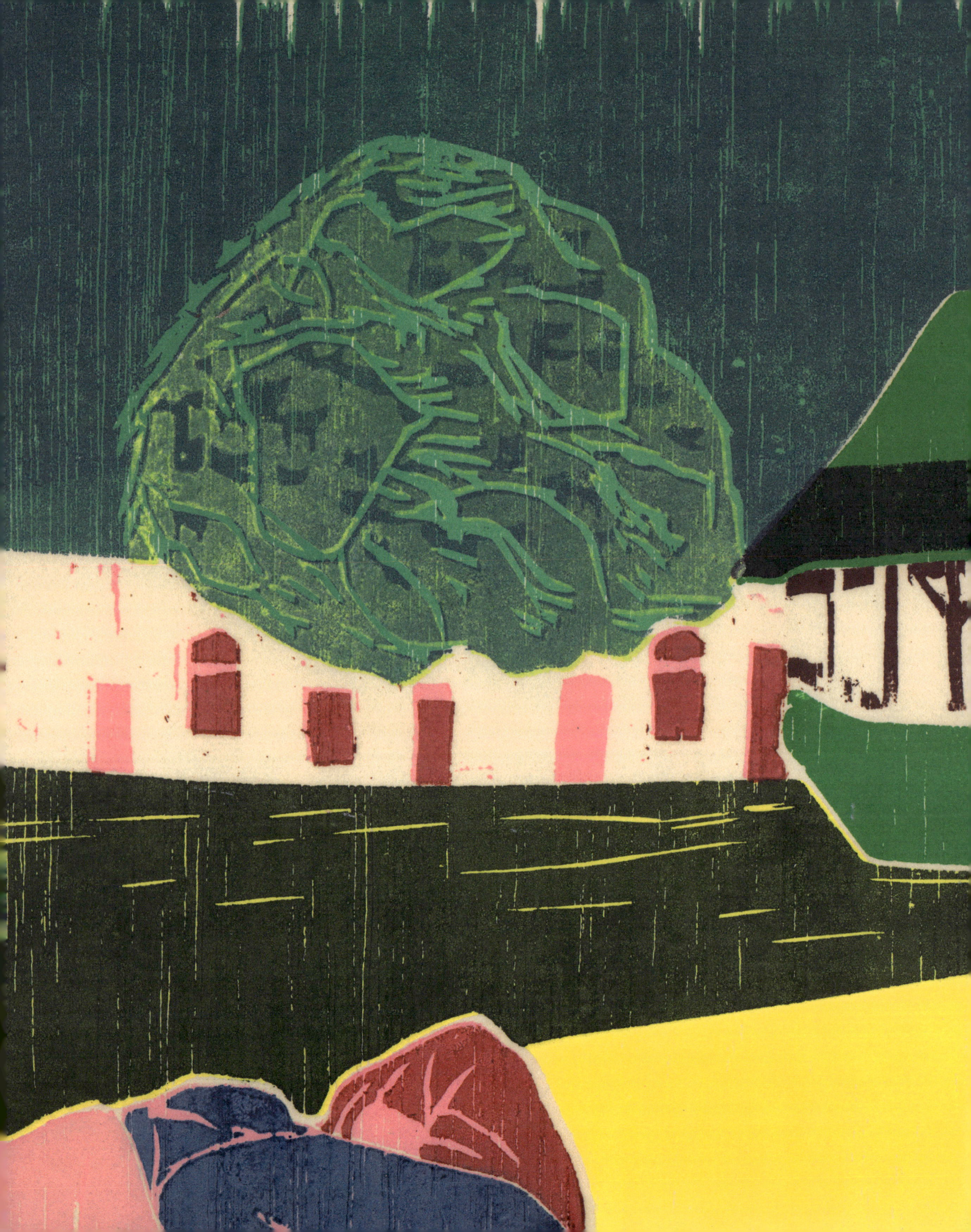

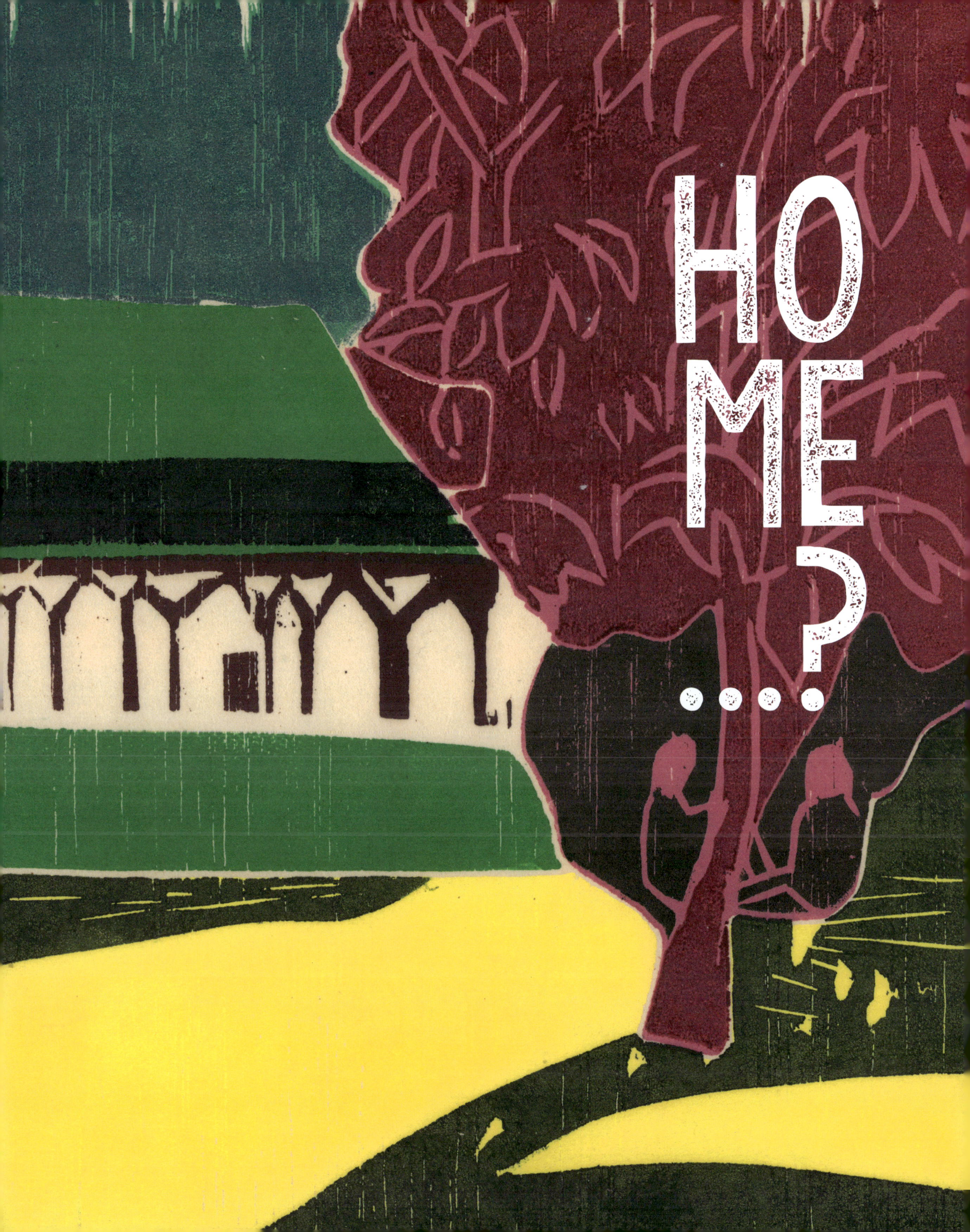

HO
ME
?
....?

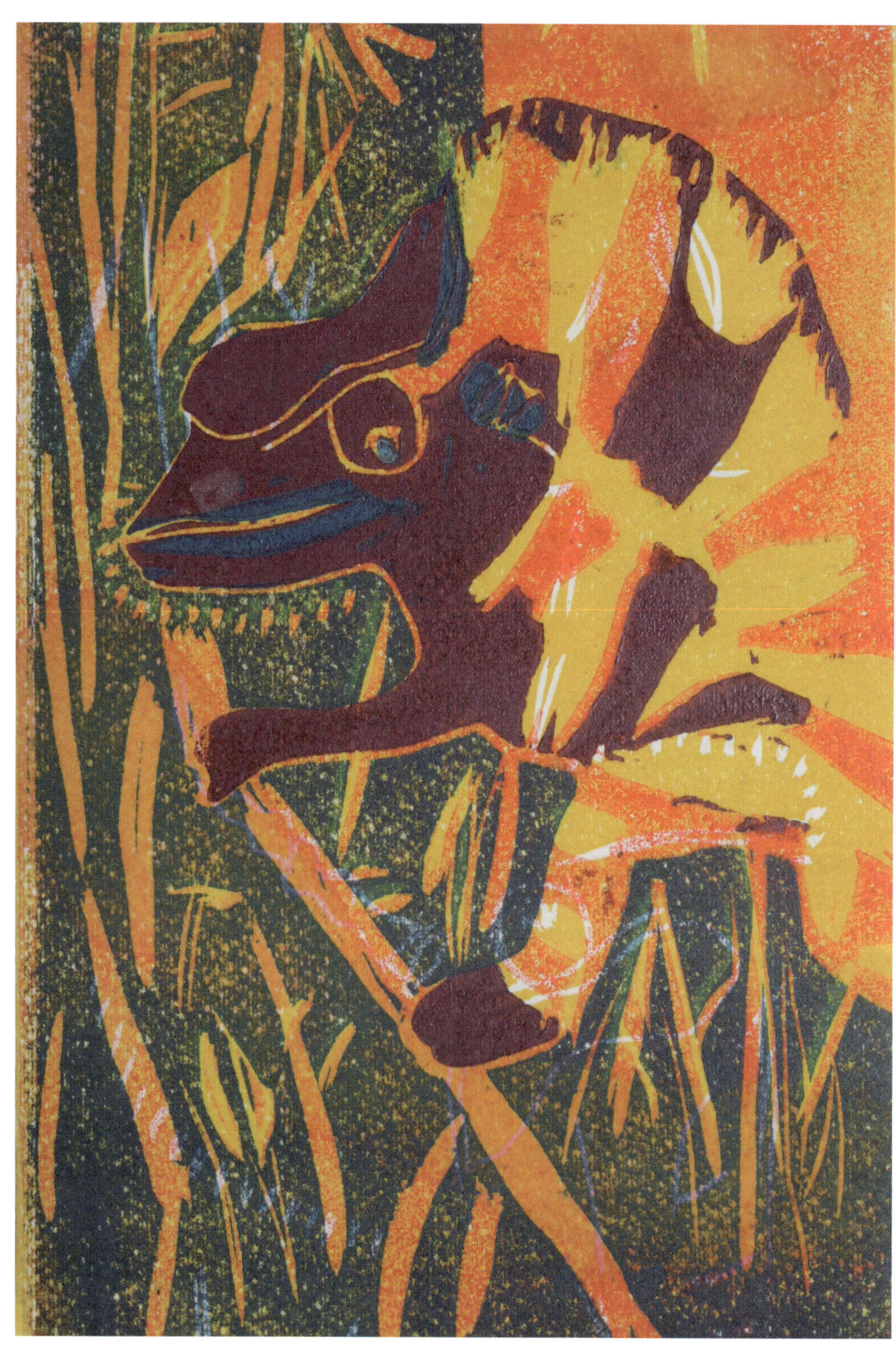

THE
CHAMELEON
PERSON
*Where does
she belong?*

[WC]

THE CHAMELEON SYMBOLISES CHANGE – changing its colours to remain hidden. I have had a lot of change in my life, so believe that this creature is a sort of comrade. During my 48 years in London, I have occupied twelve different houses, alternating between urban and suburban – suburban and urban…

Since 1972, when I arrived in London from the US (with a small baby and an English husband, I managed to have two more children – now fully grown with children of their own). I have lived in a variety of locations, each one remodelled and redecorated to my instructions. And each one falling short of my sense of settling. In the end I was able to resolve this by rooting by the river, across from Shadwell.

I see now that this was a journey to find where I belong. Looking to resolve a conflict of who I was and where I could be comfortable as a 'foreigner'. No matter how awe-inspiring this wonderful city is, there's no forgetting that you're an alien when you're in London. And perhaps because it is so diverse, one remains a non-native.

In the first instance, Camden had much appeal; we had a wonderful house and garden. As a place to bring up a family, Primrose Hill seemed perfect, with great community schools and a friendly neighbourhood. A downsize move followed, still in Primrose Hill, renting the basement, with next door's beautiful blooming magnolia never ceasing to please. When a new occupier cut it down I decided it was time to go.

My next move took me to an Arts and Crafts Coroners Court on the edge of Clapham Old Town, near to where my sons had settled. This offered me charm and space galore and I restored it to its pre-war glory. This lasted long enough (2 years) until I realised it was impossible to heat.

Notting Hill Gate then offered urban convenience but rising damp on a massive scale. Freehold occupants who refused to pay their share didn't help the matter. So a lucky escape found me in Wilmington Square, near Exmouth Market and Sadler's Wells, and close to where I began my design career. From there I reverted to suburban Dulwich in search of closer family connections and a community. This didn't last long either, and I was soon drawn back to deepest darkest urban Shad Thames and Tower Bridge to a suitable bijou arty building, outside of which twirled tourists and crowds every Saturday night, and space was at a premium.

And so it all went – providing much new adventure, and a chance to try everything I needed to try. Thankfully my twelfth landing has given me unending variety: sky, water, sailboats and an uplifting swirl of life. I am thankful every day.

Could it be that in my genes is a wanderlust?

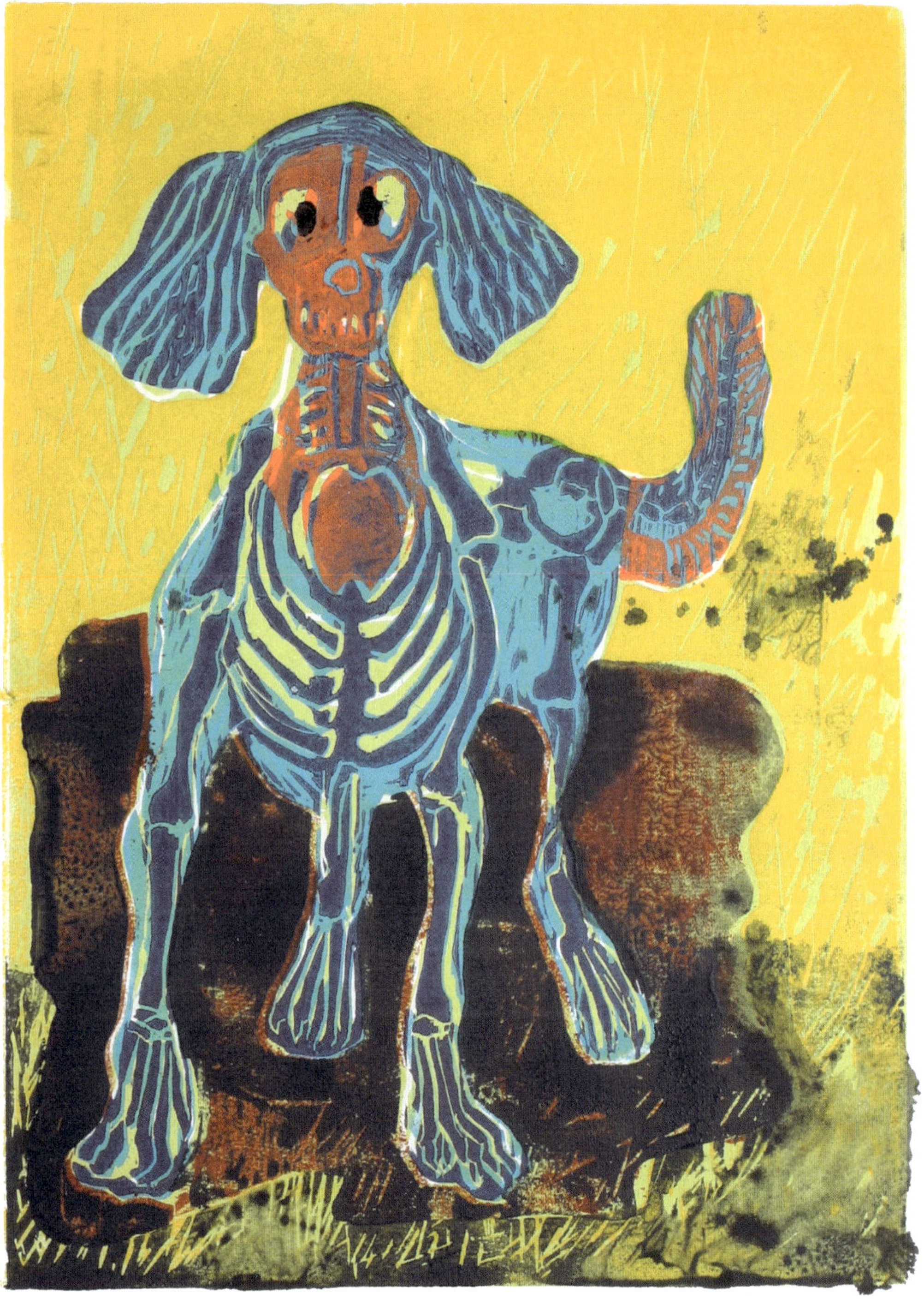

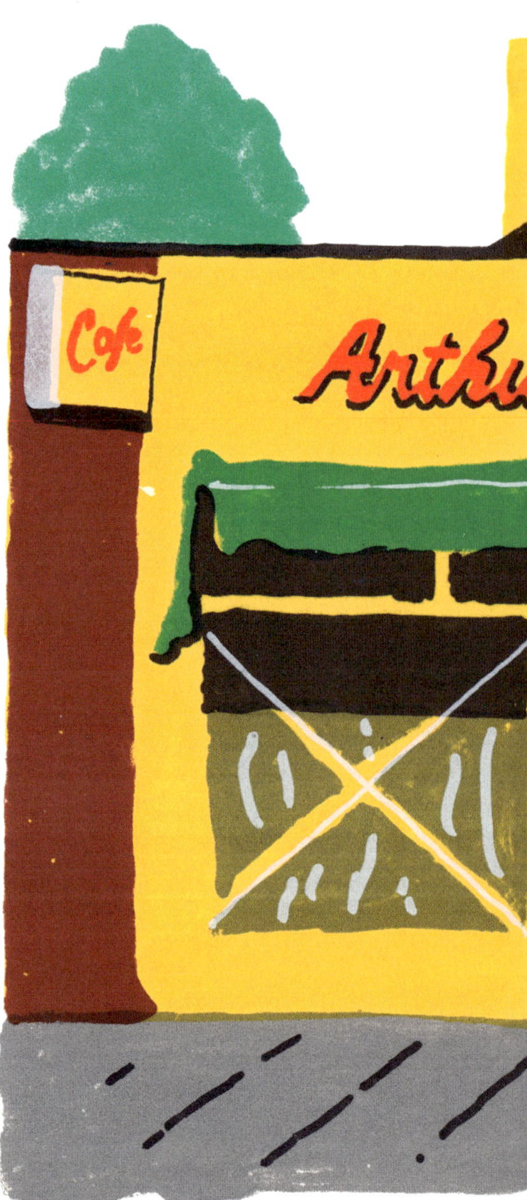

THE LOVELY COCO
– MY FRIEND AND
GUARDIAN ALWAYS

[MWC]

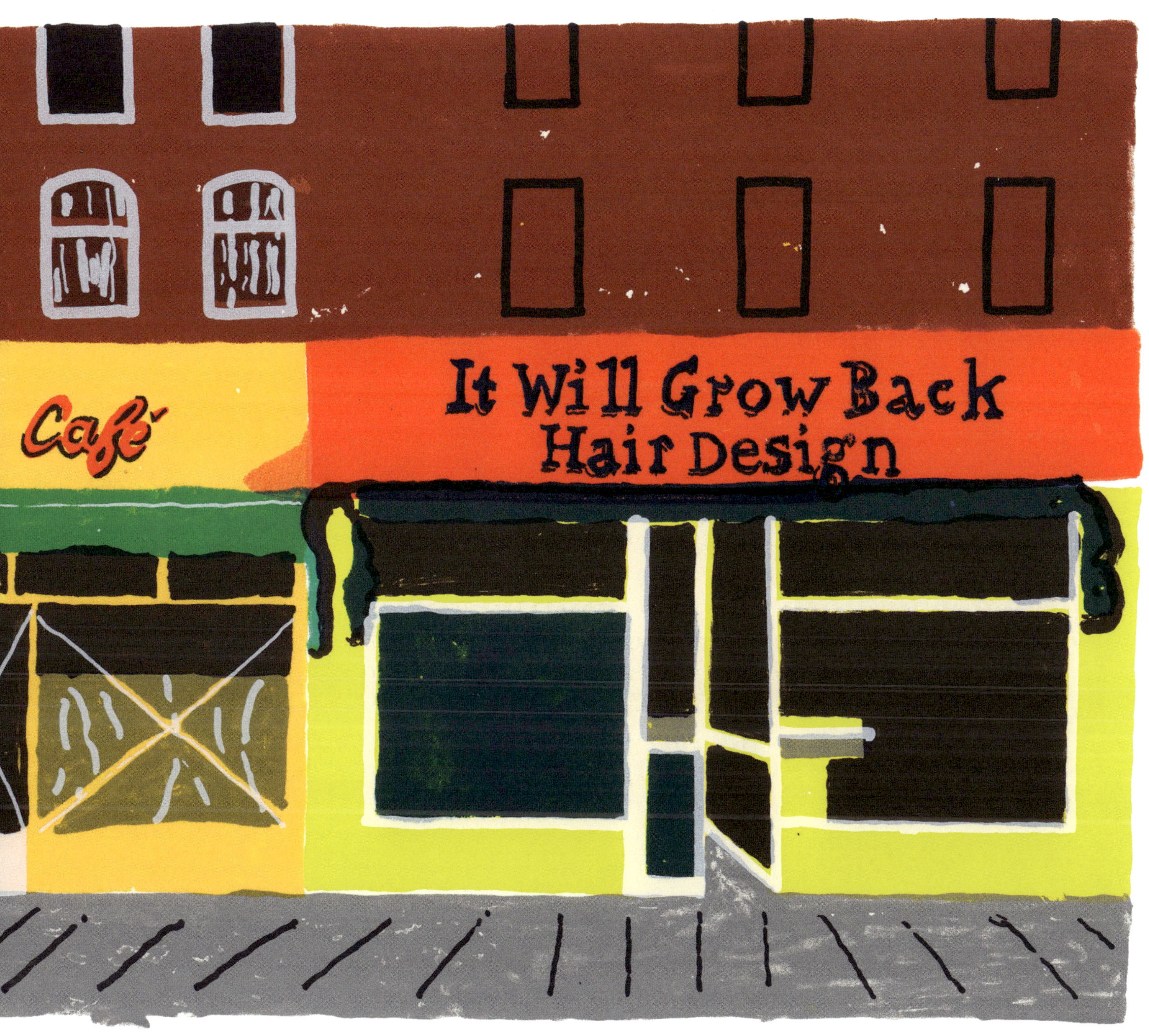

IT WILL GROW BACK,
NORTH EAST LONDON

*This Hackney run of shops
spoke of the possibilities after
chemotherapy.*

*This is a silkscreen that I made in
Brighton with colleague Ian Brown
at volcanic_editions.*

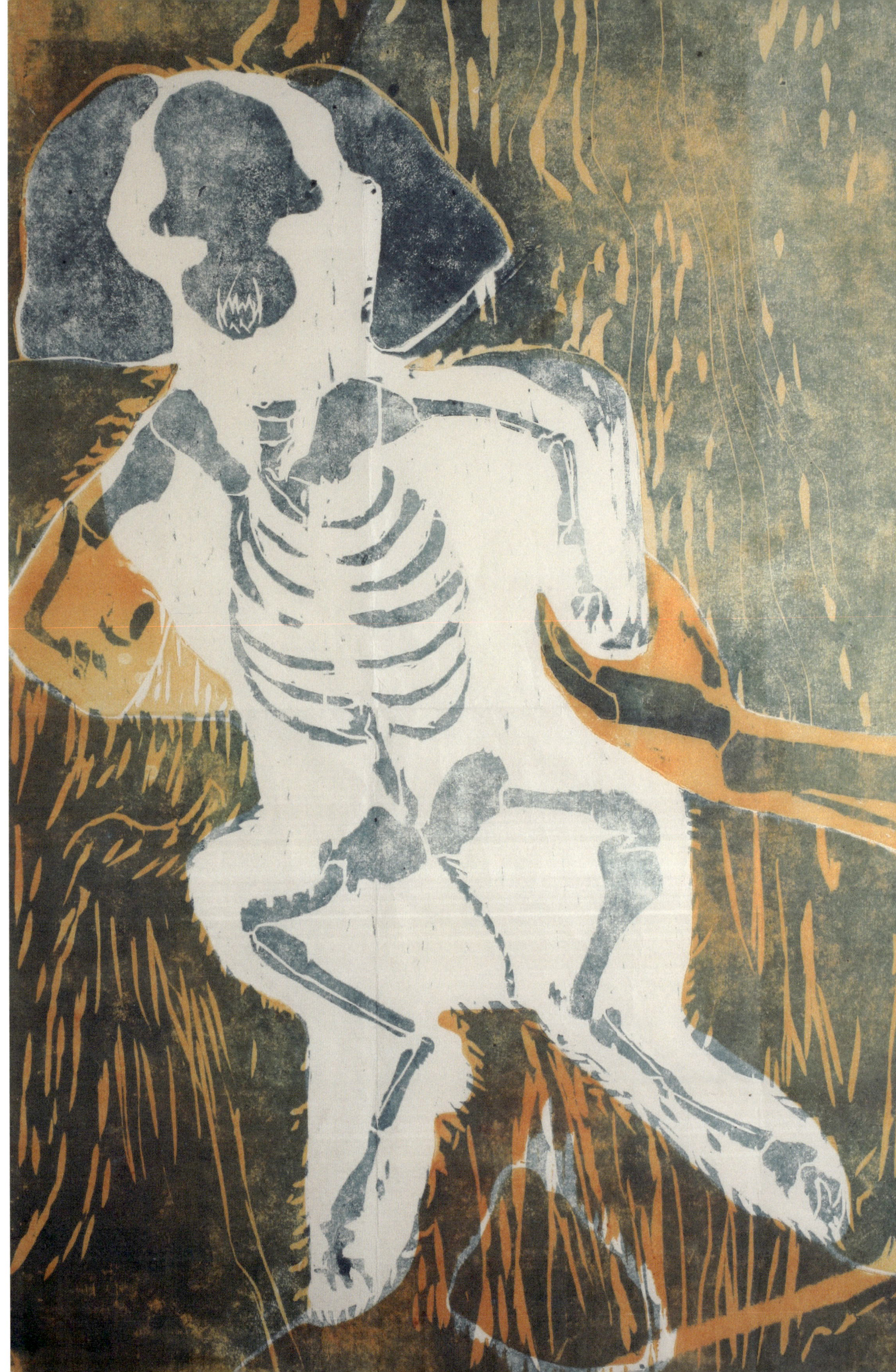

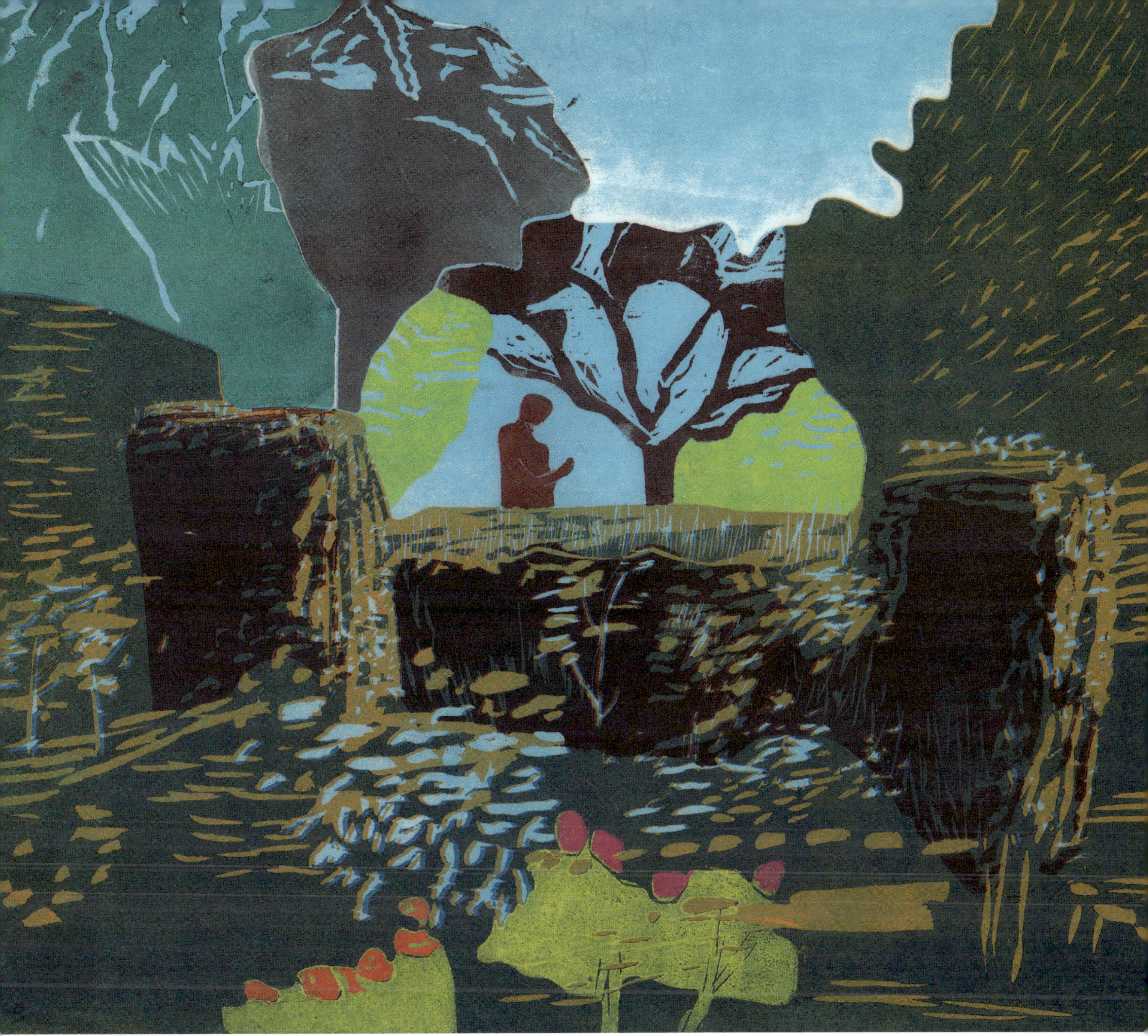

GARDEN, OXFORDSHIRE
*Our lush garden in spring,
with all its tantalising colours
and shapes.*
[RWC]

COCO #2 *(opposite)*
[MWC]

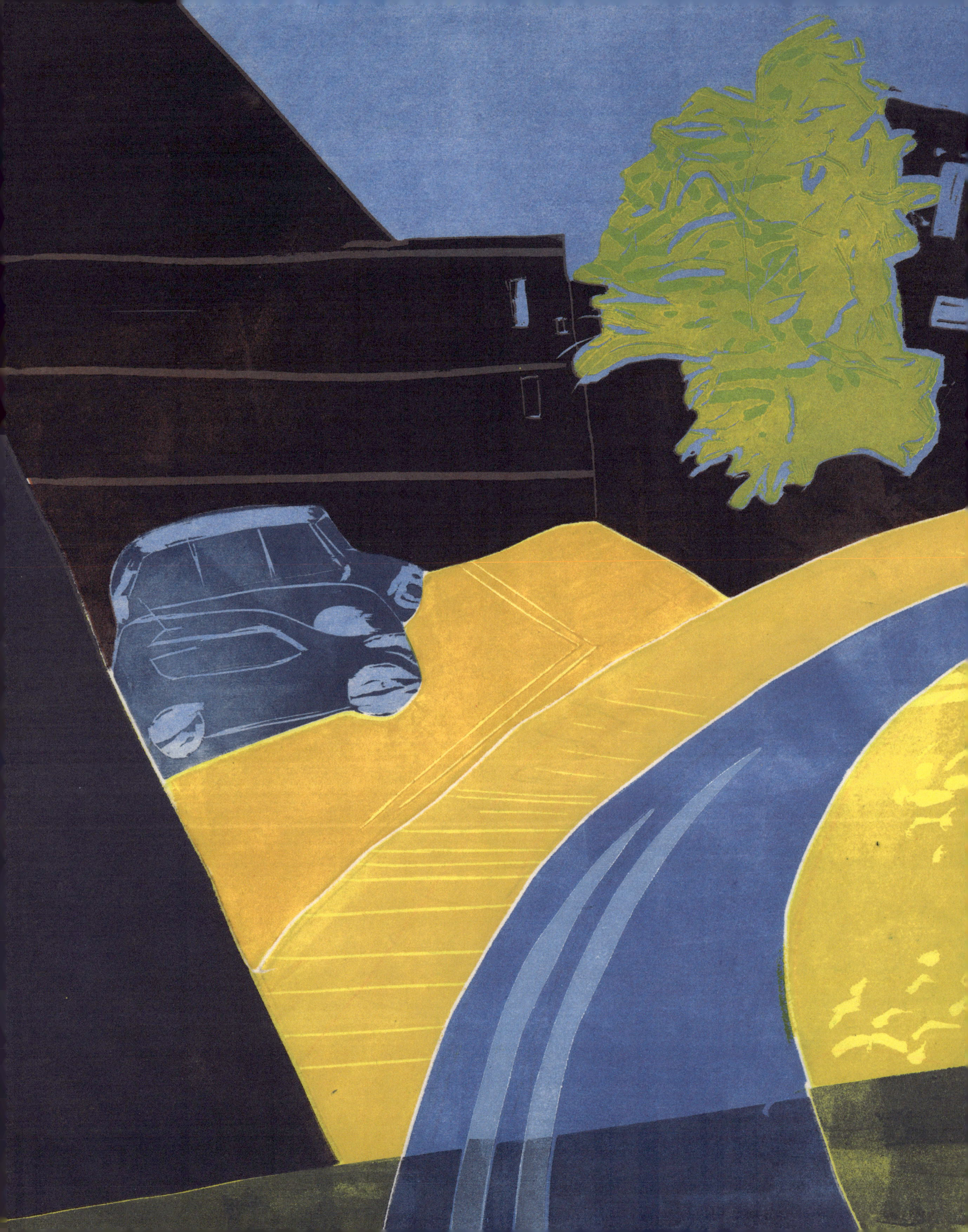

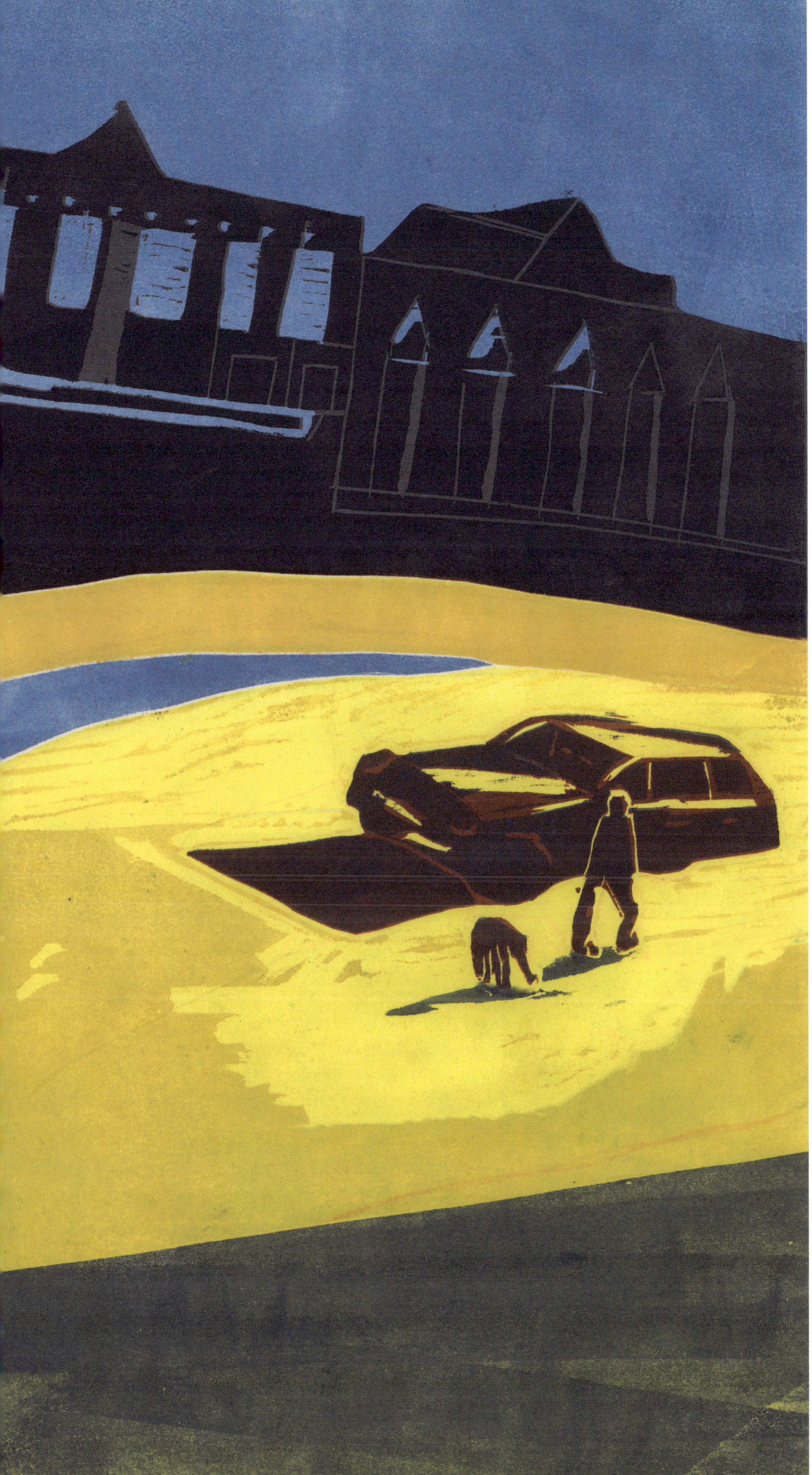

LIMEHOUSE REACH

A man, a dog and a car, in a hidden corner of East London.

[WC]

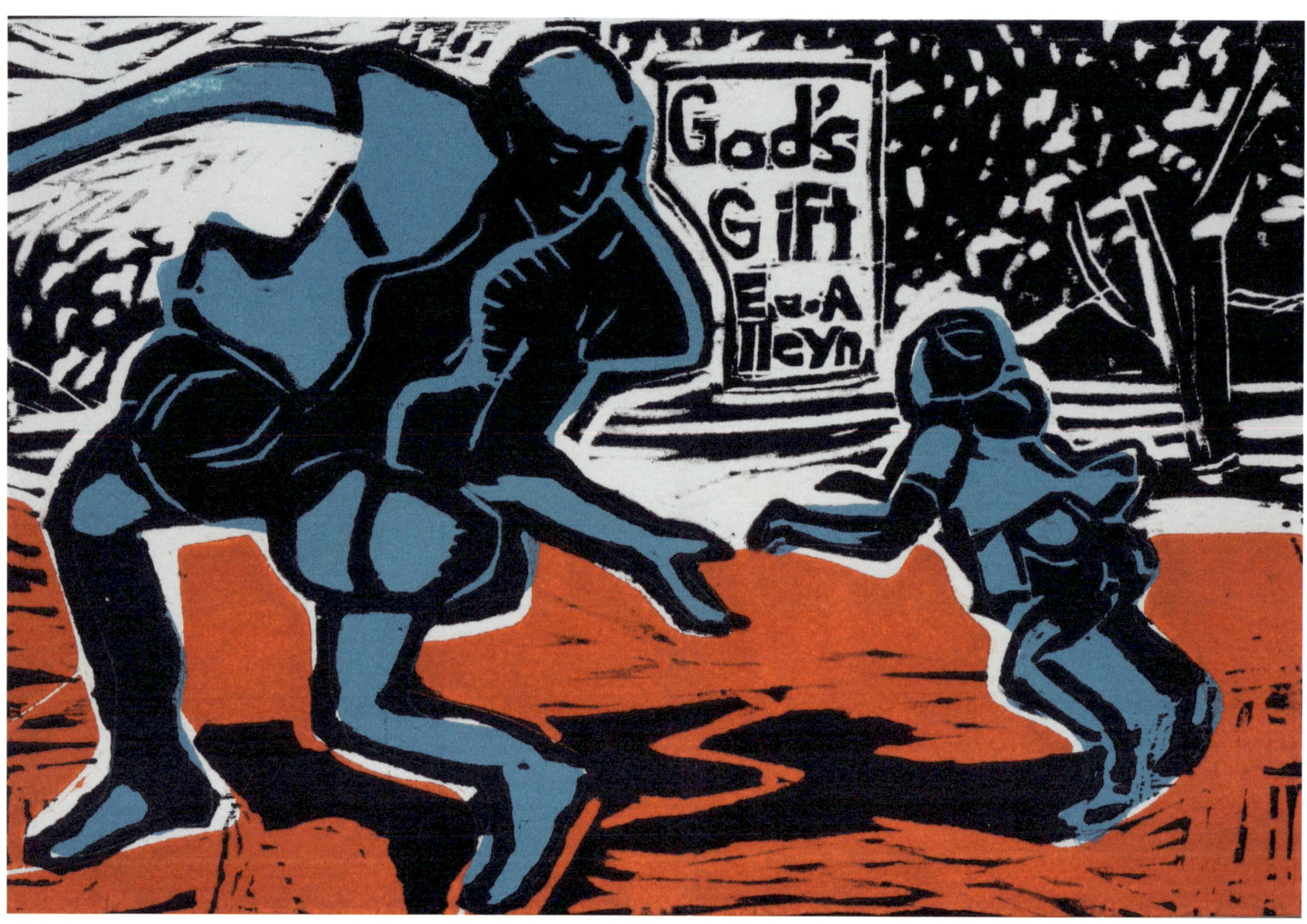

GOD'S GIFT, DULWICH

This playful image is of the statue in Dulwich of Edward Alleyn who founded Dulwich College in the sixteenth century. An actor by trade, he had made a fortune in ill-gotten gains by running bear baiting and whorehouses in Southwark. He found God and changed his evil ways while acting in a Shakespearean play featuring sprites, as seen here.

[MWC]

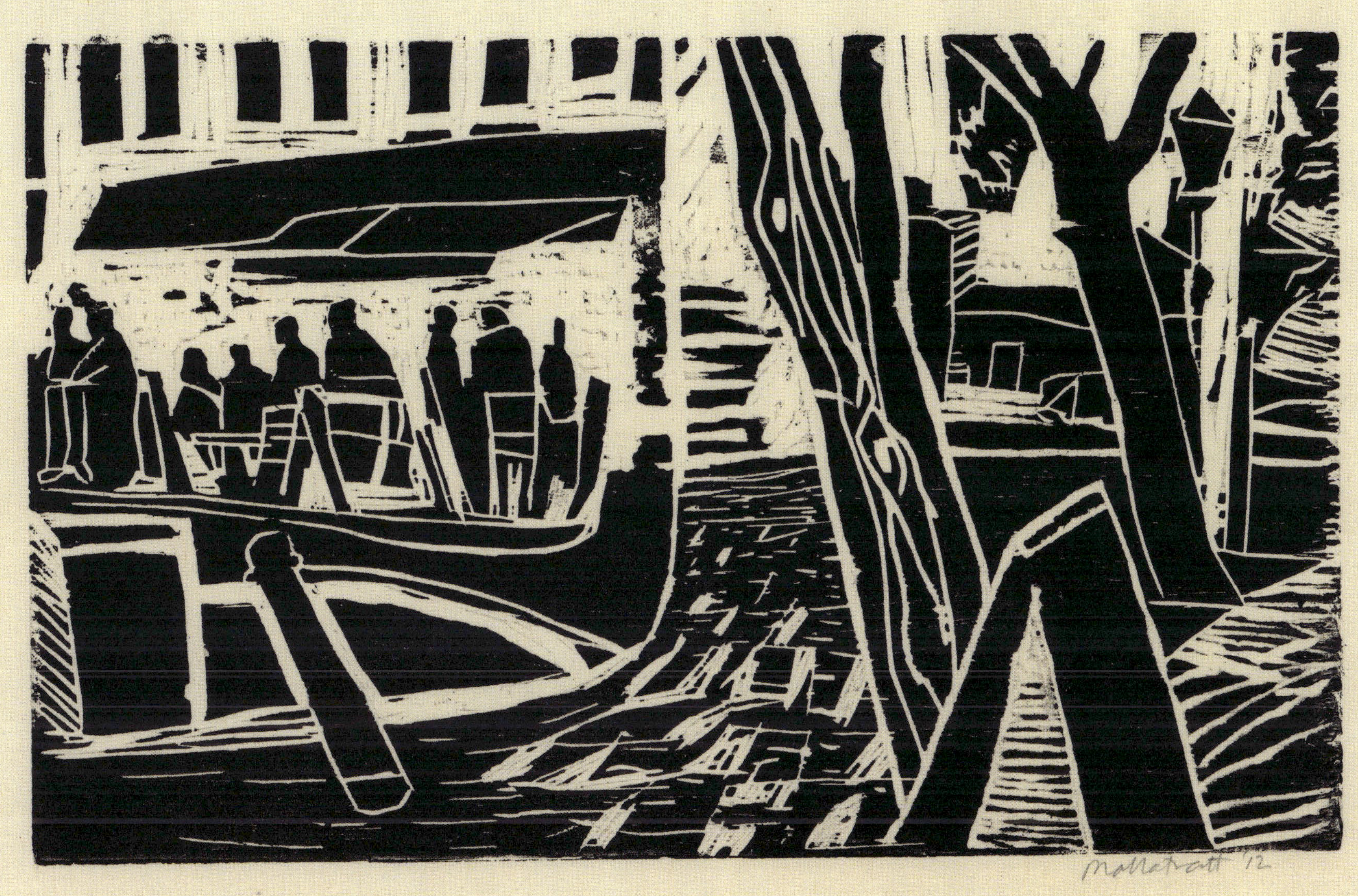

EXMOUTH MARKET, LONDON
*Always busy and buzzing, full
of history – memories, the
new emerging from the old.*
[WC]

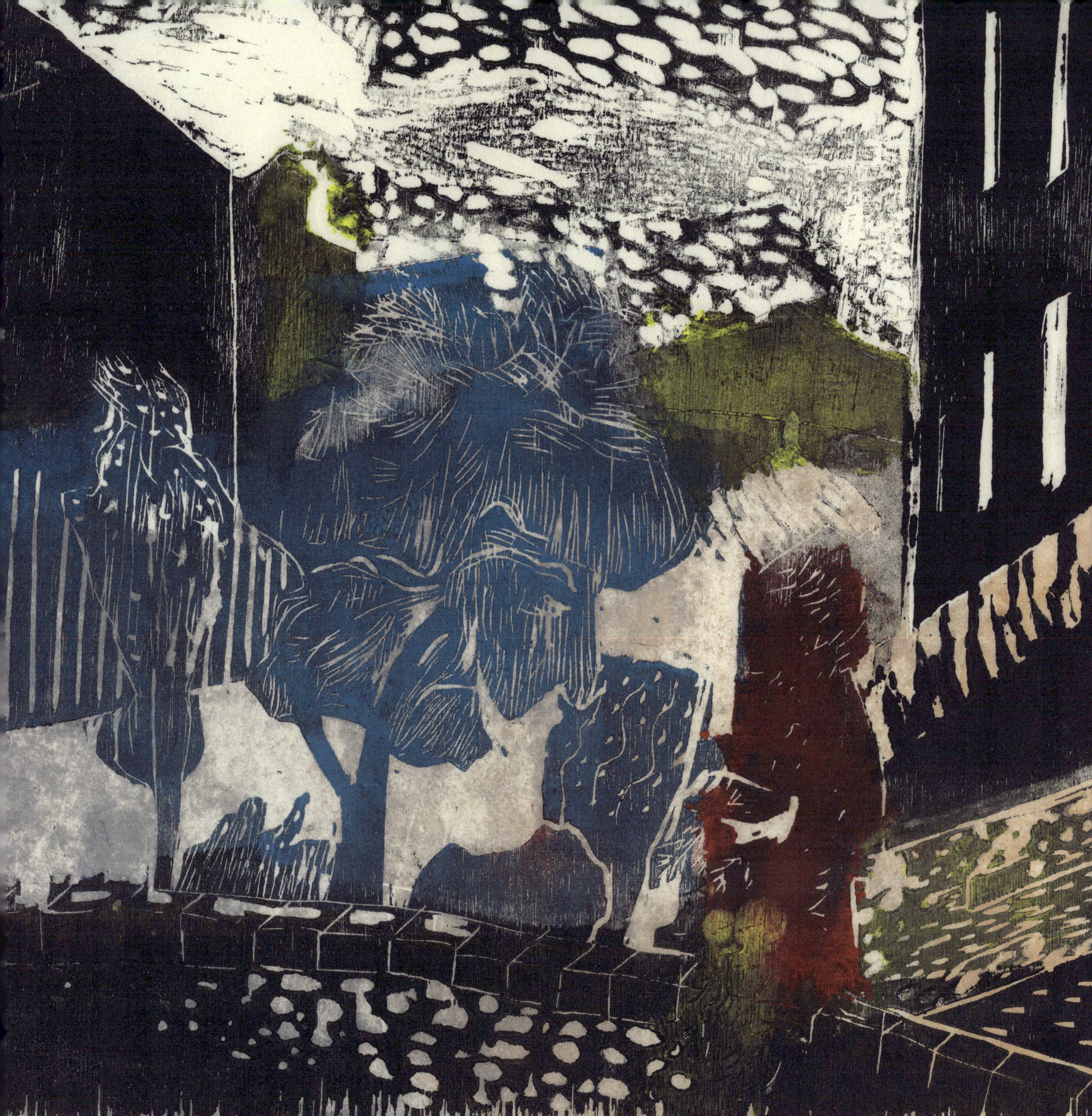

FROM THE KITCHEN WINDOW,
WILMINGTON SQUARE

*In this image I channelled
Gauguin's South Pacific woodcuts,
which were made on small boards
with black ink, simply, but to
powerful effect. I love the merging
of urban and garden.*

[WC]

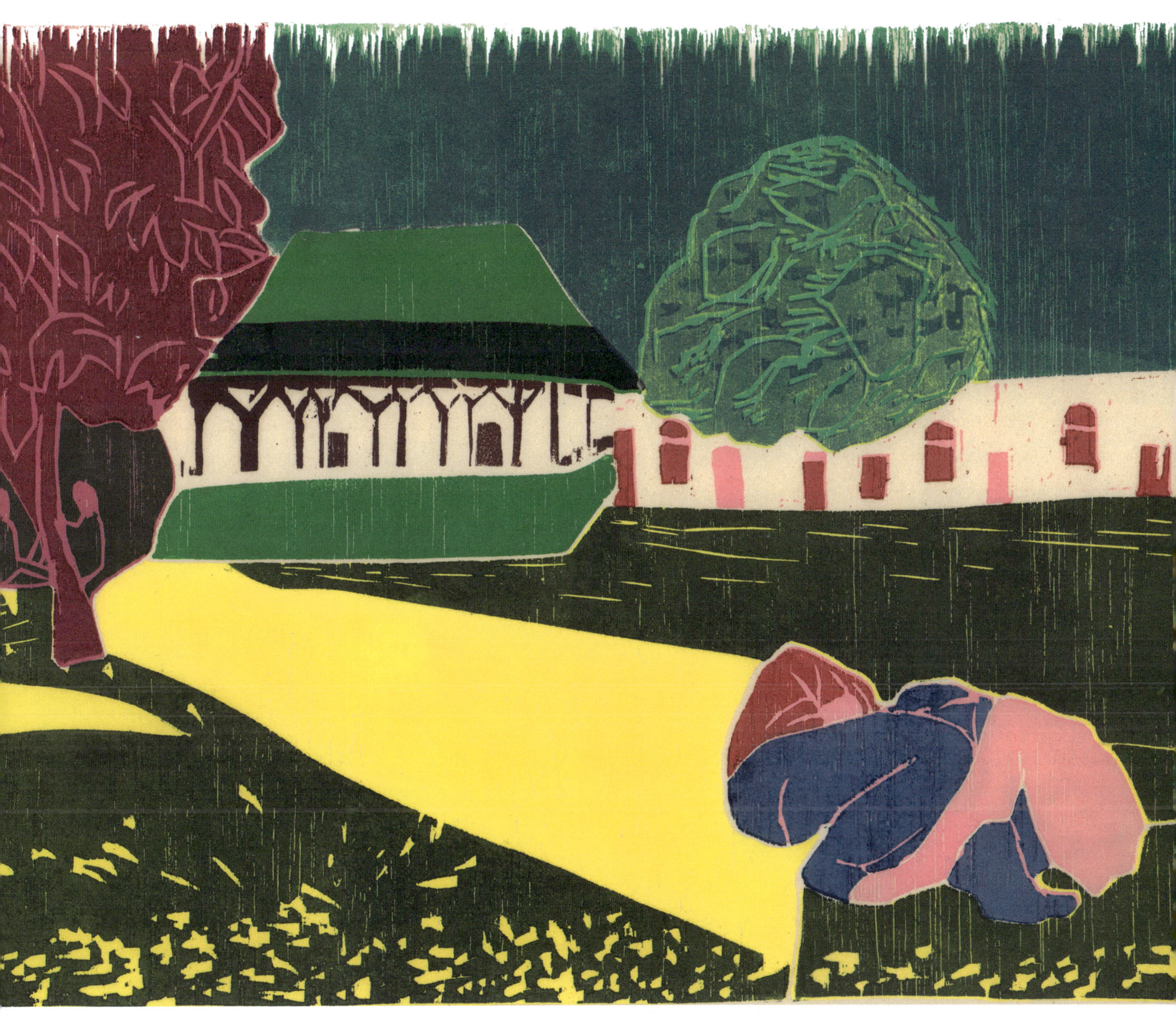

LOVERS,
WILMINGTON SQUARE

These lovers rolled around, blissfully unaware of the people in the square. The environment with them in it made an exciting composition

[RWC]

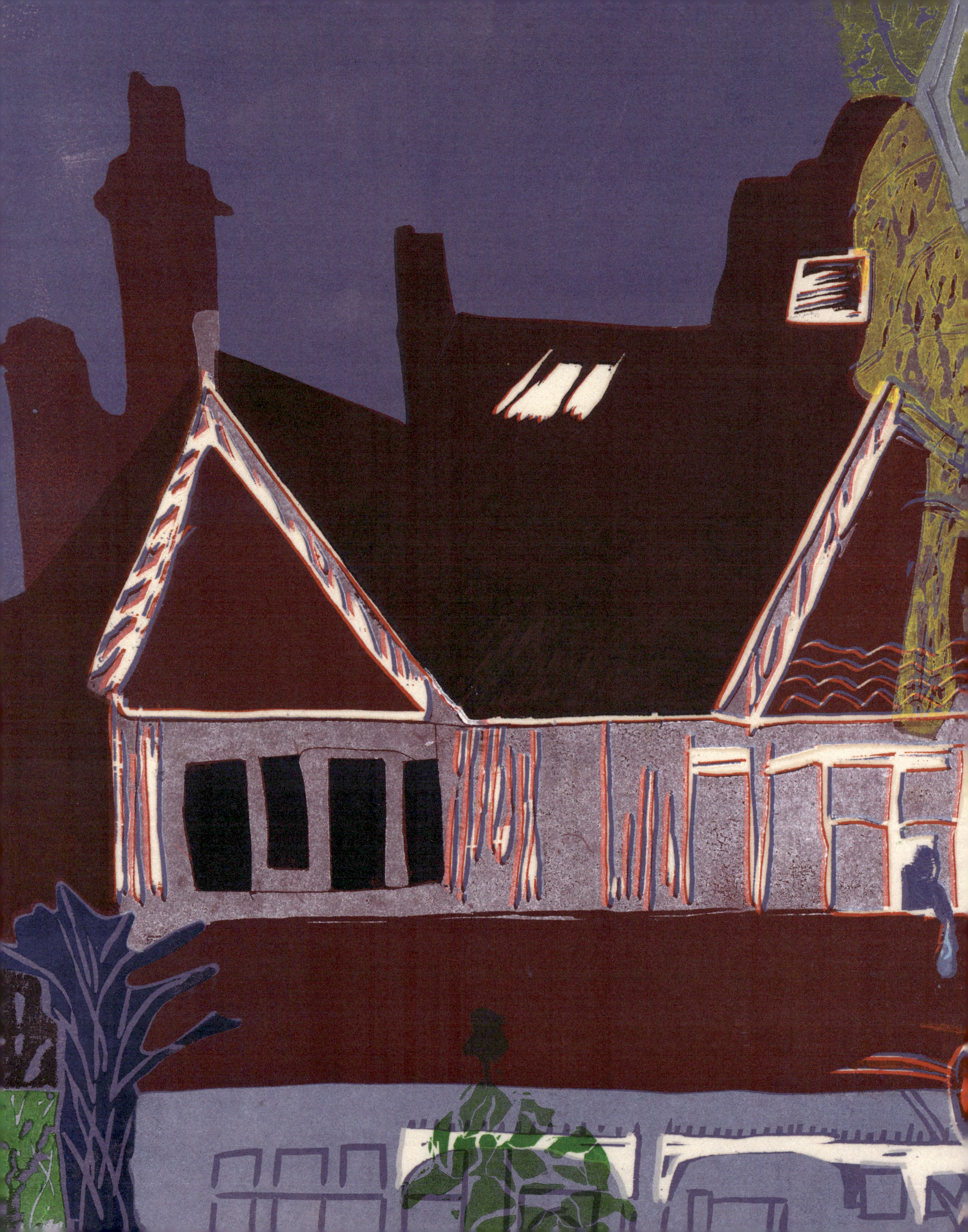

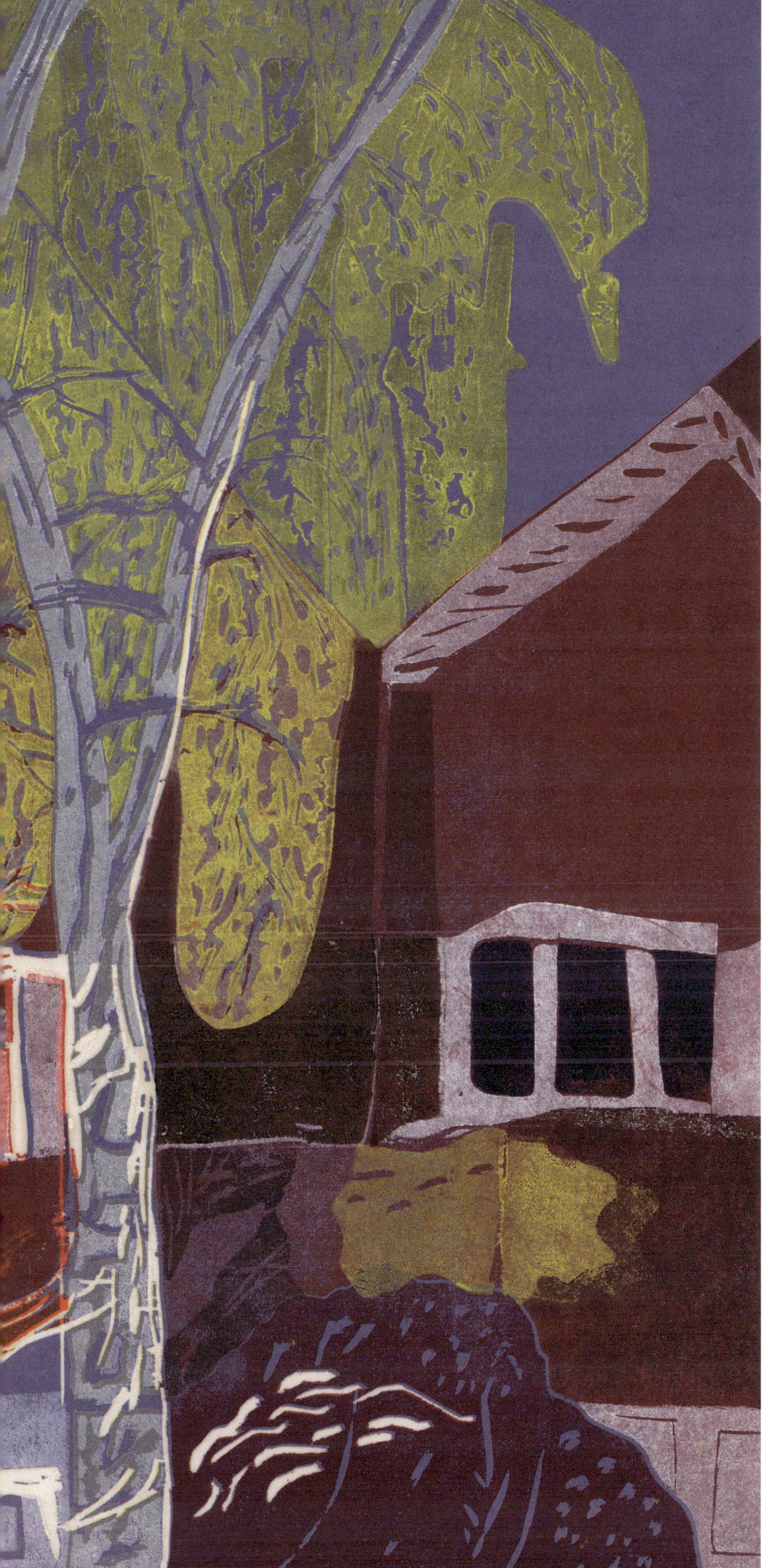

DOVERCOURT ROAD

Evening fades the light. A lady drops a bag from her window… the shadowy shapes from the chimneys above held witness to it all. Suburban life.

[RWC]

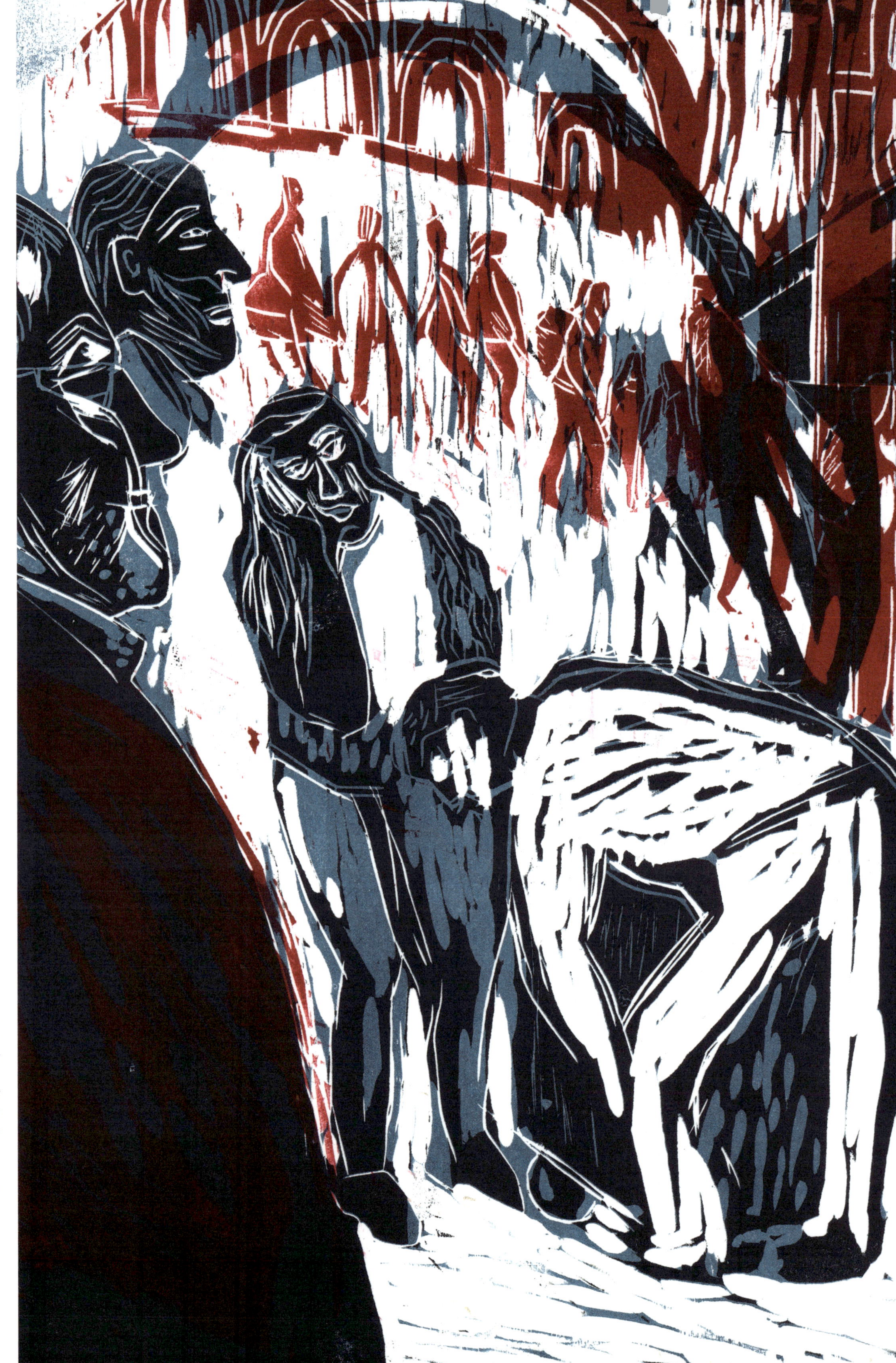

PADDINGTON
STATION, LONDON

*This was my
first woodcut.
Exhaustion, hurry
and heavy loads
to carry, suitcases
to manoeuvre…
Urban life.*

[WC]

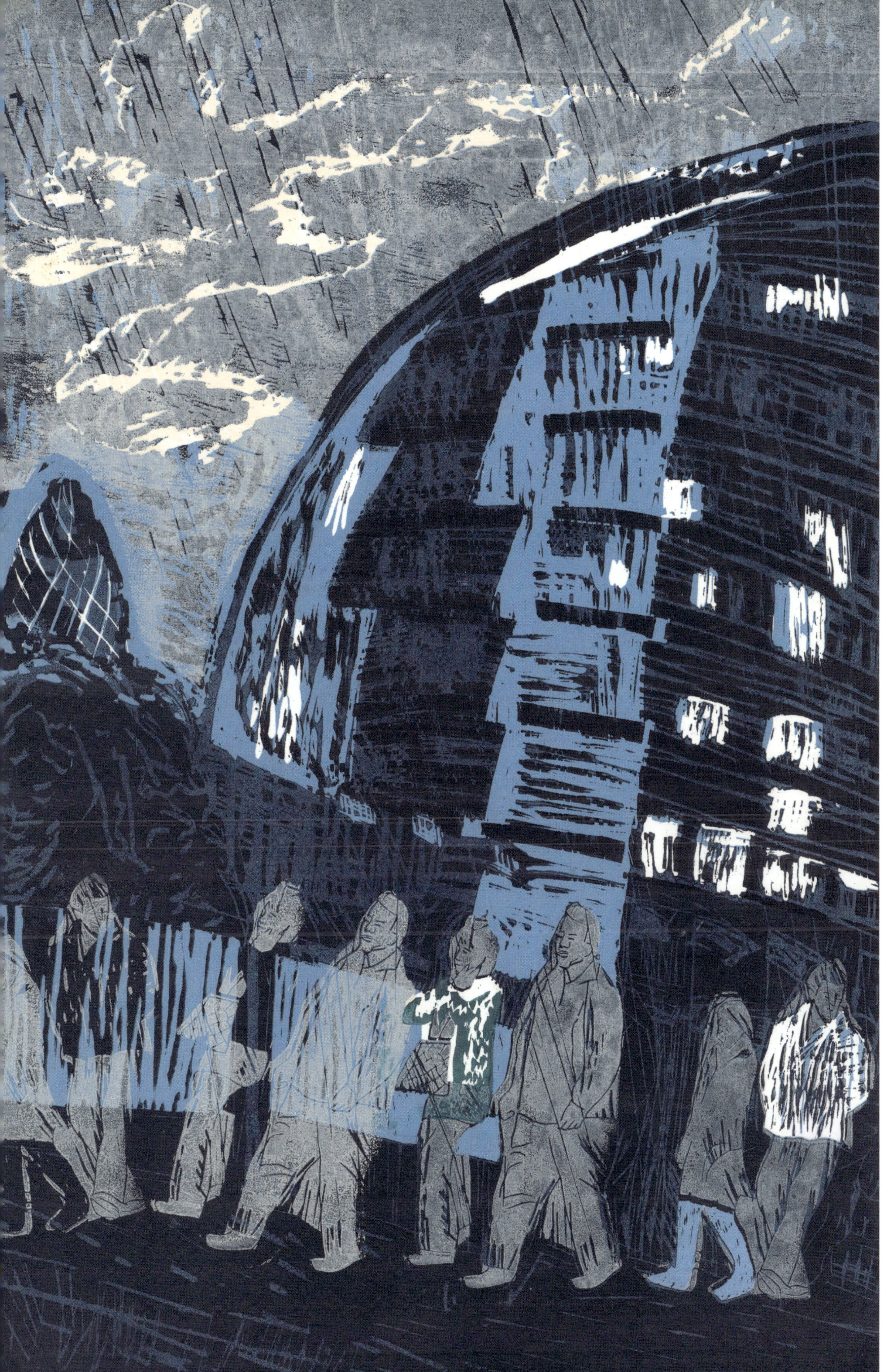

CITY HALL,
LONDON
*Rain and fog cover
the huge tilted egg
shape that is City
Hall. A weary but
determined tourist
family observes it all.*

[WC]

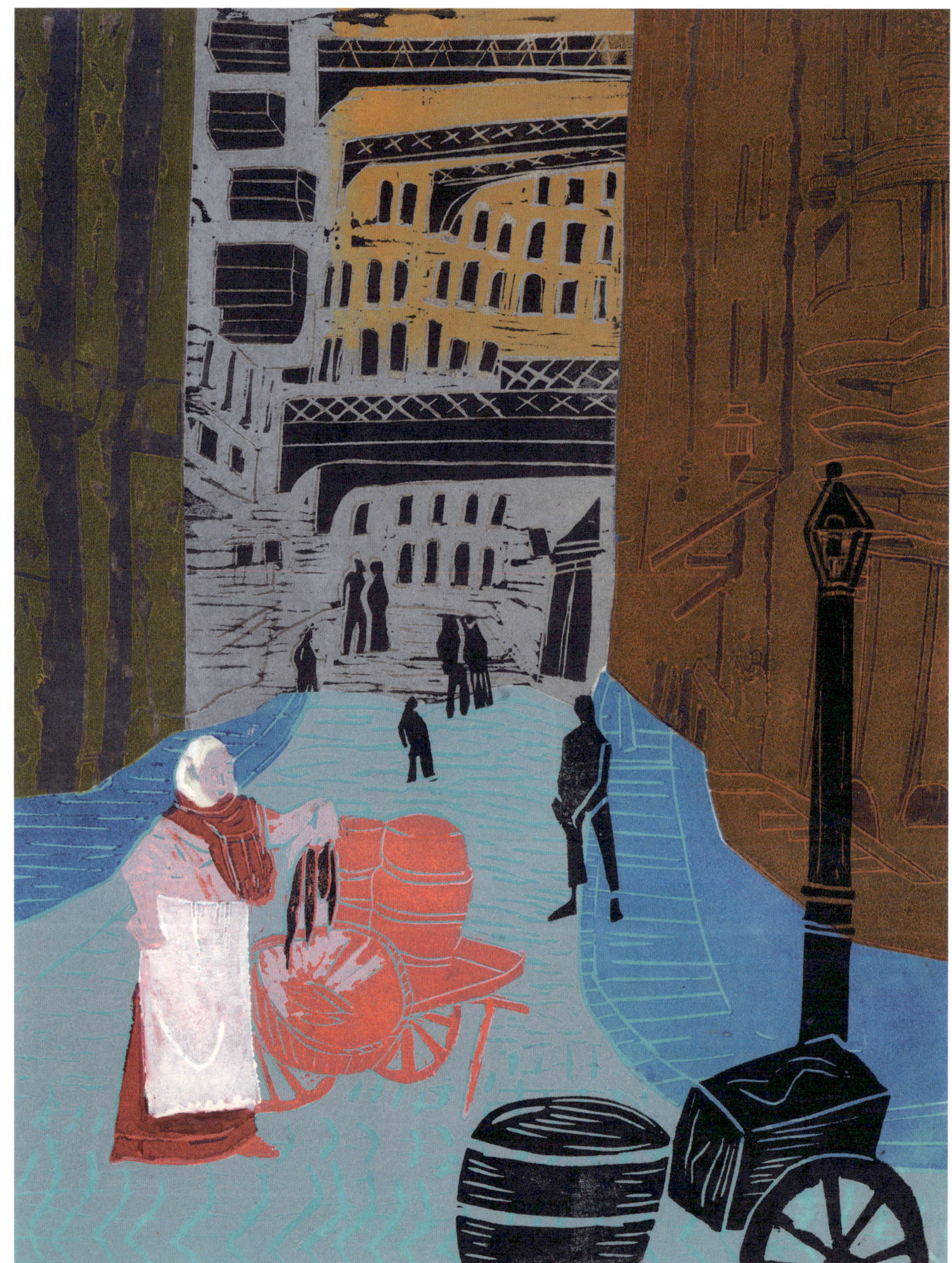

SHAD THAMES
IN THE 19TH CENTURY

*The ancient bridges for
loading produce arriving
from the Commonwealth.
England the powerful,
dominant empire, goes
about its business servicing
and receiving the world. This
humble fishmonger woman
trades for an eked-out living.*

[RWC]

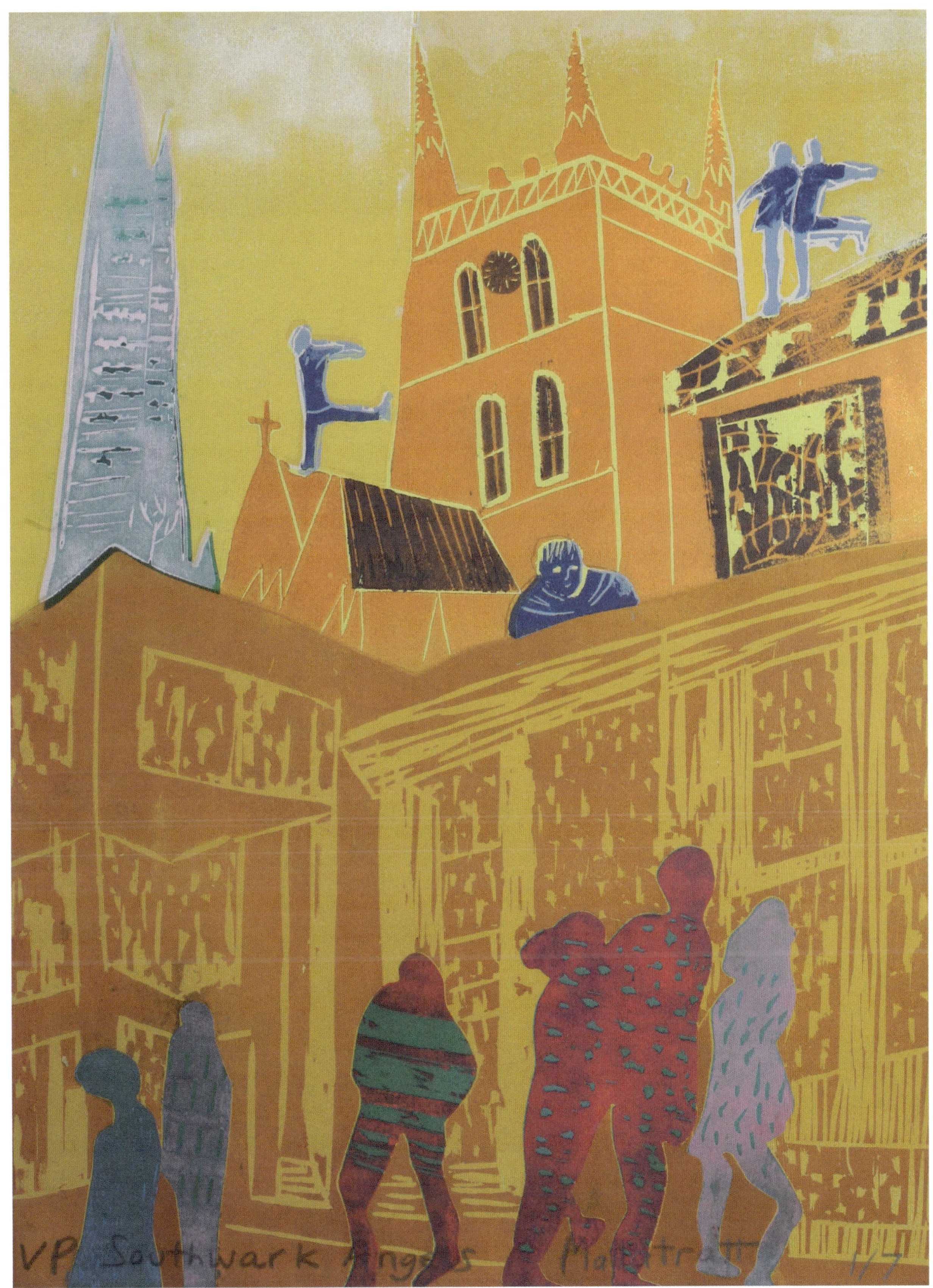

SOUTHWARK CATHEDRAL,
LONDON

*This imaginary view of the
great cathedral includes
plodding street-level
pedestrians overseen by
dancing angels.*

[RWC]

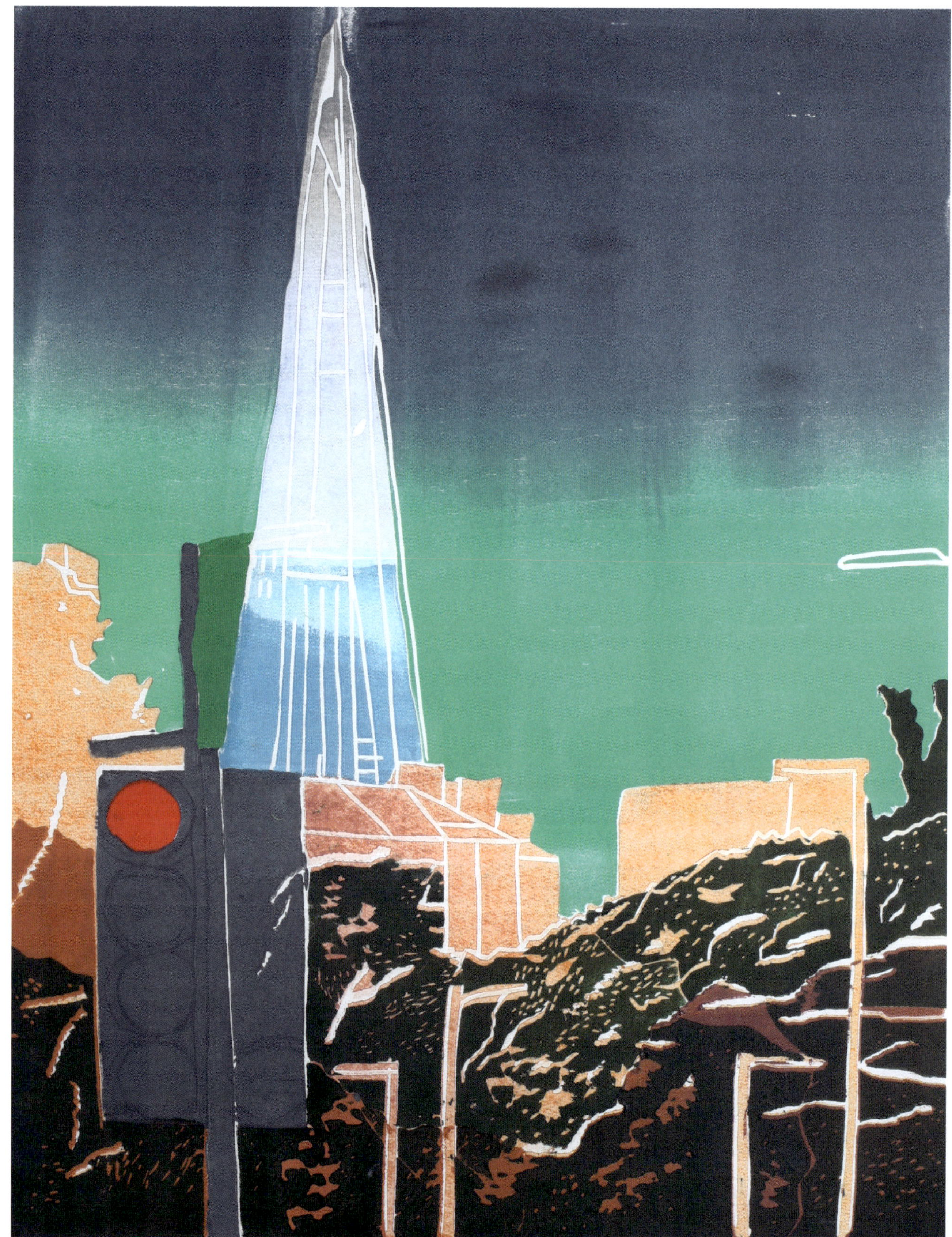

THE SHARD,
LONDON

*Shocking, ridiculous
but mighty; the
Shard landmark is
recognisable and
visible anywhere in
South London.*

[RWC]

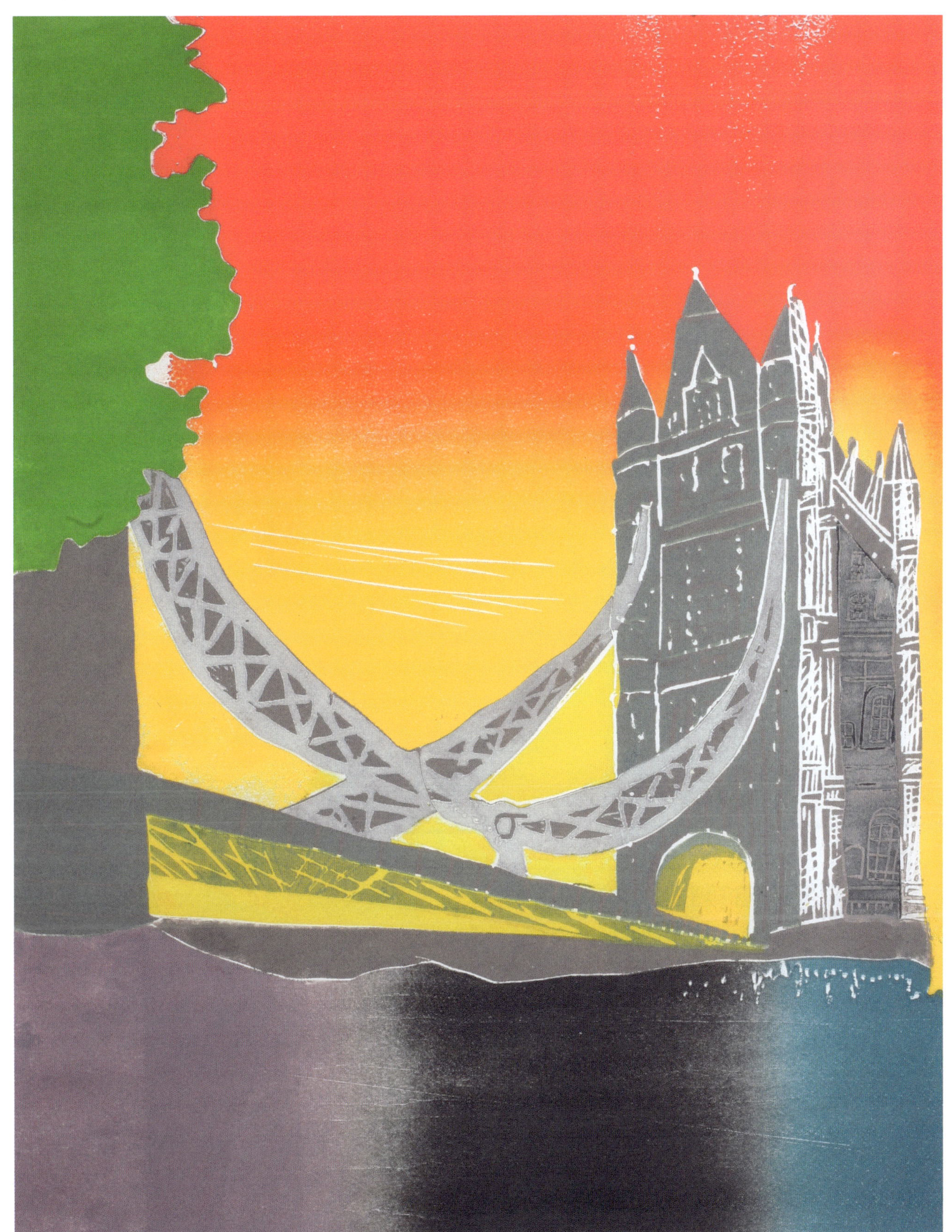

TOWER BRIDGE,
LONDON

*Old and trusty, unique
absolutely. This Victorian
bridge, looking like a
gothic fortress, was the
first to raise its roadway
to allow tall ships to
pass in and out of
London. A magnificent,
wondrous sight.*

[RWC]

LIST OF PRINTS (sizes in cm)

MEANDERINGS

HOME...?

PRINT TECHNIQUES USED

REDUCTIVE [RWC]

A method of cutting the plate with a knife or a jigsaw, then rolling on a colour and printing (using pale colours, up to dark). Next, cutting again, rolling a second colour, printing and repeating.

MULTIPLATE [MWC]

A technique using several plates – one for each colour – and printing layers of colour once each colour is dry. Ink can be diluted by a brush and white spirit, applied after it is rolled on the plate.

COLLAGRAPH [COL]

A method using cardboard sealed with yacht varnish for moisture-proofing. The card is cut or torn and colour rolled onto it. Other materials such as doilies or thin tissue can be added for texture and colour.

ETCHING [ETCH]

Etchings are achieved by using a metal plate – zinc or copper. The plate is covered in a wax ground, then drawn onto with a needle to reveal the metal beneath. The plate is then placed into an acid solution for a measured time. This may be repeated or added to, for darker lines and tones.

AQUATINT [AQT]

The plate is covered with resin or bitumen dust. The dust is then solidified with a flame. The plate is then placed in acid solution. When rinsed and dried, ink is applied by intaglio technique. This pushes ink into the grooves that have been cut by the acid. The ink is then wiped off of the surface, leaving the incised lines to be printed on a printing press.

DRYPOINT [DP]

The same method as etching, but using a plastic or aluminium plate, and without the need for acid. Ink is applied by intaglio.

The woodcuts in this book are not printed in a traditional edition, as colours are adjusted during the process. This allows a response from the effects of the press.

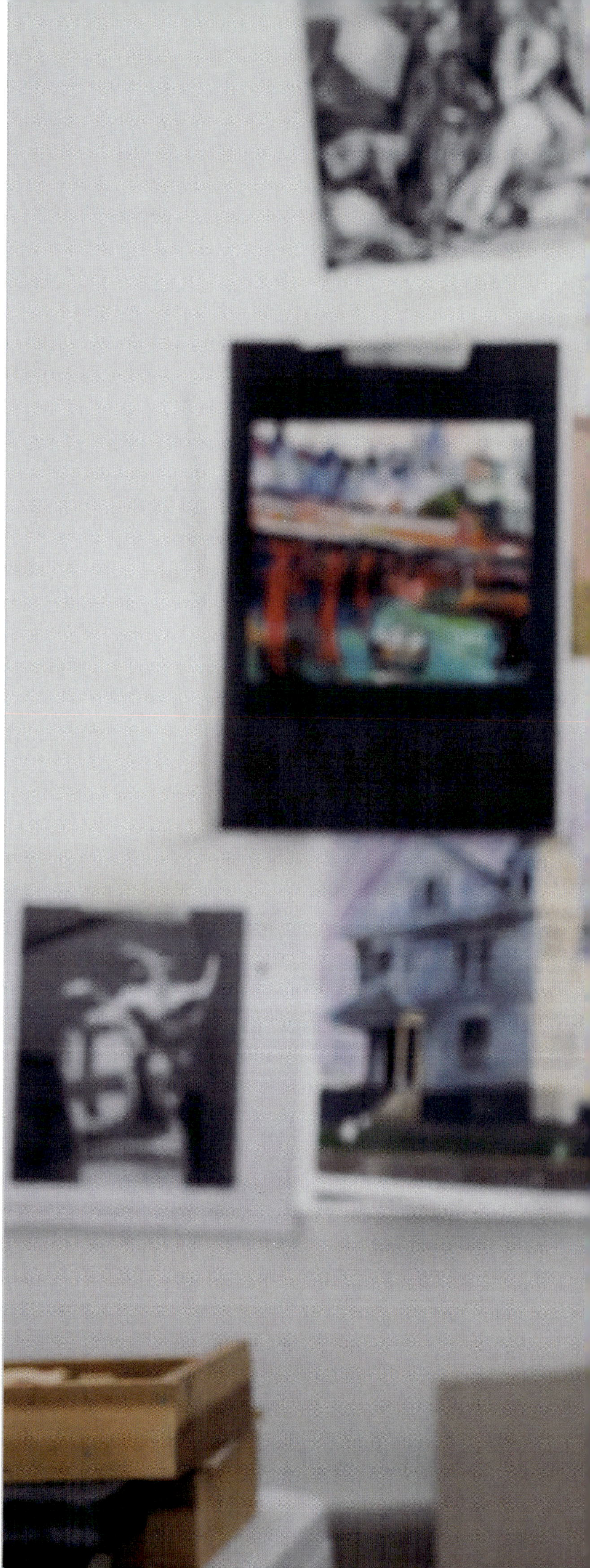

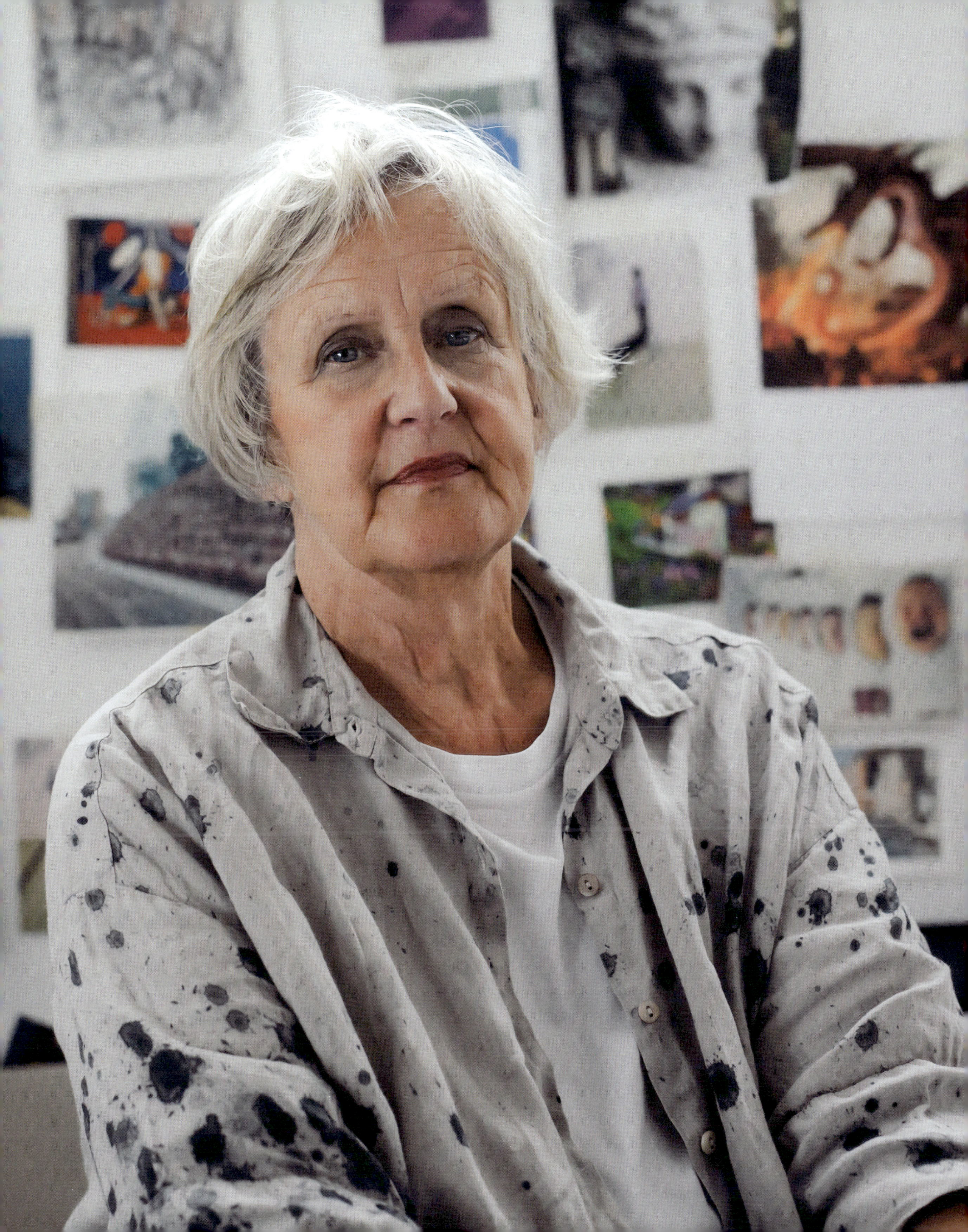

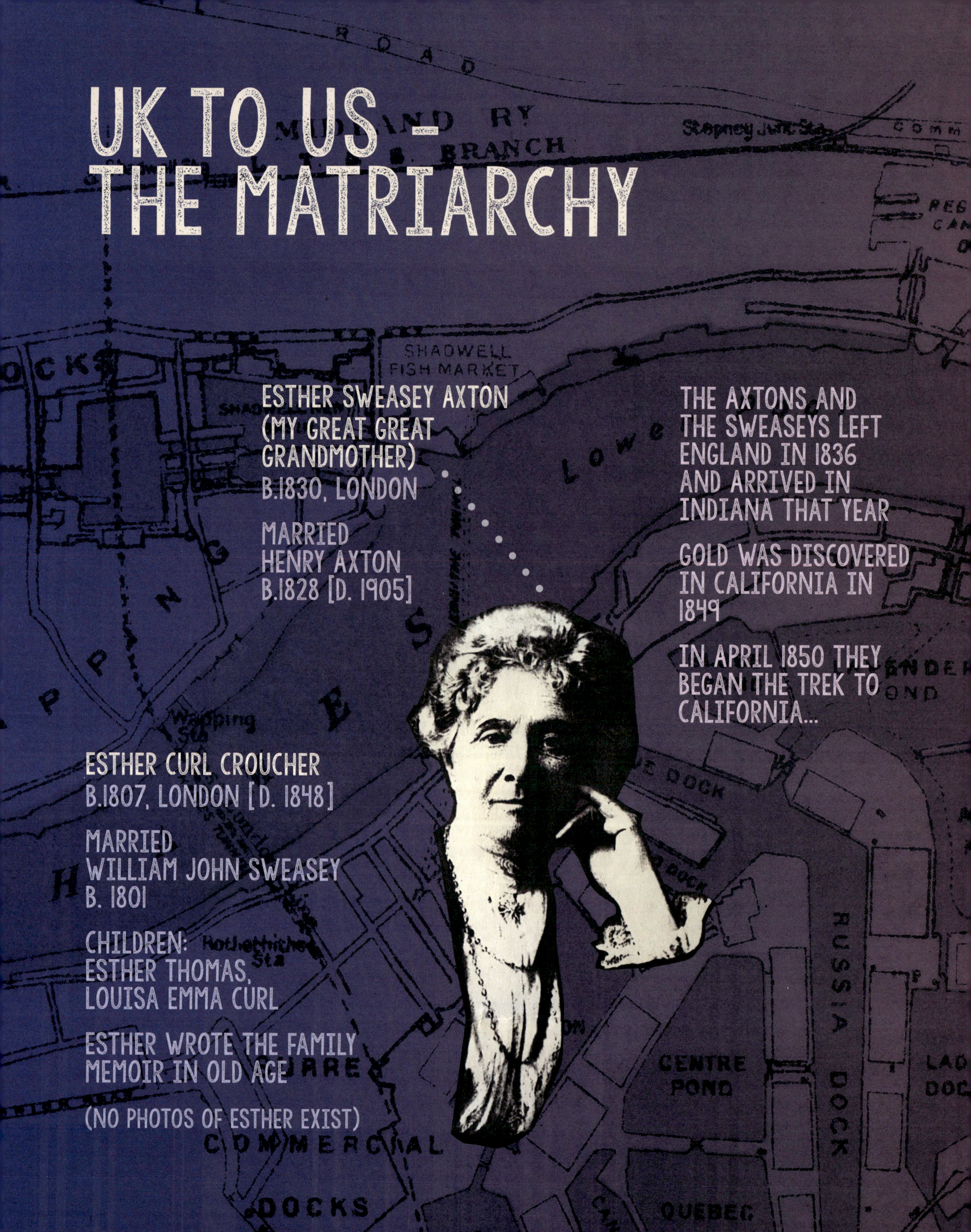

UK TO US –
THE MATRIARCHY

SHADWELL
FISH MARKET

ESTHER SWEASEY AXTON
(MY GREAT GREAT
GRANDMOTHER)
B.1830, LONDON

MARRIED
HENRY AXTON
B.1828 [D. 1905]

THE AXTONS AND
THE SWEASEYS LEFT
ENGLAND IN 1836
AND ARRIVED IN
INDIANA THAT YEAR

GOLD WAS DISCOVERED
IN CALIFORNIA IN
1849

IN APRIL 1850 THEY
BEGAN THE TREK TO
CALIFORNIA...

ESTHER CURL CROUCHER
B.1807, LONDON [D. 1848]

MARRIED
WILLIAM JOHN SWEASEY
B. 1801

CHILDREN:
ESTHER THOMAS,
LOUISA EMMA CURL

ESTHER WROTE THE FAMILY
MEMOIR IN OLD AGE

(NO PHOTOS OF ESTHER EXIST)

RUSSIA DOCK

CENTRE
POND

COMMERCIAL

DOCKS

QUEBEC

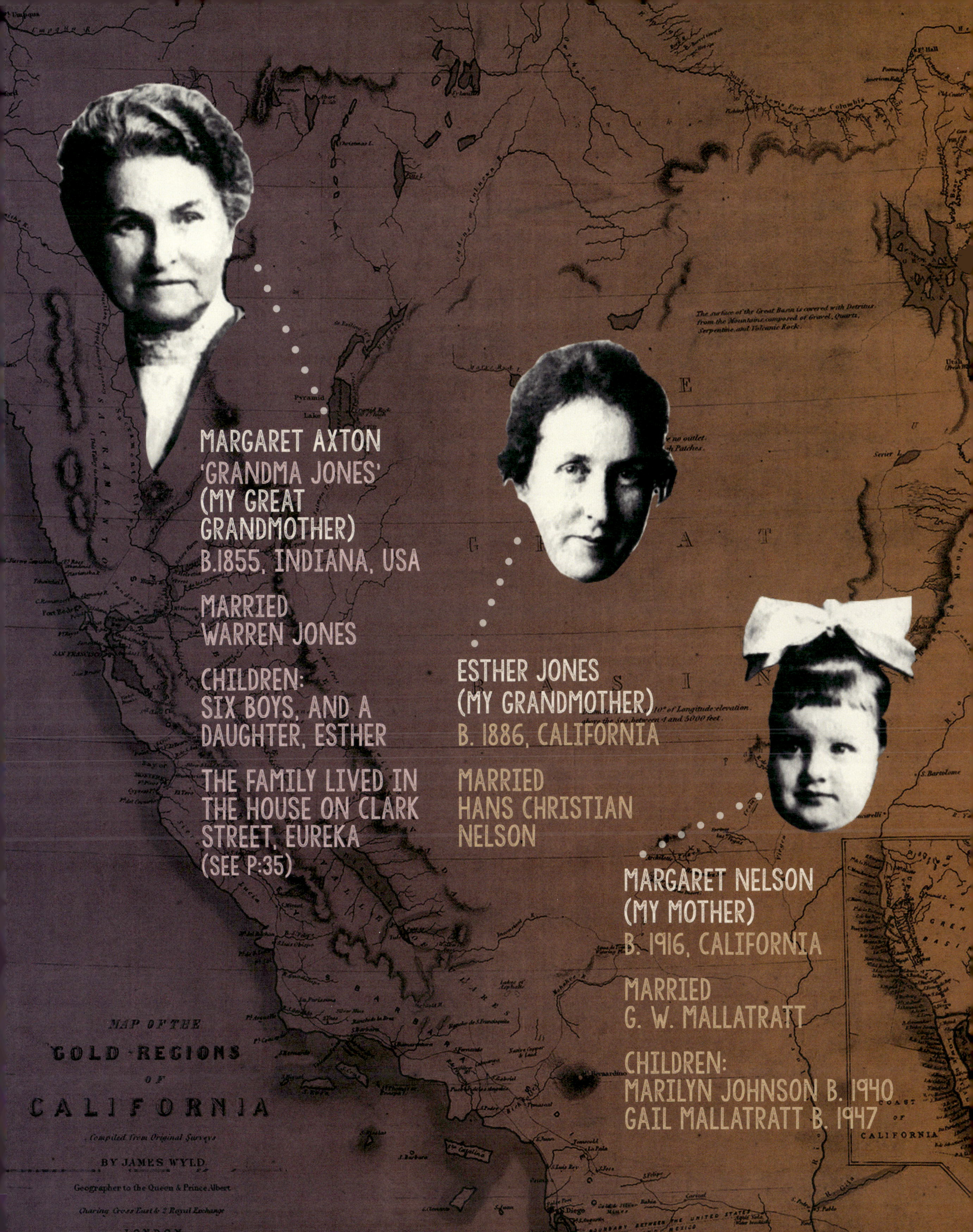

MARGARET AXTON
'GRANDMA JONES'
(MY GREAT
GRANDMOTHER)
B.1855, INDIANA, USA

MARRIED
WARREN JONES

CHILDREN:
SIX BOYS, AND A
DAUGHTER, ESTHER

THE FAMILY LIVED IN
THE HOUSE ON CLARK
STREET, EUREKA
(SEE P.35)

ESTHER JONES
(MY GRANDMOTHER)
B. 1886, CALIFORNIA

MARRIED
HANS CHRISTIAN
NELSON

MARGARET NELSON
(MY MOTHER)
B. 1916, CALIFORNIA

MARRIED
G. W. MALLATRATT

CHILDREN:
MARILYN JOHNSON B. 1940
GAIL MALLATRATT B. 1947

MAP OF THE
GOLD REGIONS
OF
CALIFORNIA
Compiled from Original Surveys
BY JAMES WYLD.
Geographer to the Queen & Prince Albert
Charing Cross East & 2 Royal Exchange

ACKNOWLEDGEMENTS

Raise a glass to all the people who inspired this book, mentioned and remembered.
To family history and life's journey, moving and searching changes,
to adventures and discoveries.

And to:
Steve Mattingly and Tony Broad, for practical and unfailing support, and kindness to me.
To Andy Stewart for skill and cheerfulness, to Diva Diana Martin Justiniano for patience,
a joyful spirit and willingness to help me out of my muddle.

Finally, and most of all, a standing ovation to Sue Smallwood for her talent,
determination, constancy and sparkle.

DEDICATION

This book is dedicated to Ian, Alexis and Zachary, and to Sam, Talia, Darcie,
Charlie, Kiran and Arun SLATTER – the next bit of family history…

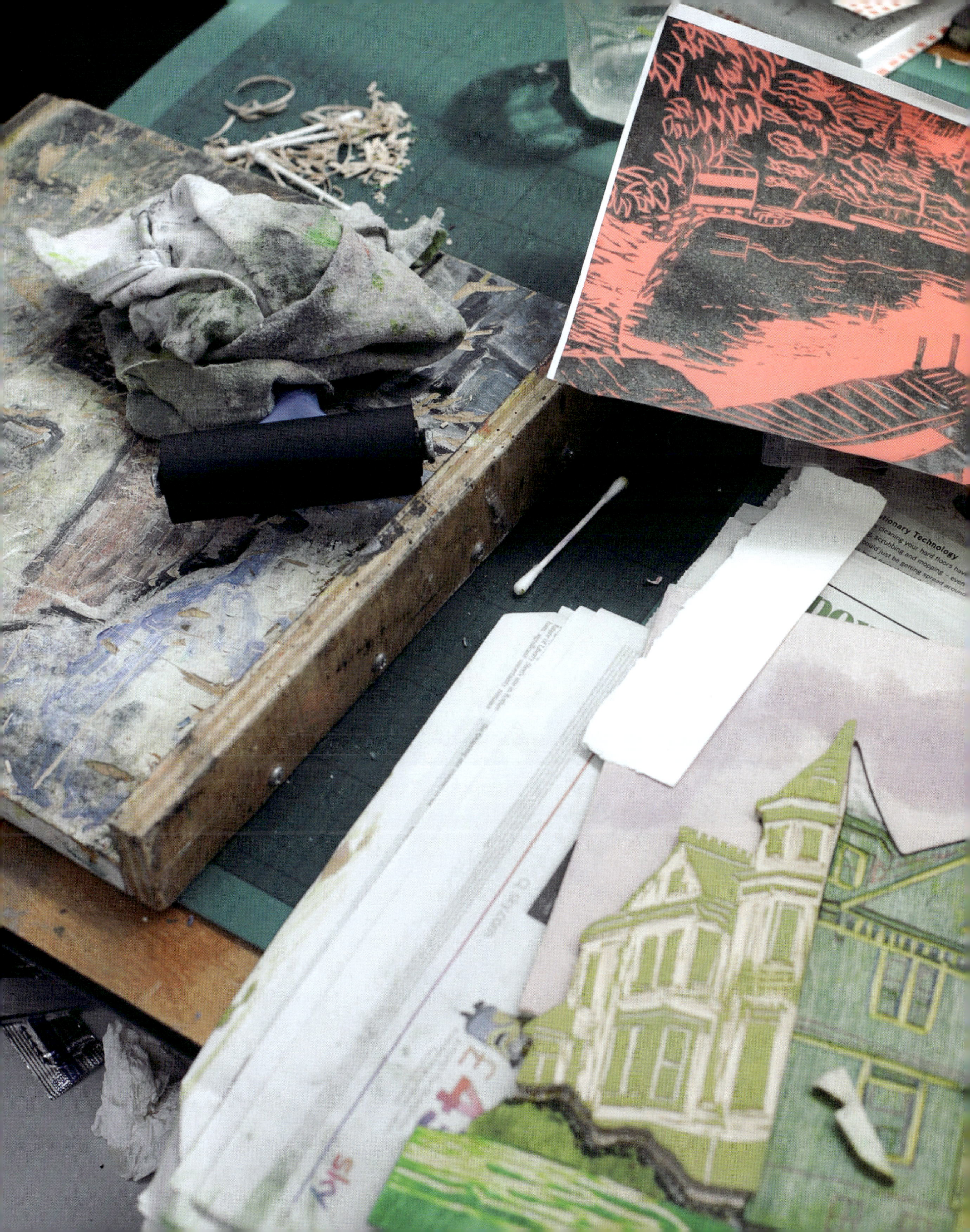

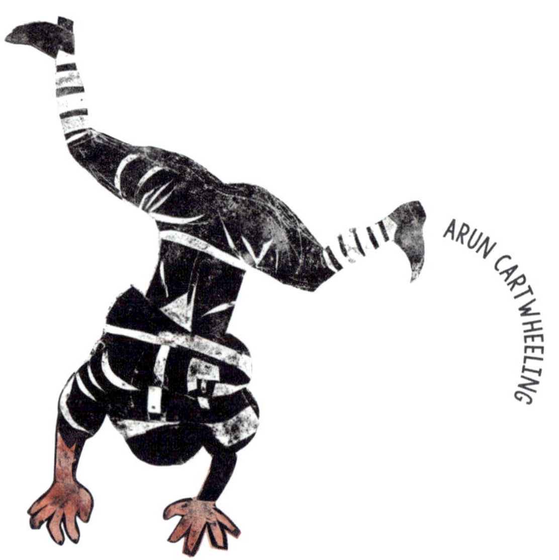

Book design: Sue Smallwood @twinsglitter productions

Prints photographed by Andy Stewart

Portraits of Gail: p.1 by Andy Stewart, p.4 by Sue Smallwood, p.107 by Diva Justiniano

PUBLISHED BY UNICORN PRESS 2022

60 Bracondale, Norwich NR1 2BE
tradfordhugh@gmail.com
www.unicornpublishing.org

Signed giclée prints of all images in this book are available, at the original print size.
Some original prints are also available for purchase.
Please contact gail.mallatratt@gmail.com for information.